Praise for *Become a Franchise Owner!*

"One of the greatest ways to claim the American Dream of business ownership is through a franchise. In his book, *Become a Franchise Owner!*, my friend, Joel Libava, takes you by the hand and walks you through all the steps. Don't make owning a franchise harder than it has to be. Take Joel's hand."

—Jim Blasingame
Host of *The Small Business Advocate Show*

"What I love about Joel Libava's style is his sensible, honest-to-goodness demeanor combined with an expansive knowledge of the franchise industry. *Become a Franchise Owner! The Start-Up Guide to Lowering Risk, Making Money, and Owning What You Do* is a testament to knowing you're in caring hands receiving the very best information so you can make your smartest decision!"

—Betsey Merkel
Process Designer, Network Strategist

"Gotham City had Batman, New York had Spiderman, Metropolis had Superman, and now entrepreneurs and future franchise owners everywhere have The Franchise King, Joel Libava. As a much needed advocate in a world full of scams, ambiguity and more sound bites than substance, Libava helps the aspiring entrepreneur navigate the franchise sea and make the best choices for themselves and their future businesses. His no-fluff style tells it like it is and clearly leads an entrepreneur through Business 101, saving them lots of money, time and heartache in the process. This is a must read for anyone interested in opening a franchise and, for that matter, anyone interested in starting a business."

—Laura Petrolino
Chief Communications Officer, Ignite Venture Partners

"Become a Franchise Owner! is the ultimate, must-read guide to anyone who has ever even considered owning a franchise of any kind. Consider the investment you're about to make in your life by opening up a franchise. If you want to make sure that you do it right the first time, read this book!"

—Jim Kukral
Author of *Attention! This Book Will Make You Money*

"It's crazy to get serious about franchising and not take the time to read this book. Franchising can be a path to success or a long unhappy journey through a dark wood; and Joel's an honest and trustworthy guide. Don't go there without him."

—Tim Berry,
Founder, Palo Alto Software

"Joel takes the guesswork out of buying a franchise by setting the record straight in an easy-to-understand way. The book takes the reader on a journey of discovery . . . about one's self, about franchising, and whether they are meant for each other."

—**Barbara Weltman**
Host of *Build Your Business Radio*

"Many failures in franchising result from the misperception that every franchise is a magic carpet to success, and that franchises never fail. The truth is that there are good franchises, there are bad franchises, and there are grab-your-checkbook-and-run franchises. Prospective franchisees need a knowledgeable, trustworthy advisor and a solid game plan. Joel Libava is that advisor, and this book provides the game plan for franchise success."

—**Sean Kelly**
President, IdeaFarm

"I applaud Joel's advice to future franchisees to plan for success and understand the franchise model before jumping into it. As a consultant to franchisors, I will recommend Joel's book as guidance for the franchise sales process. Joel's commitment to the individual success of franchise buyers not only helps them, but, ultimately, helps the industry as a whole."

—**Mark Siebert**
CEO, iFranchise Group

"If you've ever even considered entering the world of franchising, this book is required reading. You'll be able to save yourself months of work and thousands of dollars within the first fifty pages where Joel puts your personality to the test. Finish this book and you'll know for sure your very next steps."

—**Joe Sorge**
President of Hospitality Democracy and Partner, Kitchen Table Companies

"Joel talks directly to you about what's what in the world of franchising. He's not repeating the tired old stories about how great franchises are, and he's not knocking franchises with unfair criticism. He's just sitting down over coffee and telling you everything you need to know before you get involved. And he's asking the hard questions. The ones you've put off thinking about because they aren't easy to answer. If you'll do your work and answer Joel's questions, you'll find out whether a franchise is right for you, and how to make the best chance of success."

—**Becky McCray**
Publisher, SmallBizSurvival.com

"You can always count on Joel Libava to tell it like it is. He talks with candor and well-gained experience about the skills that are absolutely needed to succeed as a franchise owner. If you're in the market for a franchise business, this book is *the* place to start."

—**Flo Schell**
Founder, Franchise Coaching Systems

"Becoming a franchise owner is serious business, a life changing decision. Read this book to arm yourself with knowledge."

—**Rhonda Sanderson**
Sanderson PR

"This book is spot-on!! This is a must read for anyone considering a franchise business. This book allows you to leverage Joel's years of experience in franchise consulting to make the right choices from the very beginning; even long before you start surfing the Internet for the business of your dreams!"

—**Lonnie Helgerson**
CFE President, Helgerson Franchise Group

"Joel understands the power of franchising and his book provides straightforward information on what it takes to create a mutually beneficial relationship between both the franchisor and franchisee."

—**James Young**
President, Spring-Green Lawn Care

"When ruling a kingdom it is the king's responsibility to keep his followers safe. In franchising, it's the Franchise King, Joel Libava, that looks out for the [financial] safety of individuals interested in investing in a franchise. Regardless of an individual's background, experience, and financial net worth, Joel shoots straight and tells it like it is—whether or not an individual has what it takes to be a franchisee. In today's economic climate, with investment portfolios subject to market volatility, investors might be less concerned if Joel's philosophy was shared by their financial advisors as well."

—**Paul Segreto**
President and CEO, franchisEssentials

"There is no such thing as shopping for a franchise, which is the biggest message Joel Libava portrays to potential buyers. In *Become a Franchise Owner!* Libava walks you through how to choose the right franchise for you, what kind of investment you'll have to make, how to account for royalties and other corporate fees, and what to expect from beginning through growth. There is no other book that provides such an in-depth look at becoming a franchise owner . . . from someone who has walked in your shoes."

—**Gini Dietrich**
CEO, Arment Dietrich and author of *Spin Sucks*

BECOME A
FRANCHISE
OWNER!

THE START-UP GUIDE
TO LOWERING RISK, MAKING MONEY,
AND OWNING WHAT YOU DO

JOEL LIBAVA

WILEY

John Wiley & Sons, Inc.

Published by John Wiley & Sons, Inc., Hoboken, New Jersey.
Published simultaneously in Canada.

For general information on our other products and services or for technical support, please contact our
Customer Care Department within the United States at (800) 762-2974, outside the United States at
(317) 572-3993 or fax (317) 572-4002.

Wiley publishes in a variety of print and electronic formats and by print-on-demand. Some material
included with standard print versions of this book may not be included in e-books or in print-on-
demand. If this book refers to media such as a CD or DVD that is not included in the version you
purchased, you may download this material at http://booksupport.wiley.com. For more information
about Wiley products, visit www.wiley.com.

Library of Congress Cataloging-in-Publication Data:

Libava, Joel, 1959-
    Become a franchise owner! : the start-up guide to lowering risk, making money, and owning what
you do / Joel Libava.
        p.   cm.
    Includes index.
    ISBN 978-1-118-09402-0 (cloth); ISBN 978-1-118-17837-9 (ebk); ISBN 978-1-118-17838-6 (ebk);
    ISBN 978-1-118-17839-3 (ebk)
        1. Franchises (Retail trade)   2. New business enterprises.   I. Title.
    HF5429.23.L57   2011
    658.8'708—dc23
                                                                                    2011032159

Printed in the United States of America

10 9 8 7 6 5 4 3 2 1

This book is dedicated to my Dad, Jerry Libava, who was ethical in every facet of his life, and who made sure that this apple didn't fall too far from his tree. He left us way too soon.

Contents

Foreword

FRANCHISING IS PART of our daily lives. Every day over $1 billion is spent on franchising—and that's in the United States alone. Think about your own life. How many times a week do you spend time and money in a franchise outlet? Chances are some of the food you eat, the gas you pump, even the car you buy is transacted at a franchise location.

Do you ever dream about being on the other end of that transaction—the person collecting the money instead of spending it? Millions of people share that dream, and hundreds of thousands (there are more than 600,000 franchisees in the United States) have actually made that dream come true.

Whether you're curious and in the explorer stage or have already decided franchising is for you you've come to the right place or, more accurately, you've bought the right book. Buying a franchise can be a smart, savvy, and lucrative choice, or it could end up costing you a lot of time and money. The difference lies in doing your homework, knowing what you're buying, and getting honest insight into franchising in general, and, more specifically, your potential to succeed.

Become a Franchise Owner! The Start-Up Guide to Lowering Risk, Making Money, and Owning What You Do gives you all that—and more. Author Joel Libava, also known as The Franchise King, lives and breathes franchising. He knows the good, the bad, and, yes, the ugly. In my 30+ years covering small business and franchising, I've never met anyone more invested in helping other people make the right decision than Joel. He's so concerned about potential franchisees, so determined to help you make the right decision, you would think he's investing his own money.

In his typical approach, interweaving honesty with humor, bluntness with concern, Joel takes you through everything you need to know before you buy a franchise; he even provides a handy (though admittedly unscientific) quiz, a personality analysis, and other simple exercises you can do to make sure you're suited for franchising.

That's what sets Joel apart from most other franchise experts. He doesn't think franchising is for everyone. And even if you are suited to be a franchisee, he believes that not all franchises will be suitable for your talents, experience, and skill set. In fact, Joel takes on some franchisors for not being selective enough when selling their franchises.

There's an ongoing discussion in the franchise community about whether franchisees are entrepreneurs. This is one of the few aspects of franchising Joel and I disagree about. But our ongoing debate on this topic just underscores that Joel Libava is what I call a thought-provoker. He asks the tough questions, probes deeply, and doesn't blindly follow the industry's viewpoints.

Franchising can be the perfect solution for would-be business owners searching for the right business to start. I agree with Joel; franchising is not for everyone. If you're the type who needs to start a business because the very word *rule* gets your hackles up, then it's likely best that you steer clear of becoming a franchisee.

On the other hand, if you've longed to own a business in an industry in which you have no experience or feel you need some extra support and assistance in order to succeed as a business owner, then franchising could be the perfect solution. Those in the industry like to say when you buy a franchise "you're in business for yourself, but not by yourself." That's mostly an accurate view.

When you buy a franchise, you're really buying into someone else's system. Presumably they've worked out the kinks, learned how to attract customers, and built a national (or global) company that benefits existing franchise owners as well as new investors. But this is why it's so important you do your homework and essentially look under the hood.

There are a lot of factors you need to weigh before you actually sign on the dotted line. In *Become a Franchise Owner! The Start-Up Guide to Lowering Risk, Making Money, and Owning What You Do*, Joel shares his thorough franchise research process, so you not only know what to look for, but also how to find it. And speaking of finding things, Joel also provides an in-depth list of vital franchise resources.

Starting a business, whether you build it from the ground up, purchase an existing company, or buy a franchise, is a risky proposition. Run as fast as you can from anyone who tries to tell you differently. Buying a franchise does not eliminate the risk of start-up. But if you approach franchising the right way—the smart way—by reading this book, doing your research, checking out the numerous opportunities out there, then the risk is somewhat mitigated.

One of the biggest factors setting the franchise model apart is that, even though someone else is actually operating a specific outlet, it is the franchise's name, brand, and reputation that's at risk. Consumers don't blame John Jones or Susie Smith if their hamburgers are overcooked, their newly painted houses looks shabby, or their cars run poorly after a tune-up. They fault the company whose name is on the door of the business—the franchisor. That is why most franchises provide both initial training and ongoing support to their franchisees. And that's why, when you're in the midst of the franchise selection process, the type of training and support are key factors to assess. (I attended a training session once for Baskin Robbins' new franchisees. It was a detailed and fascinating process—and I learned there's a right way and a wrong way to scoop an ice cream cone.)

There are other aspects to consider before you make your final decision. Some potential franchise buyers are pulled between buying into an established company with a proven track record, or a new company offering perhaps a hotter concept and a willingness to negotiate. There are advantages and disadvantages to both. It's all about figuring out what's best for you, your personal circumstances, your risk tolerance, and how much money you have to invest.

To help guide you, you can follow the story of James Pennington, a downsized middle management guy with a family, a mortgage, and a deep desire to be his own boss. Does that sound like you? James does not technically exist. He's a figment of Joel's imagination, an everyman (or woman) if you will, who represents all the prospective franchisees Joel has met over his many years of working in the franchise market.

Franchise success is dependent on so many factors, big and small. Fred DeLuca, the founder of Subway Sandwiches once told me he used to sit across from potential locations, watching the flow of street traffic. (Did you know Americans apparently don't like to make left turns, and some businesses, like donut shops, do better when they're located on the going-to-work side of the street?)

It has long been the American Dream to own your own business. There is no better way to control your own destiny, to fail or prosper as a result of your own actions and not those of your boss. I think America is inherently an entrepreneurial nation; it's part of our allure as the land of opportunity.

If franchising is the path you choose to follow to make that dream come true, then *Become a Franchise Owner! The Start-Up Guide to Lowering Risk, Making Money, and Owning What You Do* is an essential guide to steer you down that path. And I can't think of anyone I would trust more to be my franchise field guide than Joel Libava.

So what are you waiting for? Turn the page and get started on your own incredible journey to business ownership.

—Rieva Lesonsky
CEO, GrowBiz Media
SmallBizDaily.com

Acknowledgments

THIS BOOK WOULDN'T have been possible without the support of my wife, Jeannine, who's been my daily cheerleader, and who, along with my daughter, Grace (The Franchise Princess), has had to endure things like my house-shaking, 144+ decibel, unique typing technique, and the extreme feelings of loneliness they must have had when I wasn't able to join them for such dynamic and culturally important nighttime television shows such as *Jersey Shore*, *Teen Mom*, and *America's Next Top Model* while I was writing this book.

To my mom, Judith Libava, who's so proud of her firstborn; my brother Jon, who's been more helpful and motivating than he knows; my sister Janet, who thinks it's really cool that her big brother is now an author; and my mother-in-law and father-in-law Lou and Lisa, who have been fantastic supporters. I'm grateful for it.

To all of my cousins, nieces, and nephews, brothers-in-law, and sisters-in-law, aunts and uncles—I think it's really cool that you've become fans on my Facebook page and that you've been genuinely excited for me to publish this book. Thank you!

To Lauren Murphy, my editor at John Wiley & Sons, who's been a genuine pom-pom shaker for the last several months; she's believed in me from day one. (Plus she follows me on Twitter!) Christine Moore and Deborah Schindlar, my copyeditors, who've had the pleasure of experiencing my cutting-edge use of commas right before their very eyes.

To my business attorney, Jack Kurant, who's always watching my back; thank you for being a trusted resource for me and for the numerous prospective franchise owners I've referred to you. It's always about them, and your work reflects that.

The following people reached out to me and gave me a shot.

To Anita Campbell, the owner of Small Business Trends LLC and a few major web properties, who put out a call for people that were small business experts in their respected fields a few years ago. She wanted to take www.smallbiztrends.com to the next level and wanted to have a team in place to help her do just that. When I didn't respond right away, she sent me an e-mail in which she explained in no uncertain terms that I was the one who should be the *Small Business Trends* Franchise Expert in Residence. She wanted me to write a monthly column for her website and be available to answer questions about franchising from her readers. When I told her that I wasn't very confident about my writing skills, she told me that she would help me become a better writer and that I needed to do it. I did, and I've been the Franchise Expert in Residence for several years now. Thanks, Anita. You're a special lady.

Jim Blasingame's people reached out to me a few years ago to be a guest on Jim's *The Small Business Advocate* radio program. It's the longest-running small business radio program in the world, and Jim really is The Small Business Advocate. I'm interviewed at least once a quarter, and I'm a member of Jim Blasingame's Brain Trust, which is the largest community of small business experts in the world. Thank you, Jim!

Jim never would have reached out to me if it wasn't for the faith that Rhonda Sanderson and Courtney Thomas from Sanderson PR in Chicago had in me. They thought that I'd be perfect for Jim's radio program and connected us. In addition, Rhonda and Courtney schooled me on public relations and its importance. I'm grateful for that and for our enduring friendship. Sanderson PR rocks. (And the three of us agree on everything—all the time.)

A special thank you goes out to Lauren, Tracy, and the rest of the gang over at Fox *Business News*. Not only did you reach out to me for my expertise on franchising, you allowed me to show off my crown while you peppered me with your tough, but fair questions on camera.

Rieva Lesonsky almost had me in tears after I read the foreword to this book that she, without hesitation, agreed to write for me. I remember seeing her picture every month in *Entrepreneur Magazine* when I was younger and always thought that it would be cool to actually meet a powerful publishing executive like her. We ended up connecting on Twitter and found out that we had lots of mutual entrepreneurial connections and friends. Well, we finally *did* meet, and she's been an amazing supporter, friend and idea-generator of mine ever since. Rieva's as genuine as they get.

Barbara Weltman, financial expert, author, and host of *Build Your Business Radio* invited me to be a guest on her very popular radio program a few years ago, and I've been able to have some great discussions about franchising with her numerous times on the air. She's become a true friend and a very loyal supporter. Thank you, Barbara.

Several people that are quite influential in small business and, in some cases, social media have, for the cost of a cup of coffee (whether an in-person coffee or a virtual one), provided their expertise when I've asked for help. As much as I think I know, I don't. I'm truly grateful for all they've done and continue to do.

Chris Brogan, the dude gets 500+ e-mails *a day*, travels around the world speaking about social media strategy, is a *New York Times* best-selling author and owns one of the most-read social media blogs around. And yet, Chris, who receives thousands of requests for help every year, has been able to squeeze in some of his valuable time to give me very helpful suggestions for my consulting business. He's a mensch. Chris, you may never know how much you've impacted my life. Your constant encouragement has been amazing, and you've helped me stay true to myself and my values. Thanks. (I wish my dad could have met you.)

Jim Kukral is a fellow Clevelander who I met several years ago at a local networking event in which he was giving a talk about blogging. His no BS approach reminded me of someone (me), and we've been friends ever since. Jim is someone who's offered his help to me dozens of times, and he's the one responsible for encouraging me (hammering on me, actually) to get The Franchise King name trademarked. Thanks, Jim!

I had a one-hour call a few months back with Liz Strauss, a Chicago area social Web strategist and community builder, who I'd met at Blogworld, an annual blogging conference. During our call, she kept asking me what it is that I wanted to be doing in my business. I was going back and forth between working with franchisors on their social media and marketing strategies or continuing my work with prospective franchise owners. She gently (not at all) helped me work through the pros and cons of each scenario. Can you guess which one won out? Thanks for helping me focus on what I'm passionate about, being an advocate for prospective franchise owners.

Barry Moltz and I became friends after we had met on Twitter. Another Chicago-area small business powerhouse, Barry has offered to assist me with my business more times than I can count. I think I even took him up on his offer once. Barry is a great guy and a great connector of people. Thanks for always checking up on me, Barry.

I'm not sure what it is about Chicago that produces really smart people (Lake Michigan's water supply, maybe?), but I'm adding Carol Roth to the Chicago mix. Carol (who I met through Barry Moltz) has kind of taken me under her wing. (At least that's how I look at it.) Carol wrote an amazing book, *The Entrepreneur Equation,* and, like me, tells it like it is. During our first phone call, I distinctly remember telling her that I thought that she was the female version of me—a fearless, in your face, I really don't care what you think of me, type of person. In one way I was right; in another way, I was wrong. Carol's much more than a blunt businesswoman; she's an expert at fixing what needs to be fixed and has led me down the path of right ever since we met. Carol's another one who always asks how I'm doing and tries to make sure that I'm doing things right for things that are very long term in nature. Thanks a lot for helping me take things to another level, especially in my writing.

Finally, I'd like to acknowledge all the people who have made both my personal and professional life exciting and meaningful. You've helped me more than you know with your loyalty, plus your belief and trust in me. I consider you to be my friends. Thank you so much! In really random order:

David Siteman Garland, Steve King, Joe Sorge, Guy Kawasaki, NEENZ, Gini Dietrich, Lisa Gerber, Shonali Burke, George Nemeth, Michael DeAloia, Margaret Box, Kevin Goodman, Brad Kleinman,

David Toth, Tom Sudow, Rick Taylor, Ken Sachs, Nada Norval, Mike Milby, Eric Kim, Kelly Kim, Rob Goggins, Butch Gladden, Steve Gemlo, Barney Greenbaum, Keld Alstrup, Staci Wood, Cali Yost, Gila Fox, Jerry Wilkerson, Suzanne Vara, Lisa Hoffman, Ronna Delson, Anita Cohen-Williams, Laura Petrolino, Rush Nigut, Jay Berkowitz, Charles Internacola, Glenn Hudson, John Jantsch, Niall Devitt, Priya Ramesh, Todd Weiss, Jerry Darnell, Liliane Rausch, Shannon Davis, Marshall Reddy, Brent Leary, Jim Coen, Paul Segreto, Deb Evans, Elza Gennicks, Rush Nigut, Charles Internacola, Greg George, Missy Ward, Shawn Collins, Ace Conway, Mike Barrett, Dick Russ, Howard Wayne, Sarah Wilson-Jones, Erika Kerekes, Melinda Emerson, Roberta Frieder-Holzer, Ivana Taylor, Staci Wood, Abbey Gannon, Eve Tahmincioglu, Carol Tice, Sara Wilson, Ann Handley, Christine Perkett, Greg Pitkoff, Heidi Cool, Brad Nellis, Steve Millard, Matt Dickman, Jodi O'Neill, Jill Miller-Zimon, Eve Lopez, Jeff Shuey, Scott Hepburn, Bob McDonald, Jennifer Decker, Adina Genn, my Uncle Al, John Renner, Paula Tresger, Ivan Walsh, Craig Slavin, Jon Tokar, Ron McDaniel, Glenn Hudson, Mike Michalowicz, Rita Braunek, Martin Lindeskog, Fred Leo, Howard Kass, Dawn Rivers, Eric Percell, Cathy Larkin, Brian Layman, John Marcus, Lila Hanft, Tracy Previte, Doreen Kukral, Ramon De Leon, Jeannie Walters, Cindy Hartman, Mike Hartman, Elaine Lipman-Barnes, Hillary Cable, Dane Carlson, Molly Cantrell-Kraig, Rachel Kabb-Effron, Dave Van Horne, Shawn Hessinger, Gordon Dupries, Dana Devereux, Derek Arnold, Kristen Kaleal, Dan Schawbel, Betsey Merkel, Eric Olson, Rob Reuteman, Lisa Kanarek, Joe Bono, Steve Shenberger, Zane Safrit, Caron Beesley, Shashi Bellamkonda, Tim Berry, Gary Schoeniger, Shonali Burke, Lee Tenenbaum, Laura Bennet, Jeff Nischwitz, Bruce Levin, Jason Kealey, Chris Wisbar, Barry Benjamin, Becky Benjamin, Danielle Smith, T.J. McCue, Kimberly Kitchen, Margie Toombs, Ray Toombs, Mike McCormack, Gloria Ferris, Steve Cadwell, Patrick McCoy, Mike Burzminski, Kristi Hines, Brian Clark, Gloria Luzier, Cathy Hay, Don Hay, Paul Hay, Travis Campbell, Derek Halpern, Angie Swartz, Ed Epstein, Roy McKinney, Christopher Ernst, Philip Lathrop, Dickson Dawson, Kelly Brown, Ellen Rowan, Dan Hanson, Doug Hardman, Eric Nusbaum, Andrei Neimanis, Phil Madow, Larry Carnell, Linda Zucker,

Bonnie Diczhazy, Deborah Levinsky, Michael Lamb, Larry Schulman, Melissa Koski, Paula Schleis, KiKi L'Italien, John Heaney, Joseph Grossi, Donnete Smith, Drea Knufken, Scott Allen, Benjamin and Halle Barnett, Josan Garcia, Debbie Obermiller, Chuck Corsillo, Mark Leventhal, Tony Ramos, Peter Vadas, Tom Turner, Mark Geyman, Mark Saige, Anne Barr, Rohit Bhargava, Mari Smith, Peter Biro, Larry Brauner, Mark Siebert, John Siebert, Leslie Carruthers, Keith Clem, Lea Bailes, Anna Sary, Carole Cohen, Mary Patton, Donald Cranford, Diane Thurmann, Sean McGarry, Terry Starbucker, John Crickett, Shara Karasic, Sue Keith, Rene Rodriguez, Diane DiPiero, Brian Sokol, Brian Rosenfelt, Janet Dodrill, Todd Taskey, Jim Evans, Mel Urick, Bridget Ginley, Anne Hach, Andy Halko, Lizette Pirtle, Abby Hawke, Diane Helbig, Matthew Shay, Duncan Campbell, Jerry Herman, Carol Staiger, Julie D'Aloiso, Ted Cligrow, John Sternal, Stephanie Hicks, Kate Hubben, James Young, Sonia Simone, Becky McCray, Susan Wilson-Solovic, Peter Shankman, Susie Sharp, Ursula Petula Barzey, Susan Oakes, Beth Schmitz-Biegler, Flo Schell, Denise Wakeman, Jonathan Fields, Jason Falls, Denise O'Berry, John Warrillow, Darren Rowse, Thursday Bram, Tim Ferris, Justin Jason, Astacia Carter, Shama Kabani, Angie Pohlman, Linda Daichendt, Sue Keith, Sean Kelly, Marcia Pledger, Will Kessel, Barbara Payne, Adrienne Leigh, Wayne Liew, Grant Marquit, Joe Mayer, Ted Jordan, Drew McLellan, Steve Shenberger, Jack Monson, Amber Naslund, Lisa Dilg, Amy Nichols, Regina Olbinsky, Katie O'Toole, Liz Page, Robert Brady, and Nellie Akalp.

Thank you so much.

BECOME A
FRANCHISE
OWNER!

Introduction

IF YOU'RE READING this book, it must mean that you're considering becoming your own boss: congratulations! As they (whoever *they* really are) say, it's all good. In fact, I love franchising. I love its potential. I love being closely involved in the industry. I guess you could say that I'm just a franchise love child.

But before you go quitting your job or selling your house, let me clarify. Just because *I* love franchising doesn't mean that *you* should, too. It is important—vitally important—for you to feel confident that franchising is the right decision for you. Luckily, I'm here to help.

I liken the business of franchising to this: just because your neighbor owns a very successful chain of dry-cleaning franchises doesn't mean that *you* should. After all, you see your neighbor's life from the *outside*. You don't know whether he's in debt up to his eyeballs or if he's a debt-free millionaire. One thing is for sure, he's not home much.

With owning your own business, you'll experience freedom and control like you've never had. You'll probably wish you would have made the decision to become an entrepreneur a lot sooner. You'll expand your business. You'll build equity—*real* equity. You'll rub elbows with other highly successful business owners, and you'll have a blast—*most times*. Other times, small business ownership is just plain ugly. Aardvark ugly. Losing your home ugly. Divorce ugly. Heart attack ugly. You get my drift. UGLY. And *that* is why I wrote this book—to help you avoid ugliness (you're welcome).

1

But before we roll up our sleeves and dive in, it's important for you to know who I am, where I came from, my motivations, and my style.

I like to say that I'm a recovering franchise broker. (Hey, if former attorneys can call themselves *recovering attorneys*, I think that it's okay to borrow part of their term.) Part of my success in helping folks figure out if becoming a franchise owner is really for them has to do with my own experience being a lousy franchisee. I didn't want to follow the system. I felt that *my way* of doing things was better. I used up a ton of energy trying to change the way the franchise operated, but it wasn't really mine to change.

I even developed a franchise quiz of sorts to help you find out if prospective franchise owners should even look at franchise ownership. (You'll have access to this free quiz later in the book.)

My franchise brokering career, sometimes called *franchise consulting*, spanned 10 years, and during that time, I met with hundreds of prospective franchise owners in person and over the phone. My role was that of a matchmaker; I carefully paired together interested *candidates* to franchise concepts that were a fit, based on specific criteria.

I helped a lot of people find opportunities in franchise ownership. Most of them are still in business today.

When the time was right, I became an independent franchise consultant and could choose which franchisors I wanted to work with.

I found that being an independent consultant was a better fit for me. So although I'm *not* a commission-based consultant-broker anymore, I do still work with aspiring franchise owners . . . but in an advisory capacity.

I also help the franchise community with content and social media services. I set up blogs. I help franchisors tell their own unique stories so that they can start attracting high-quality franchise owners. It's something that I've been doing more and more of.

In 2006, I was encouraged to start a blog about franchising.

Being among the first to start a franchise business blog helped establish my brand. I looked at it as a way to differentiate myself and build a loyal following, and it did.

In 2007, I renamed it (in keeping with The Franchise King brand), and it's been The Franchise King Blog ever since (www.thefranchiseking .com/blog). It's really been a game-changer for me. That said, I encourage you at this time to bookmark this page and take a moment to perform an online search for franchise blogs. (After you do that, don't forget to come back to the book!) Did you see where The Franchise King Blog ranked in the results? I've put lots of important information about franchising in the 1,000+ articles that are featured on the blog. Why do *I* get to call them *important*? Because the geniuses at Google, Inc. think they are (if they didn't, the Franchise King Blog wouldn't have a top position in the Google search engine).

Having a top-rated franchise blog has other perks, too.

I made friends with influencers who helped expand my platform. I'm called the Franchise Expert in Residence by Anita Campbell over at Small Business Trends (www.smallbiztrends.com). My annual report on the Top Franchise Trends is one of the most widely read pieces on current franchise trends anywhere.

I'm also a writer for Open Forum by American Express (www.openforum.com), another award-winning small business site, and SBA.gov (www.sba.gov), the U.S. Small Business Administration's website.

When Wiley Publishing approached me about writing a much-needed new book on becoming a franchise owner, I knew exactly what I wanted the book's focus to be on: helping prospective franchise buyers not lose their money in a franchise business, so that they could increase their odds of success. That's my goal for you, and everything that I've included in this book has been designed to do those two things. For example, you're going to meet James Pennington, who, after being downsized from his positions in middle management, sees an advertisement for a franchise opportunity and ends up investing in one. However, James may hold the world record for the number of things he did *wrong* during his search for a franchise and how he went about making his decision to move forward with it.

I feel that history is a great teacher; that's why I've included a brief history of franchising in this book. I hope that you find it interesting, but more importantly, I hope that you'll be able to get a real appreciation for what the early pioneers in franchising did for the franchise industry. After all, if it wasn't for them, you wouldn't be reading this book, contemplating taking your shot at The Dream.

Just because you *want* to become a franchise owner doesn't mean that you *should*. Do you even know if you'd make a good one? In order to help you find out, I've provided a free quiz that will do just that. (I'll even grade it for you, personally, and we'll review the results together.)

Do you know what franchising is? Really? The business model of franchising is very unique, and it's important for you to know all the pieces and all the parts of it. Don't worry; there's a chapter devoted to the business model and the amazing benefits that come with it.

What are your top professional skills? What are you really, really good at? What professional skills do you possess that are just average? I'll help you find out so that you'll only hone in on franchise opportunities that will allow them to shine, which will increase your odds of success.

All of us have a unique set of personality traits (that's part of what makes us unique). I'll show you how to identify the ones that you can use to your advantage in a franchise business. Then you'll learn how to combine those traits with your skills, so you can start to look for a match.

And just how much time *do* you want to spend looking? Do you realize how much of a time-suck you have the potential to be in just by typing the word *franchise* in your favorite search engine? I'm going to show you how to be a laser-focused franchise searching machine so that you won't spend every waking hour searching endlessly online for that *perfect franchise*.

Do you know how much money you should invest in a franchise? Do you know how to do a net worth statement? How much of your own money will you be expected to pony-up? Can you get a grant? All the answers about *the money* will be revealed. You'll see.

Have you ever heard of a franchise broker? Sometimes known as franchise *consultants*, if you're looking for a franchise, you'll eventually run into one. That's because they troll the Internet looking for people just like you. They want nothing more than to offer you their *free* services. You're going to find out why their franchise matchmaking services are free, and more, in a very revealing chapter devoted to that segment of the franchise industry. I know what I'm talking about because I used to be one myself!

If you do *this* right, you'll be able to sleep well at night. I'm talking about franchise research. It's the most important part of the franchise buying process, and it's the longest chapter of the book. I'll be showing you a step-by-step way to do proper franchise research. It's not difficult, but it does take time (if you want to do it right). If you're at all tempted to skip a chapter, don't make it *that* one.

You'll learn all about Discovery Day. This is the day that you pay a visit to the headquarters of the franchise you're really interested in. But you can't just pay them a visit. You'll have to be invited. And, if you *do* happen to get invited, should you always show up? You may be surprised at my answer.

If you think that you'll need a small business loan, don't even think of walking into your local bank without a business plan. What's the matter? You never wrote one yourself? Did you know that there's free help available to help you do just that? I'll show you where and how.

Lawyers. Did you know that a franchise contract is more than one-page long? It's actually 20 to 30 pages in length, and there's almost always some legal Latin thrown in to confuse and amuse. I'm kidding; why would any legal document ever be written up for the express purpose of confusing the reader? After all, everyone who's ever wanted to become a franchise owner has gone to law school and has a complete understanding of legalese. The bottom line is that you're going to need a lawyer and not just any lawyer. You'll see.

Decision Day. That's right; eventually you're going to have to make a yes or no decision on becoming a franchisee of the franchise that you've been laser-focused on. I'll walk you through it and more.

I'm primed and ready to give you the best advice on franchising out there. I've lived in the trenches following up and reporting on the trends in franchising for years. I've been able to help lots of people get into franchise businesses as a broker and, more recently, as an advisor. At the beginning of this brief introduction, I told you that I really love franchising, that I love its potential, and that maybe I'm a franchise love child. Well, perhaps *franchise love child* isn't the right term. As a matter of fact, I don't think that I'm a franchise love child after all. Perhaps, just perhaps, I'm the Franchise King.

1

About James

"Learn from the mistakes of others—you can never live long enough to make them all yourself."

—John Luther

THERE'S ONE HUGE mistake that most prospective franchise owners make when they start searching for a franchise business to buy, and it is the following: *They start their search for a franchise by searching for a franchise.*

Read that over again.

Are you with me?

I didn't think so.

Maybe if I tell you a story. . . .

James Pennington only had four jobs in his 20-year career—the one he got right out of college and the ones he got after that. After receiving his business degree at The University of Chicago Booth School of Business in 1990, he scored a nice management position at the Spring-Flash Lighting Company. He excelled there and started moving up the company ladder. James married his college sweetheart, bought a small house in the Chicago suburb of Northbrook—complete with a white

7

picket fence—and settled down. A couple of years later, he and Marcia (his wife) had their first child, and a year later, their second.

James enjoyed the work he did at Spring-Flash and gradually received an increasing amount of responsibility—including the added stress that went along with it. However, he was fine with the stress; his ever-growing paychecks made it more palatable.

Back at home, things were happy, but a little cramped. James and Marcia's three-bedroom home didn't have a lot of extra room for storage and such, so the Penningtons put it up for sale and bought a larger home less than a mile away.

Shortly after they moved in to their new home, James was offered the position of vice president (VP) of sales for a new lighting division being launched at Spring-Fast, which he gladly accepted. This new role put James in charge of getting some new and very cutting-edge products into the hands of key decision makers at all of the major lighting chains. Hs job involved lots of travel and lots of product presentations. These new products were getting great reviews, as was James.

One Tuesday morning, James's administrative assistant Janet connected him to a call from someone who wanted to pay him a compliment regarding a recent presentation he made at one of the lighting industry conferences. James took the call from an individual who began the conversation this way.

"James, your name has been mentioned to me several times in the last few months, and I hear that you are really one to watch."

James was flattered, of course, and replied, "Thank you so much. Our new products are doing really well, and I'm grateful to be involved."

The man continued. "My name is Tim Adams, and I'm an executive recruiter with CCM. We specialize in finding great sales executives for companies that need to get things to the next level, which is why I'm reaching out to you today. We're working with a company that I feel could use your expertise, and may be a nice fit for you. Are you interested in learning a little bit more about this possible career opportunity?"

"I'm not really sure. I get one or two calls a month from folks like you, and I'm pretty happy with my situation."

"I understand. But would you at least be open to learning more about the position and this cutting-edge company?"

"I'm just not sure. The opportunity would have to be pretty amazing for me to even consider leaving Spring-Flash."

"This *is* one of those amazing opportunities, James. It's with a publically held company, and they're offering a generous amount of stock options . . . for the right candidate, of course. Their salary package is . . . well . . . amazing, too."

"I guess it wouldn't hurt to spend some time learning a little more about this position."

"I was hoping you'd say that, James."

Two months later, James left his successful 16-year career at the Spring-Flash Lighting Company for *greener* pastures. You see, ComfortLites, Inc.—the young company that had recruited him—was headquartered in Portland, Oregon.

Thanks to the generous salary, sizeable amount of stock options, and wonderful relocation package, James didn't have too difficult a time convincing Marcia that they had to take this shot. While their kids weren't too enthusiastic about leaving their friends behind, the Penningtons assured them that they would make wonderful new friends in Portland.

Things went pretty well for the first year or so. James secured some great new (and *large*) customers for his new employer, and the family was getting used to their new community, just outside of Portland.

Then things started to get a bit strained during James's second year at ComfortLites. First, his division's president was abruptly let go. Word on the street was that ComfortLites had stolen the idea for one of their hottest products directly from a competitor and that a lawsuit was in the process of being filed against them.

This lawsuit *was* filed later in the year, and it was the first of many that would be filed against ComfortLites. They were prohibited from selling any of the lighting products in question until the matters were settled in court.

Eventually, James's division was closed down, and he was downsized. He received a ridiculously low severance package—and unless the company would be able to pull out a last-minute miracle, his stock options were going to be absolutely worthless.

As one can imagine, things at home were a bit tense for awhile with James out of work. However, he was able to secure a management position, after only six months of being unemployed, at a Portland area packaging company called Mingley Packaging. He wasn't hired as a VP, but he *was* in middle management, and the salary package wasn't too bad.

James traveled quite a bit in his role as sales director. He was in his element, which involved making lots of high-level presentations and securing new customers for the company. He performed well enough to eventually be promoted to the VP of sales, a position that had recently become available.

James ended up staying at the packaging company for five years, until they downsized—and he was once again let go. This time, it was "because of a slowing economy," according to the rather timid human resources director—the person who gave James the bad news. James was so absolutely shocked that he was just let go and stormed out of the office, briefcase in hand. After all, James thought to himself, he had brought his company Mingley well over $15 million in new business during his tenure. The "slowing economy" didn't seem to be affecting the company all *that* much.

So, once again, James was job hunting and managing to land a couple of interviews. However, things felt a lot different during the interviews this time around. He tried to put his finger on it, but couldn't.

When James mentioned these feelings during one of his job-search networking activities, several people told him that his age was probably starting to play a negative role in his interviews.

He couldn't believe it; he was 49 years old, in pretty good physical shape, and even looked a lot younger than 49. He wondered aloud if "this is how it's going to be now?" He was angry. He was also getting depressed.

One month later, however, James landed a job.

The Portland Lighting Warehouse certainly wasn't his first choice in a new job; however, it was available. He was hired on as shipping and receiving supervisor and would be taking a 40 percent pay cut. But the hospitalization plan was great, and his office was only 10 minutes from home.

However, James's dip in salary couldn't have come at a worse time; his oldest child, Marie, was deciding between two good universities, both of which were pretty expensive. Though Marie would be getting a little scholarship money, it would barely make a dent. Things were tight. And the atmosphere at home was *electric*.

Of course, the wattage *really* increased when—after only seven months of working at his new position—James was let go once again. His supervisor told him that Portland Lighting Warehouse was cutting staff because of the recession but that "they really liked him." James was instructed to "exit the building," which he did, with one flimsy cardboard box in hand. He knew that his 10-minute ride home would feel a lot longer that day.

He didn't even bother to call Marcia while on his way home. Actually, he pulled into the parking lot of a local fast food chain and turned off his car. He sat there shaking his head and wondering out loud, "How could this happen to me? *Now* what am I supposed to do?" It was well before lunch, so there was really no one else around.

James sat in the quiet of his car and relived the last 24 years of his professional career. Things had started out really well. He secured a great job right out of college and learned a lot about business in his 12 years at Spring-Flash. He had been promoted a few times and was pretty happy there. He got so good that others in his industry were taking notice; heck, an executive-level recruiter called *him*! The job for which he was recruited was a great one, with impressive pay and even stock options. He liked the fast pace and entrepreneurial spirit that the young company had, that is, while it lasted. Too bad that job only lasted two years. And those stock options—well, they were worth about $200 now, and he was thinking of cashing them in—and fast.

He felt lucky to get his next job after only six months of looking; Mingley Packaging was a pretty good place to work, and it enabled him to learn about the shipping industry. He liked it there. He did a great job for the company and brought in many new customers—customers that Mingley Packaging might have never had a chance to even present to. But it wasn't enough, he supposed, because he was let go from that job, too.

And now this; how was he going to tell Marcia that he got fired yet again? What would he tell his kids? He was absolutely dreading going home.

James knew that things would settle down in a few days at home and that he'd have to pick himself up by his bootstraps and get another job. Ugh. That thought alone made him *not* want to start his car and head home. He really didn't feel like updating his resume (again!). He didn't feel like doing what he called *The Interview Shuffle*—putting on his suit and shuffling from one job interview to the next, knowing that although most of them were probably a total waste of time, he still had to show up looking perfect and pressed.

James was just about to start his car when another unwelcome thought entered his mind: his age. He wondered just how many companies in the area were anxiously waiting for a 50-year-old, recently fired middle manager to appear for an interview. And the question of just how he was going to pay for Marie's college education was also appearing in the Top 10 "What the heck am I going to do now?" hit parade that was currently going on inside his head.

He knew it was time for him to head home.

■ ■ ■

Marcia was really angry—not at James, though. She was angry at the situation. She knew that her husband was incredibly smart and talented; after all, they had done pretty well through the years. Amazingly, Marcia wasn't freaking out (totally) about money. They had managed to save some over time, which was something that really helped her cope (at least initially) with her husband's firing. Though reality began to settle in a few months later when they wrote a $20,000+ check for Marie's first year of college; they *were* able to work through that process together by taking lots of deep breaths.

Having some money in the bank allowed the Pennington's to breathe a bit; the issue was that they weren't collecting any income to replace it. The $400 a week that James received in unemployment benefits only paid for their electric bill and part of their cell phone bill. It was, of course, a mounting problem.

And there was another problem brewing: James was angry. He'd worked really hard for over 20 years. He was an honest a guy who'd always put in the extra effort required to excel at all of the jobs he'd ever had. Now he felt like he had nothing to show for it. As a matter of fact, he felt like a big, fat loser.

James was also starting to get resentful. He resented the fact that it didn't seem to matter how well he had performed at any of the corporations at which he worked; they still let him go whenever they downsized, which was something that really troubled him. How was it that he brought these companies serious profits, which helped their bottom lines, but they sent him packing anyway? He started to question if it was all worth it anymore.

For the next few weeks, he did the usual things that people must do when they're out of a job; he updated his resume; he attended networking events; and he had lunch with folks that he thought could help him in his job search. He spent a couple of hours on his computer every day, scouring the online job boards, visiting LinkedIn, and engaging in other assorted job-seeking online activities—all to no avail. It was tough out there now, and the U.S. economy was sinking even more deeply into a recession. James was getting worried. He started to wonder if he'd ever find a job.

One day, while searching online for some ideas, he came across an advertisement proclaiming the following:

Don't Get Another Job

Become a Franchise Owner Instead

Become Your Own Boss!

James hadn't really thought of not getting another job although the way things were currently going, it just might work out that way. The reality of the situation was that James wasn't getting any younger, companies weren't presently hiring, and his measly unemployment checks were about to stop coming.

James thought to himself that maybe he *should* look into owning a business. He approached Marcia with this idea.

James: Honey, maybe I should look into owning a business.
Marcia: Oh really? Like what?
James: No idea, really. Probably a franchise of some type.
Marcia: So, like a Subway, or a McDonald's?
James: Maybe. Heck, I don't know. *Something.*
Marcia: Why are you thinking about this all of a sudden?
James: Because the job market is terrible right now, and I'm getting nowhere in my search.
Marcia: So—why a franchise or, for that matter, why a business? And exactly how much money are we talking about here, Mr. Trump?
James: Well, I haven't really gotten that far yet.
Marcia: Let me know when you do. I'm sure you understand that I'm a little nervous about this idea of yours.
James: I know. I know . . . but I don't really know what else to do.

Now that James had Marcia's permission (really?) to start looking around for a franchise, that is just what he did. He spent hours every day looking at all of the different franchise websites. He even managed to gather up enough courage to request a couple of brochures from some franchise companies. He essentially put his job search on hold and began getting excited about the possibilities. He found it incredibly energizing to participating in something so totally different from the typical corporate job search in which he'd engaged so many times before. As a matter of fact, he pretty much had lost his desire to even look for a job; he knew what he wanted. He wanted to be his own boss!

He didn't bother telling more than a couple of people of his new idea because he was a little worried about it getting completely shot down. James was a man on a mission!

Though James had entertained occasional thoughts about opening up his own business throughout the years, he never really investigated anything. After all, he really didn't have to; he was bringing home some nice paychecks.

Marcia pretty much let James do his own thing in regard to looking around for a franchise business. He had told her that if he got serious about something, he would share it with her at that point, which seemed fine with her.

For some reason, James was attracted to food franchises—sub shops, ice cream shops, and pizza places. These types of franchises popped up all the time on websites and even in magazines and newspapers. He had no problem visualizing himself running a food franchise. He pictured himself rolling up his sleeves and pitching in when his store was shorthanded or had just gotten a rush of new customers bursting in the door. He also had pictures in his mind of his wife and kids pitching in and helping out; heck, they could even work there! James was bursting at the seams and couldn't wait to get started with something.

Now that he had a nice image in his head of the kind of franchise he wanted, he started to request information from several food franchises. As his brochure collection grew, he tried to figure out which one or maybe even which two to pick out and contact. Though he had received calls and e-mails from almost all of the franchise salespeople, he wasn't ready to call them back. He wanted to look at their brochures and learn all he could about them.

So far, James was focusing most closely on two food franchises; a big-name submarine sandwich shop and a pizza franchise that looked pretty interesting. He contacted both of them and awaited their calls back. The pizza franchise sales representative called back first; actually, he called James back about a half hour after James called him.

This man, Tim Pierce, seemed pleasant enough; he gave James a basic rundown of the opportunity, including some history, where some of the current locations were, and total costs involved. James would have to invest between $250,000 to $350,000 for this franchise. There weren't any 23-Topping Pizza franchises in the suburban Portland area as of yet, so he would have first dibs in his choice of location—something that would be a huge advantage, according to Tim.

Teresa Blair from the big-name submarine sandwich chain called the following day. She wanted to schedule an online webinar for James to attend. She explained that the webinar would really help James understand how things worked in their franchise and that there would even be a question and answer (Q&A) session with a couple of current franchise owners at its completion. James told her that he'd attend it and added it to his online calendar.

Meanwhile, Tim from 23-Topping Pizza had sent James an e-mail with more information, including something called a *franchise disclosure document* (FDD). Tim had explained that he was required by law send this to James; James even had to sign an online form acknowledging that he'd received it. The FDD was almost 250 pages long. Tim told James that he'd eventually want to print it out but to look it over in the meantime and write down any questions he'd have. James looked over the FDD for about an hour and then went back to reading the shiny brochure again.

James also attended the webinar with the submarine sandwich chain, which he found pretty interesting. He learned that the company had over 25,000 franchises throughout the world and that they wanted a lot more. The people running the webinar were really aggressive and seemed pretty hard-sell. They also came across like they were plenty busy and shared as much. They stated that they were only interested in talking to people who were "really ready to pull the trigger on buying a franchise" as they had plenty of people inquiring. It kind of turned James off, truth be told. He talked with Teresa after the webinar was over and told her that he'd think about the opportunity some more and get back to her.

However, James really had no intention of calling Teresa back, nor did he have to "think about the opportunity." He didn't like the way the folks at corporate headquarters came across, so he eliminated this franchise opportunity. Plus, he was really starting to like 23-Topping Pizza—a lot.

James spent the next week using various Internet search engines to find out all the information he could about 23-Topping Pizza. It actually didn't seem as though there was a lot of information available.

He discovered that they had been around for about five years and that they currently had 25 franchises scattered throughout the United States, mostly around the New Jersey area, because that's where their headquarters were located. He also searched to see if there were any complaints registered with the Better Business Bureau and didn't find anything—which he took as a positive sign.

James told Tim during their next phone call that he was very interested in the opportunity and wanted to know what he would have to do to get the ball rolling. Tim informed him that the next step he'd have to take would be to schedule a visit to franchise headquarters for a Discovery Day. James didn't know what a Discovery Day was, but he agreed to attend one anyway. Tim came up with a couple of dates, and James told him that he would have to check with his wife and get back to him.

That night at dinner, James told Marcia that he had found a franchise that really interested him. He explained that it was a pizza franchise out of New Jersey and that it looked like a winner. The concept featured 23 topping combinations, and that was one of things that set it apart from all the other pizza franchises. He went through some of the other particulars, including how much it would cost, how long it would take to open up, and a few other interesting tidbits about the franchise itself. When Marcia asked him what he knew about pizza, he told her that the important part of the business was the *business* part—not the pizza-making activities.

In fact, the question that Marcia asked concerning his knowledge (or, in James's case, his utter lack of knowledge) about pizza kind of bothered him. He thought that it was a strange question and shrugged it off as a result of some nervousness that Marcia was probably experiencing.

Tim suggested that James bring Marcia to the Discovery Day as it was important for her to see the operation and meet the principals. James asked Marcia if she wanted to fly out to New Jersey to attend it, but she told James that this was his baby and stayed at home. She figured that she'd learn more than enough about it when James came back to town and told her everything about the franchise.

Tim and James had one more call before James's Discovery Day. Tim explained that the day would include a tour of headquarters, short meetings with the executive staff, and a couple of stops at some up and running 23-Topping Pizza franchise locations. Tim also mentioned that James would be leaving with a franchise contract to look over so that he could make a decision on whether to move forward as a 23-Topping Pizza franchisee. James felt a little twinge in his stomach during the last part of that phone call with Tim; however, it quickly passed, and he figured that it was normal to be a little nervous about investing money in a business.

Tim's Discovery Day came up really fast, and, as his plane landed at Newark Liberty International Airport, he reflected for a moment. It felt a little strange to be going out of town on business, but in a totally different way. The "on business" part had to do with potentially *his* business. Wow. Double wow, actually. His pulse started racing and he felt himself breaking out in a bit of a sweat; was he nuts? What was he thinking? He had a mortgage, a spouse who didn't work, and two beautiful children—including one that was just starting an expensive private college. $250,000 was a lot of money. What if this pizza franchise turned out to be a total bust? Could he, a 50-year-old man—recover from a $250,000+ loss in enough time to have *some* semblance of a retirement? Would Marcia resent him forever if he failed at this business? Maybe this was a crazy idea, and he should just turn around and go home, so he could start his job hunt again, this time in earnest. It sounded a lot safer all of a sudden.

As promised, a driver was standing by to take James to the 23-Topping Pizza headquarters—a ride that took about 45 minutes. Although he was still feeling a bit nervous, a smile started to appear on his face. The thought of not working for someone else was starting to overshadow his fear of failing and losing money.

Tim greeted James at the main door to headquarters, and they proceeded inside. Tim asked James some polite questions about how his flight was and so on and then showed James into a well-lit conference room. Tim sat down next to James and laid out an agenda for the day.

- Tour of headquarters
- Meet and greets with the chief executive officer (CEO) and other members of the executive team
- Private meeting with the CEO

- Lunch at the 23-Topping Pizza flagship restaurant
- Two-hour personal meeting with a franchisee at his location
- Back to headquarters for a recap/Q&A
- Presentation of the formal franchise contract
- Transportation back to Newark Airport

The Discovery Day went by incredibly fast, and the highlight was the two hours that James spent with Jimmy Fanzika, who owned two franchises of 23-Topping Pizza. Because James had arrived after the lunch rush, there was plenty of time for him to look around and ask some questions. Jimmy shared his story of how he came to be a franchise owner of 23-Topping Pizza and how things were going with his two restaurants.

Jimmy came from a long line of restaurant owners. His parents had owned a local restaurant for 40 years, and Jimmy worked there until he started college. Though he liked the business, he wanted something that he could call his own. After college, he decided to open up his own pizza restaurant. He did, and his little restaurant did pretty well until about three years before. A couple of other stores located in the strip center where his store was located went out of business, and the landlord was having problems filling the empty spaces. The recession was just around the corner, and not too many people were launching new businesses. Jimmy's restaurant suffered—big time, that is, until someone from 23-Topping Pizza stopped by and made Jimmy an offer that he couldn't refuse.

The offer was this:

23-Topping Pizza would come in and convert Jimmy's independent pizza restaurant into a 23-Topping Pizza *franchise*. Because most of the equipment needed for operating a 23-Topping Pizza was already in place, Jimmy would only have to pay the $30,000 franchise fee, invest in an interior makeover (to match the colors of 23-Topping Pizza), and change the signage. So, instead of coming up with around $250,000 for a brand new 23-Topping Pizza franchise operation, he would only have to invest in a *conversion franchise*, and he could be up and running in no time flat!

Jimmy told James that he felt that he really didn't have much choice, and that's why he became a franchisee of 23-Topping Pizza. He shared

James's fears about becoming a franchisee; he was used to being the one running the show, which included doing all of the marketing, coming up with new menu ideas, and the like. He liked his independence.

And then there was his family. While they certainly supported his dream of starting his own restaurant from scratch—and even helped him with his initial investment—they also knew that he was struggling lately. He told James that at first, his family wasn't too fond of the idea of turning the restaurant into a franchise. But times were tough, and they didn't want Jimmy to have to close his restaurant. So they gave Jimmy their blessing—along with about $50,000.

Things ended up working out pretty well for Jimmy; he recently opened up his second location and really likes the product. Jimmy also was nice enough to verbally share some of his profit and loss data with James during his visit, along with some other pertinent information about marketing, operations, and personnel.

The driver outside of Jimmy's restaurant who was waiting to take James back to franchise headquarters beeped a couple of times, signaling that it was time for James to get going. He thanked Jimmy for his time and left for his final couple hours of Discovery Day.

James's mind was racing almost as much as the car in which he was riding; it was a whirlwind of a day so far and more than a little overwhelming—but in a good way. He got to taste the food. He got to visit privately with a current franchisee, who shared some of his franchise's financial information. Now it was time for the serious stuff: the franchise contract. Though James knew that he wasn't expected to sign it that very day, he was starting to feel uptight about the legal ramifications of franchise ownership, not that he was all that well-acquainted with what those were.

James sat down with Tim in a small private office, where they went over the 25-page franchise agreement methodically. Tim asked James if he had any questions. He didn't really have any about the franchise agreement right away, but he did have a question about four lawsuits that he had read about in the FDD a couple of weeks before.

Tim told him that three out of the four lawsuits were against franchisees that weren't paying their agreed-upon royalties. These franchisees were supposed to be paying 6 percent of their gross sales to corporate, but they had all fallen behind by several months, so 23-Topping Pizza sued and won. Tim also told James that one franchisee stayed around after that and was currently doing pretty well. The other two went out of business.

The other lawsuit was over a location—or a lack thereof, as Tim explained. He shared that a husband-and-wife team had purchased a franchise that they were planning to open up in Lansing, Michigan. The couple looked at 10 potential locations at which to open their franchise but couldn't decide which one would be best. They had called corporate headquarters for suggestions and got a couple; however, no one there really knew too much about that part of Michigan. After about a year of failing to decide upon a spot for their store, the couple sued 23-Topping Pizza for "not working hard enough helping them find a suitable location." Tim told James that the two settled out of court and were no longer franchisees. James asked Tim why corporate didn't help more, and Tim told him that they did all they could, but the couple was "just kind of wacky."

James then asked Tim a couple of questions about the franchise contract, which Tim was able to answer satisfactorily.

On his way out the door to grab his ride back to the airport, Tim shook his hand and told him that if he liked what he saw during his Discovery Day visit, he should get the signed franchise contract back to him within a week or two, along with his check for $30,000 for the franchise fee. James said, "okay" and got in the car.

James could hardly contain his ear-to-ear smile during his ride to the Newark Liberty International Airport. His decision was made; he just had to do a bit of selling when he got back home.

After James shared details of his Discovery Day, he told Marcia that he really needed and wanted her support in this venture. Marcia was not entirely convinced. On one hand, she believed in her husband. He was a hard worker who didn't take lots of risks. Plus, it wasn't like his phone was ringing with amazing job offers. On the other hand, the prospect of investing a quarter of a million dollars into a pizza franchise—with no guarantee that it would even be successful—frightened her. But she didn't want James to sense her fear.

Before they signed the franchise agreement, James thought it best if he had an attorney look it over. Marcia's uncle—a corporate attorney—told James that he'd be happy to look at it; however, he also warned James that he wasn't really very well versed in franchise laws. James faxed it over to him and awaited his call back.

Two days later, Marcia's uncle called him and told him that he really didn't see anything strange on the contract. As far as he could tell, everything looked pretty standard. James thanked him for getting to it quickly and made a mental note to make sure that he asked Marcia to send him a nice package of Omaha Steaks (or something in that genre.)

At dinner that evening, he told Marcia that her uncle didn't see anything out of the ordinary and that he really wanted to do this. Moneywise, they had access to the $30,000 he would need for the franchise fee. The other $200,000 or so he could get from a combination of stocks that he could sell and a business loan that he should be able to secure at their local bank. It would still leave them in *pretty* good shape for his daughter's college education costs.

The next morning, both James and Marcia signed the 23-Topping Pizza franchise contract and sent it to Tim—along with their check for $30,000.

The first bank that Marcia and James visited declined their small business loan application, and told them that they wanted more collateral. Five stressful weeks later, an out of town bank approved their request for a $225,000 loan.

At that point, James started scouting out locations. He was now working with Blake Dannon, the director of operations at 23-Topping Pizza. Because 23-Topping Pizza didn't have a real estate department, Blake handled the franchise's new location openings. He was good at operations, for sure; however, Blake himself was still kind of learning the ropes about commercial real estate and all of the complexities involved therein.

Blake had contacted James right after his small business loan had been approved and told him to start driving around to see if he could find any suitable space for his new pizza franchise. So that's exactly what James did. He wanted to find his location, and fast. He had visions of customers standing outside the door of his brand new franchise and wanted to make them a reality as quickly as he could.

James came upon a couple of what he thought were good places to open a pizza franchise. The next thing he did was to contact the commercial real estate brokers whose names and numbers were right on the windows of the empty retail spaces he was interested in. These individuals called back in rapid fashion, and James set up meetings with each one of them at the locations they were representing.

The first location that James visited was really nice. It had been a restaurant until about a year ago, but the broker told James that it had closed down because the owner was having health issues. The broker gave James the particulars, including the price per square foot and the types of leasehold improvements that would be needed to make it right for his franchise. James told him that he'd think about it and went on to see the second location that he liked.

The second location was a lot smaller than the first; however, it was situated in a new strip mall center. It was a brand new space, and the broker told James that he had been looking to place a restaurant of some type in the space. The two discussed prices and also talked about what it would take to build-out the space and make it into a pizza restaurant. James really liked the second space that he saw.

James reported back to Blake with his findings, and Blake told him that he thought that James's second choice (the newer space) may be too small. Blake said that the larger one would probably be better, but because he didn't really know the area, he wasn't sure about the location itself. He said he would talk to the CEO and get back to him.

James really liked the newer retail space; it smelled good inside, and the strip center itself was really sharp. There were several eclectic shops up and down the strip center, and, even though they didn't look busy that day, the broker assured him that they were most of the time.

Blake got back to James a couple of days later and told him that the CEO agreed that although the space in the newer location was kind of small, the final decision was up to James. They would approve the location as long as James liked it and felt the area would be good for a

23-Topping Pizza franchise. James signed the five-year lease for the space (the smaller space) in the strip mall a few days later.

The flight to New Jersey seemed to go a lot faster than the last time. James couldn't wait to attend the one-week training class at 23-Topping Pizza's headquarters because, when training was over, he would be just about ready to open for business. He was ready!

James felt that the training was very thorough that week; he learned how to make pizza, of course. He also learned about inventory control, cash management, payroll, marketing, advertising, and human resources—along with a few other things that he couldn't really remember all that well. It *was* a little overwhelming, but he kind of figured it would be and didn't mind that his head was spinning as he got into the car that would be taking him to the Newark Airport so that he could catch his flight back to Portland.

He had a lot to do; he had to make sure that his restaurant would be ready by April 19, the day of his grand opening.

James was able to pull it off; he opened his new franchise business on April 19, as planned. It was a festive day as the mayor and several other local dignitaries showed up for the official ribbon-cutting ceremony. Lots of backslapping took place, and everybody seemed to love the restaurant and, of course, the free food.

Marcia was there every day at the beginning; she kept the dining area looking spotless, scheduled the staff, and generally helped to make sure things ran smoothly. She usually stayed until the lunch rush was over so she could get back home in time to see her teenager, who usually got back from school around 3:00 p.m. or so. She would hang out with them for a little while and then get back to the restaurant in time for the dinner rush, which was mostly take-out—but she helped keep things humming along. Sometimes one or even both of their kids (when their daughter was home from college) would come back with her and help out.

James, however, was there all the time. Fifteen-hour workdays were the norm. He was exhausted when he came home, but he didn't mind it too, too, much; after all, this is what he wanted. He wanted to be his own boss.

For awhile, that is.

It wasn't the 15-hour days, seven days a week that sent James over the edge. It wasn't even the fact that he hadn't had a day off for seven months (not that he was counting). It was the kids. Not his own kids, mind you. It was the 10 part-time, pimply-faced terrors that were his employees and who had a 30 percent tardy rate combined, that is, when they even *bothered* to show up.

James was near the end of his rope. He had already been through almost 50 employees since opening in April. It seemed that he spent most of his time hiring, training, or firing his employees. Even worse was the fact that he was starting to get the feeling that his current crop of recruits was about as good as it was ever going to get.

James was one extremely stressed franchise owner. When he first started considering this opportunity, he was focused on becoming a successful multi-unit franchise owner. Now he couldn't even *begin* to think about a second location; he never seemed to have enough employees to run his current one, which meant that he couldn't leave his restaurant long enough to do anything, let alone start looking for a second location in which to open.

Adding to James's stress level was the fact that Marcia was starting to hint that she wasn't feeling exactly enthusiastic about coming in every day. She told James that she didn't mind helping but that it was starting to be a real grind. James asked Marcia if she would hang in there for a little longer, for which he received a very unpleasant eye roll in return.

Marcia *did* hang in there for the entire first year that they were in business. That was good. Nothing that followed, however, was anything that a casual observer of the situation would call "good."

The 23-Topping Pizza location located in the Portland Commons shopping center had reached a milestone of sorts; it was still in business exactly one year after being open. The problem was that James didn't feel like celebrating; he just wanted to sleep for two weeks straight.

James and Marcia really had no idea just how hard the food service business was. James was still putting in 15-hour days, seven days a week—and he was *tired*. Marcia had just about had it and was starting to worry about her husband's health. She told James that he needed to get some more help so that he could take off at least a couple of hours every day. She also told him that she couldn't work there anymore unless it was an emergency. She hated dealing with all of the employee hassles and customer complaints; plus, their house was a pigsty because she was hardly ever home.

James had one more, fairly substantial problem: the restaurant was losing money. He couldn't seem to get ahead. The expenses—including what turned out to be a very expensive lease—and other things like rising food costs, employee turnover, and average (at best) sales, were starting to add to his already elevated stress level. Plus, he had already blown through $40,000 of a credit line he established when they opened the doors. Then there was his small business loan. His last payment was two weeks late, which caused his banker to pick up the phone to say hi. (Marcia didn't know anything about that.)

He was barely talking to the folks in New Jersey. You see, James was also two months behind in his royalty payments. So far, he had been pretty successful at avoiding their phone calls. Actually, he was pretty successful at avoiding *lots* of phone calls by this time.

James was able to keep his pizza franchise open for six more months—until he was forced to close up shop. He certainly didn't *want* to close his doors; this would affect 12 other people because they would be out of a job. He felt bad about that. He felt a lot worse about the $300,000 that he just lost—not to mention two years of looking for and then opening the business.

Marcia felt pretty bad, too. She felt sorry for her husband; he had stepped up to the plate, big time. He was at the business all the time. He tried like hell to take care of his usually flaky employees, all the while attempting be a good husband throughout this experience. (It was too bad he was so tired all the time.)

The following few months were brutal as James tried to work things out with the bank. He had to *lawyer up* and deal with the royalties that he owed 23-Topping Pizza Corporation. His lawyer also had to help him with the strip center's landlord. He owed him some money, too. Actually, if you want to get technical, James owed rent for 3.5 more years. (Remember, his lease was for five years.) Of course, the state wanted their unemployment and sales taxes. And the Internal Revenue Service (IRS) needed James to write a couple of checks, too. The pressure was on. "Hey," he said to himself. "At least college was half paid for."

Oh, and one more thing; he had to get his resume pressed and cleaned for what was sure to be an exciting time for this 50-something year old former executive and middle manager.

He decided that he needed to go somewhere—anywhere. He got into his car and just started driving. He cranked up his favorite radio station and cruised around for about an hour. It was like he was on autopilot.

He really had no idea how he ended up in the parking lot of the same exact fast food chain that he had been in just two years earlier. He turned off his car and reminisced for a little while. The last time he sat in this parking lot he had just been fired. He was full of fear and wasn't quite ready to go home and tell Marcia that he lost his job—again. It had been a tough day.

This time, as he sat in his car, he thought about his decision to be in business for himself. His motives were good; he was sick of the corporate thing, and he wanted to take a chance at The Dream. Now his dream was shot; he had lost a lot of money, and it was going to take a long time to climb out of the financial hole that he had created in just two short years. He wondered if he was ever going to be able to make up for a $300,000 loss.

As James looked back on his franchise ownership experience, he started wondering what he did wrong. Was it all his fault? Did he choose a lousy franchise concept to buy? Was it too expensive? Did he select the wrong location? Should he have asked Marcia to become more involved in the daily duties? He pounded the dashboard of his car and yelled out, "What happened?"

■ ■ ■

The above was a work of fiction. I don't know a James or Marcia Pennington. There is no pizza franchise called 23-Topping Pizza. The companies mentioned in the story don't exist. The University of Chicago's Booth School of Business does; as does the community of Northbrook, Illinois. Portland, Oregon is real, too.

The story above is sort of a mash-up of the kinds of things I've seen happen with people just like James over the years. Lots of folks that I worked with in an advisory role were downsized executives. Lots of the folks that I *didn't work with* were, too. But they decided to seek out franchises to buy on their own.

Some of people that chose to go at it alone actually ended up contacting me again. However, it was usually too late for them by this time. Their franchises were failing, and they were looking for a way out.

I wonder if they were sitting in their cars much like James was when they called me, hoping that I could come up with a miracle of some type, to help save them from financial ruin.

James made a ton of mistakes. Deciding to go out and find a franchise to buy *on his own* was the first one.

Now I'm sure that there are lots of very successful franchise owners who were able to find and research franchises pretty much on their own. That's fantastic. Some of their success has to do with luck. Some of it may have to do with amazing business acumen. Some of it was probably timing or even geography. It happens to some people some of the time—and I wish for their continued success!

However, this is not the norm. Most people who are considering opening a franchise do exactly what James did; they start looking at different franchises, get some brochures (online and offline), and then try to figure out what's what.

That's a mistake. As a matter of fact, this was James's second mistake. He started his search for a franchise by searching for a franchise. I don't want you to do that.

Once you determine that franchise ownership is for you, I'm going to teach you a much better way of going about selecting and researching franchises. The great thing is that if you commit to following all of my suggestions that are contained in this book, you'll increase your chances of success as a franchise owner.

You're okay with that, right?

Let's move on to the next chapter. I'm going to show you where to start your search for a franchise business and how to customize that search—just for you.

2

A Brief History of Franchising, Briefly

"In the business world, the rearview mirror is always clearer than the windshield."

—Warren Buffett

OUR JOURNEY INTO the history of franchising starts in a much simpler time. It was a time when automated teller machines (ATMs) and iPhone apps didn't exist—a time in which lots and lots of give and take was needed merely to survive: the Middle Ages.

The Middle Ages weren't known as the best of times in human history, and in all honestly, it probably wasn't a very pleasant time to be alive. There were hundreds of famines in Europe, a continent who lost a third (perhaps even more) of their population to the Black Death plague. Working class folks who didn't feel they were getting paid fair wages were constantly staging violent uprisings, and there was a great amount of discontent and conflict having to do with religion.

The Middle Ages also happened to be when the business model of franchising started to appear. (At least one positive event occurred amid all that suffering.)

Back then, some of the local governments granted high church officials (and others considered to be important) a license to maintain order and assess taxes. Medieval courts or lords gave these individuals the right to operate ferries, hold markets, and perform business-related activities. These *franchisees* paid a royalty to these lords in exchange for, among other things, protection that was essentially considered to be a monopoly on commercial ventures. Over time, the regulations that governed franchises became a part of European Common Law.

The Colonial period was the next period during which franchising really started to take hold. It also happens to be my favorite part of franchise history, as it involved *Franchise Kings*. The local sovereign or lord would authorize individuals to hold markets or fairs, operate the local ferry, or to hunt on his land. This concept extended to the kings, who would grant a franchise for all types of commercial activities including building roads and even brewing ale. European monarchs (who were technically close enough to being kings themselves) even bestowed franchises upon entrepreneurs who agreed to take on the risk of establishing colonies. Once these colonies were created, their founders were able to gain the protection of the Crown in exchange for taxes or royalties.

Let's take a quick break on the topic of the history of franchising and take a walk down the hall to the language arts wing. The word *franchise* is derived from the Anglo-French phrase that means "liberty" or "privilege or freedom." The *Free Merriam-Webster Dictionary* defines *franchise* as follows:

1. Freedom or immunity from some burden or restriction vested in a person or group;

2. a: Special privilege granted to an individual or group; *especially*: the right to be and exercise the powers of a corporation; b: A constitutional or statutory right or privilege; *especially*: the right to vote; c: (1) The right or license granted to an individual or group to market a company's goods or services in a particular territory; also a business granted such a right or license; (2) the territory involved in such a right

3. a: The right of membership in a professional sports league; b: A team and its operating organization having such membership

Your language arts lesson is now complete. Let's return now to the history wing and continue where we left off in our lesson on franchising's background.

The modern franchise business model can be traced back to an entrepreneurial giant by the name of Isaac Merrit Singer. In the 1800s, there was nothing automatic about manufacturing clothes. Everything was stitched together by hand, in not-too-ideal working conditions. The women who did the sewing worked incredibly long hours—and, of course, everyday housewives had to do a good deal of sewing, too. It was a tedious process for anyone completing it.

Isaac Merritt Singer was the founder of I. M. Singer & Company and the first person to patent a practical, widely used sewing machine. Though these machines started to appear on the scene in the mid 1800s—and worked pretty well—Singer came up with an idea that made them work even better: a *lot* better. So he started selling them, and, despite the fact that the sewing machines were fairly expensive (about $125 each), Singer established a system that would make them far less cost-prohibitive for the people who needed to buy them the most. One of his partners came up with the idea to introduce the first-ever payment installment plan, which required customers to pay $1.15 per day over the course of a month for their brand-new sewing machines. This pay-per-day method allowed people who couldn't afford the somewhat hefty price tag all at once to purchase the product within their means—and initiated a system that is still widely used today.

The other technique that Isaac Singer and his business partners utilized to speed up distribution was something called a *licensing arrangement*. They would find businesspeople who were interested in owning the rights to sell these amazing machines in certain geographical areas and get these businesspeople to pay an up-front license fee. Isaac and his partners also required licensees to teach consumers how to use the machines that they had just purchased. This arrangement allowed the partners to use money garnered from the licensing fees to fund more manufacturing. They now had a new distribution network—consisting of licensees—all ready to go.

Most franchise experts agree that Isaac Singer's technique was the spark that created franchising as we know it today. However, mass production of sewing machines was just one part of the story taking place in America in the mid- to late 1800s. There was another item being made in bulk that would prove to have even more impact on our current way of life.

Imagine living in a time in which most of America's roads were made of dirt. A little over 100 years ago, paved roads were unheard of and unnecessary, that is, until the automobile was invented. Then the creation and ultimate mass production of this new form of transportation changed everything. It was an exciting time because there was finally a way for people to get from location to location a lot faster than they ever had.

The entrepreneurs who were producing automobiles must have known that they had a life-changing product in their midst. However, they might not have appreciated the extent to which they were pioneering an entire new industry.

As a mounting number of people became interested in and wanted to purchase automobiles, the individuals selling cars had to find a way to distribute them. For awhile, some automobiles were sold in mail order catalogs. Some were even sold by salesman who traveled around trying to find buyers. However, neither of these systems was very efficient. Members of the industry needed to find some other way—some type of distribution system that could help these new car companies reach the next level.

In 1896, a couple of risk-taking entrepreneurs got the ball rolling in the right direction. The first of these was a man by the name of William Metzger, who built and opened the first independent automobile dealership in Detroit, Michigan and became the first auto dealer. He sold an electric automobile called a Waverly for around $1,000. (As a side note: Isn't it interesting that over 100 years later, automobile manufacturers are starting to sell electric automobiles again?)

The second entrepreneur to get involved in the automobile distribution was H.O. Kohller, who opened the first automobile franchise in Reading, Pennsylvania, where he sold Winton motor vehicles.

As the industry continued to grow, demand started to outpace supply. Another entrepreneur then came onto the scene and helped solve that problem—a man named Henry Ford.

As you likely know, Henry Ford invented the assembly line. This was a hugely significant development and was exactly what the automobile manufacturers needed at the time. The assembly line enabled Ford's famous Model T to be put together in about an hour and a half, as opposed to the 12 hours it took before his system was introduced. There was now a definite and widespread need to find a way to distribute these automobiles—and Henry Ford (and, to some extent, the folks at General Motors) filled this need. They introduced franchises/dealerships to daring entrepreneurs in cities and towns throughout America.

In fact, these first franchisees didn't even have to pay for privilege to utilize this system. According to *The American Car Dealership* by Robert Genat:

> A franchise to sell new automobiles didn't cost anything to obtain. It was granted to a person, who in the manufacturer's estimation would be a good representative of the company and its products. The contract was at most two pages of uncomplicated "legalese." The territory claimed by the franchisee was spelled out in detail and often a map of the area was attached to the contract. While giving the dealer a defined territory, it was not exclusive. The company retained the right to grant another franchise in that territory or to make sales in that territory from company stores (sales outlets owned by the manufacturer) (Motorbooks International, October 1999, pp. 17–18).

In other words, it was a real give and take; franchisees didn't have to pay an up-front franchise fee for the right to sell automobiles, which was a huge benefit. They were able to significantly lower their total capital outlay. They just had to weigh that against the real possibility that the automobile manufacturer could add additional franchises anywhere they wanted to. Considering how popular automobiles were getting at the time, it was probably a risk worth taking.

The following section from Genat's book also provides a look at some of the rules back then that still apply to franchising today:

There were requirements in the contract to have a facility from which to sell and service the products represented. Proper signage was [required] in order to identify the building as an authorized dealer. Rules for the early dealers were simple—sign an agreement to sell cars, and a territory would be assigned. Most of these agreements required that the franchisee also stock spare parts and offer a repair service for the cars sold. Today's automobile franchises (for the most part) have the same business model, and a major amount of revenue comes from the sales of parts, and the maintenance and repair of vehicles. (p. 18.)

There was also a by-product of all the automobile franchises that were springing up during the automobile's early years: the gasoline service stations that were needed to keep these new cars fueled and in good working order. Some of these became franchises as well. It's tempting to wonder if Henry Ford knew how much impact his invention was going to have. For instance, did he envision the massive amounts of products, services, and new business types that would evolve because of the popularity of the automobile—offerings and establishments such as the following:

- Gas stations
- Transmission repair shops
- Auto painting shops
- Convenience stores
- Drive-thru restaurants
- Motor lodges (motels)

Do you see anything in common with those five businesses? That's right; lots of them are franchise businesses. Some company names include the following:

- BP gas stations
- AAMCO

- MAACO
- 7-Eleven
- McDonald's
- Howard Johnson's

Isn't it amazing how the invention of a single product—and, ultimately, its mass production and distribution—changed *everything*?

However, it's important to keep in mind that before automobiles started to crisscross the country, people generally tolerated below-average roads. The folks who used horses for their transportation needs didn't really need a perfectly smooth road surface. They rode their horses to their destinations and kicked up some dust (of course, when it rained, it was a muddy mess). However, bicycles were also a pretty popular mode of transportation in the late 1800s and early 1900s, and the people that rode them complained a lot more about the dirt roads than the people who used horses.

Those complainers were actually a fairly well-organized bunch. This was due in large part to the fact that they had formed bicycle clubs with lots of members, and, as many of us know, sometimes it takes the power of a group to stimulate necessary changes. To that end, the Good Roads Movement was formed in 1880, mainly as a result of increased pressure by bicycle clubs. Bicyclists—along with engineers, farmers, and other interested parties—got the ball rolling by encouraging the U.S. Government to start improving the roads. This was perfect timing for all of the automobiles that were just about to pounce onto the scene.

So, what does this all have to do with franchising?

The answer: *everything*.

To delve further into this, let's pretend for a moment or two that you're living in 1920. You're 25 years old, married, and the proud father (or mother) of three beautiful children. You work incredibly hard, make an average wage, and enjoy your family time on the weekends. Recently, you purchased a brand new Ford Model T—a very nice automobile. Your family was so excited when you first brought it home, and that first "family drive" was magical—a truly life-changing experience for all of you.

This same life-changing experience was repeating itself over and over again, all across America as more and more people were buying cars. (That's because Henry Ford was building them really, really fast, and he was committed to manufacturing automobiles that were very affordable.) So, naturally, you wanted to drive your automobile more. You felt a newfound freedom. What used to be a really small world all of a sudden became bigger; trips that used to take days now took mere hours. You came up with a list of all the places you wanted to go and all the people you wanted to see. It was almost like all the new paved roads that were being built were being built just for you.

That is exactly how this first franchise changed not only the history of American business, but the experience of everyday Americans as well. If you agree with me on this, then the next person to whom I'm going to introduce you will make perfect sense. (Even if you disagree, it's okay. Just follow along.)

Raymond Albert Kroc is my personal franchise hero and someone who *should* be a hero to everyone who is part of this industry. Franchise owners everywhere owe Kroc a debt of gratitude—from franchisees that own 100 or more units, to the solo franchise owner in a small town, to the Idaho farmer who's one of the lucky few able to sell his potatoes to McDonald's.

Of course, if it wasn't for Ray Kroc, there wouldn't be a McDonald's to begin with.

Born in 1902, Ray Kroc was a sales guy with incredible vision. He started out selling milkshake mixing equipment and even mortgaged his home to become a distributor of the Multi-Mixer—a hot product during that time that could make five milk shakes at the same time. Kroc traveled all over the country, meeting entrepreneurs in the food industry and selling them his products.

During his travels, he had heard about two brothers from California named Dick and Mac McDonald. The McDonalds owned a very busy hamburger stand at which they were using eight of Kroc's milkshake mixing machines—*simultaneously*. Kroc drove to California because he had to see this for himself. What he observed there was an assembly line-like system being used in—of all places—a restaurant! The

McDonald brothers appeared to have this procedure of theirs down to a science.

Kroc had an epiphany after seeing this amazing restaurant operation firsthand: he envisioned these restaurants being built all over the country. As it happened, the McDonald brothers happened to be looking for a franchising agent to sell franchises across the country, and, as someone who'd been a salesman for the past 30 years, Ray Kroc was just the guy for the job.

Kroc cemented a deal to be the McDonald brothers' exclusive agent and started selling franchises. At the same time, he also opened the first duplicate of the McDonald brothers' California restaurant in Des Plains, Illinois. Kroc saw something big in the making and tried to convince the brothers that they should start thinking bigger, also. A few years later, the three owned multiple restaurants. However, Kroc was the one that wanted to build the eateries into a true empire. He recognized that it was the perfect time to introduce a chain like this, as automobile travel was becoming increasingly popular in the 1950s, and freeways were beginning to be built in a big way.

Now you can see why I said that the mass production and mass distribution of automobiles truly changed *everything*. Increased automobile use increased the need for paved roads, which paved the way for businesses to open up along these new roads—businesses that could support these drivers' (and automobiles') needs. In other words, now that automobiles were common all over America, businesses were sprouting up everywhere that people traveled.

Ray Kroc knew what he wanted. He pictured the McDonald brothers' hamburger restaurants dotting the landscape and knew that the people traveling all over the country by automobile needed places to stop and eat. Kroc ended buying out the McDonald brothers for a paltry $2.7 million. With the less-than-motivated McDonald brothers out of Kroc's hair, he was free to bring this idea of his to the next level.

And so he did.

By 1963, McDonald's had grown so much that its signs boasted information about "One Billion Hamburgers Sold"! By this time, McDonald's had just hit its 500th restaurant mark, and it was uphill from there—to say the least.

Both Henry Ford and Ray Kroc helped put franchising as we know it today on the map.

Ford played a huge part in the actual design of the franchise model. Once he was able to get mass production down to a science, he knew that he had to hone in on the distribution side of the business, which he did by creating a franchise (dealer) network all across the country.

Kroc's contributions to franchising had to do with uniformity and cleanliness. A McDonald's franchise located in Sacramento, California, will have the same menu items and will most likely be just as clean as a McDonald's franchise located in Dubuque, Iowa. A world without automobiles and Big Macs—I can't fathom it.

"The two most important requirements for major success are: first, being in the right place at the right time, and second, doing something about it."

—Ray Kroc

3

Take the Franchise Quiz!

"If one does not know to which port one is sailing, no wind is favorable."
—Lucius Annaeus Seneca

BEFORE YOU BEGIN reading, I should let you know that this is a *really* important chapter, and you'll be quizzed at the conclusion of it.

But first, I want you to do something and that is to go ahead and simply do what most prospective franchise buyers do by taking the following steps:

- Go online, and type the word *franchise* into a search engine.
- Click through all the results like a crazy person.
- Find a franchise website or two that you like.
- Spend a few days—maybe even a few weeks—looking around.
- Don't bother to really learn more about the franchises that interest you.
- Don't request an information packet from those franchise offerings.
- Get frustrated with the process.
- Talk yourself out of the idea of owning a franchise.
- Just get a new job instead.

If that sounds like something you've either done in the past or something that you'd rather *not* do, then you've chosen the right book.

Some people go through frustrating exercises, like the one I just described, several times during their professional careers. They get burned out at (or even lose) their jobs, and they start looking at other options. Sometimes, those options include possibly becoming a franchise owner.

But often, they're merely spinning their wheels and completely wasting their time—because they don't know what they're looking for. More important, they don't even know if franchise ownership would even make sense for them.

The likelihood is that they've only *heard* things about franchises—things like:

- Franchises provide a proven system, so they can be real money machines.
- To be successful, all you have to do is follow the franchise's system.
- Franchises have lower risk than regular businesses.
- Franchising is easy because everything is all set up for the owners.
- Franchises are turn-key businesses; in other words, all you have to do is turn the key to the door of your franchise business every morning because just about everything's been set up for you already by the franchisor.
- Franchise companies help you with everything.
- You'd have to be a real idiot to fail in a franchise.
- Franchises put you in business *for* yourself, but not *by* yourself.

You've heard some of those too, right? And I have a sneaking suspicion that one or two of those statements might have a lot to do with why you're considering franchise ownership. Yet even if those eight things were all true (which, as you'll discover shortly, they're not), you could *still* fail miserably at being a franchise owner.

Let's go back to the scenario I described at the chapter's beginning—the one that describes what most prospective franchise owners do. Now think about what *you* may have done with regard to checking out some franchises before you even picked up this book. Come on; are you going to try to convince me that you haven't been looking around? I'm going to assume that you *have* been doing so—for a while. Have you found a few that sound pretty interesting? Are you able to see yourself as the franchise owner in one of more of them? Great! At least you're getting a feel for what's out there. It's really important that you do some franchise shopping, right?

Wrong.

Whenever I speak with someone who tells me that they're "shopping for a franchise," I immediately stiffen up and enter the stress zone. My blood pressure rises, the vein in the middle of my forehead starts to throb, and I know that it's time to hold my tongue. Please, please, please, don't be one of these people who goes franchise shopping. There's no such thing. It's not like looking for a new car or new washing machine. It's *so* different.

For example, if you make a mistake on your choice of washing machines, you could probably just exchange it. Or (worst-case scenario) you could just go out and buy another one. You'd be out several hundred dollars, *but you'd get through it.* You might even find someone to purchase the machine you have but don't want to use. Investing $100,000 of your own money in a franchise business, on the other hand, is an entirely different ballgame. If you make an error or two in your research or, even worse, in your franchise selection, you could lose your entire investment. That would be a little more difficult to get though.

In case you haven't figured it out already, I'm trying to teach you something here. I'm trying to make sure that you're well aware of the difference between shopping and then investing $100,000 of your own money into a franchise business of your own and shopping and then investing $400 to $500 in a washing machine.

Now I know that you *know* the difference in your head, but do you *know it* in your gut, too?

I mean, how much heart-pounding fear is involved when you're shopping for a new washing machine? How much are you *really* going to research one? I'll even go a little further. Even if you're really, really careful about your washing machine research, how much time and energy are you really going to spend on this little exercise? How much stress are you really going to be feeling?

If you're not getting your undies in a bunch just *thinking* about going out and *shopping* or, I'm taking a big risk here, even *buying* a brand new washing machine, then you're okay in my book.

My point is this: starting to explore opportunities in franchise ownership is not a shopping expedition. It's a *major life decision*. It's big stuff. If you think buying your first house was big, you're right. Buying a franchise business is just, well, bigger! I highly recommend that you have a plan. As motivational speaker and Dean of Personal Development Earl Nightingale said, "All you need is the plan, the road map, and the courage to press on to your destination." This book's purpose is to provide you with such a plan right now. Reading it chapter by chapter will give you the direction you need, and the first step of this plan is to truly figure out what goes into owning and operating a franchise. And I can almost guarantee that it's a lot more complicated than you think it is.

To that end, let's go back and consider that franchise *shopping* you're doing. (Gosh, I really do hate that word!) I had asked if you had found any interesting franchise opportunities. Let's assume for a moment that you found a couple—or even just one—and for whatever reason, you're attracted to it.

Close your eyes for a moment. Take a deep breath. Feel your bliss and excitement about starting this franchise. Okay. Do you have a nice mental picture of that opportunity? Are you able to picture yourself as the happy, extremely successful franchise owner?

Good!

Now erase that picture. Forget why you're attracted to this franchise (or franchises). As a matter of fact, I don't even want you to *look* at any franchises yet. Doing so would be crazy. Crazy, I tell you!

You're wasting your time. It just doesn't matter yet.

You're putting your cart before your horse.

The first step in the process of choosing and researching great franchises has nothing to do with looking at franchises. *You just think it does*.

And no, it doesn't matter which ones you've looked at or whether you feel that you've found the perfect location for that terrific franchise business that you found. I even want you to forget the names of the franchises you've discovered, what they sell, and the services they provide. None of this matters—*yet*.

You need to begin your franchise discovery process with a clean slate. Spend a few minutes with a damp rag and clean it. Don't worry; I'm going to help you figure out this franchise thing. You just need to make sure that you're starting in the right place.

Start in Your Head

"If your head tells you one thing and your heart tells you another, before you do anything, you should first decide whether you have a better head or a better heart."

—Marilyn vos Savant

The place I want you to start your franchise discovery process is in your own mind. That's right; it's time for you to do some serious introspection. You're going to have to take a deep look into yourself and figure out exactly who you are as it relates to the business model of franchising. You need to start with *self*-discovery, before you can move on to *franchise* discovery.

It's time for you to have a serious and candid conversation with yourself, and to find out if you're even right for franchise ownership. Yes, that's right; there is a chance that owning a franchise is absolutely the wrong thing for you to even consider, let alone do.

What if it turns out that you're *not* a match for the business model of franchising?

Will you be disappointed? Or will you be grateful?

And, what if you just wasted money on this franchise book? I'm kidding, of course.

Here's one sentence that I need you to focus on right now: *It's their system, so they get to write the rule book.*

In order for a franchise business to work, it *has* to have rules. If franchises didn't have rules, then they wouldn't be franchises; they'd be independent small businesses. Don't get me wrong; there's nothing wrong with an independent small business. They're just a lot different from a franchise business.

So the first thing you need to consider is whether you are okay with rules.

In other words, how has the *rule thing* worked out for you in the past? For example, have you been a rule follower in your previous positions? Were you able to abide by your company's line of thinking? Did you follow procedures as they were laid out? Were you okay with the parameters they set?

Or were you resistant? Did you *fight* the system? Were you and *are* you still a rule *breaker*? While I'm not suggesting that it's entirely unacceptable to break the rules, I am trying to help you figure out at which point of the rule spectrum you actually fall. It's pretty basic; either you're generally okay with following the rules, or you're not. But only *you* know the answer. That's why it's so important for you to look inside yourself by starting in your head, and you must endure this process before you go back online—or wherever you're thinking of going—to search for that perfect franchise.

The bottom line is this; if you're generally comfortable with following someone else's rules and have a strong desire to be in business for yourself, franchise ownership is an option that you should explore. However, if you *don't* have a very good track record of toeing the line—and instead really prefer to make your own rules—then becoming a franchise owner may not be the way to get into business for yourself.

But there *are* some exceptions to this.

Cyborgs

I've consulted with hundreds of prospective franchise owners. Almost every time I ask the question, "are you okay with following rules?" these people answered yes. They *generally* considered themselves to be rule followers. I say generally because none of them *seemed* to be Cyborgs; I'm pretty sure that they were real live humans—ones who have choices. Sometimes, the choices they make go against the grain. In this case, these humans may not have followed the rules *every* time. In general though, they did, so they considered themselves rule followers. Got it? Good.

Now if they shared with me that they *didn't* consider themselves to be rule followers, I *generally* didn't meet with them. As far as I was concerned, there was no reason to because they would have made really lousy franchisees. I usually let them know, as gently as possible, that they needed to get a job or maybe look into buying an *independent* business because they weren't *franchise material*. Some of these folks—the ones with whom I didn't meet—got pretty angry when I told them that; however, *I* was okay with it. I was also fairly confident in the fact that I probably saved them a couple hundred thousand dollar mistake! They just didn't know it. Heck, they should have thanked *me*!

I was always tempted to ask these individuals if they thought that they could will themselves into a complete personality change. Now it is probably true that most of us can probably change *some* of our personality traits when needed. For example, if you're a really impatient person whose Saturday afternoon routine includes grocery shopping at what's usually a very busy store at that time, you can probably thumb through *US Weekly* or use your smartphone to check your e-mail while waiting in an especially long line. However, while these two activities may *temporarily* help you become more patient, you probably couldn't call the adjustment in your demeanor a *total* transformation.

Maybe your current job (if you have one) requires you to work lots of extra hours, perhaps because your company is short-staffed. You might be sick of working extra hours and are starting to get seriously burned out. You become more resentful as each 60-hour week passes. However, looking for a new job is out of the question right now, and you have bills to pay. So you suck it up and adapt as best you can. You know that the situation is probably *temporary*. You're able, for the most part, to keep your head on straight and your attitude in check. It's just what you have to do.

But if you're a prospective franchise owner who hasn't exactly had a glorious history of following the rules in your professional life, do you really think that it would be wise to invest $200,000 or so into a franchise type of business, which, at its core, is a rule-based business model? (I'll wait a couple of minutes for you to digest that question.)

I mean—do you **really** posses enough power to do a total personality transformation? (If so, please send some of that power my way. Thank you.)

Of course, you could be someone who's living in some type of franchise fantasyland. You may well assume that you'll be able to go out and buy a franchise and then just pretend that there are no rules or that maybe they just won't apply to you. That'll be an enjoyable experience for you and your family. Please let me know how that works out. I'll include it in this book. Don't worry; I'll have plenty of time to include a chapter about you because your franchise ownership experiment will only last months—perhaps even days—not years. Just send me your story, and I'll have my publisher insert it into the digital edition.

Are you picking up what I'm putting down? In other words, are you starting to get a feel for the types of people who are right for the business model of franchising and the types who aren't? I hope that this is becoming clearer to you. Now just in case I haven't confused you yet, I think that it's time for me to do so. I'm going to throw you a little curve.

I *have* consulted with a handful of prospective franchise owners over the years who weren't who I'd call *ideal franchise candidates*—at least on paper. (I'll get to the paper part soon.) But they *were* worthy of my time. I simply didn't meet or consult with *most* of the folks who contacted me. Either they didn't qualify financially, they weren't right for franchise ownership because of a little problem they had with the rules, or I just didn't *feel* that I could assist them. In addition, and I know that you'll find *this* hard to believe, some of the folks were a tad unrealistic about things like how long it would take them to replace their incomes if they invested in a start-up franchise and some other pretty insignificant details. (I'll be getting into franchise owner income possibilities and the like later in this book.)

My consulting meetings generally consist of guiding clients through the proper franchise business selection and research process. While I still do meet with a select number of would-be owners, there were a few folks with whom I met that didn't really look on paper as though they should even *consider* becoming franchise owners. These folks were either current or former independent small business owners; in both cases, they were used to making their own rules. They *had* to. But something had changed in their companies that compelled them to start looking into some alternate options—one of which was investing in a franchise.

These folks were coming to me from a very different place than the typical prospective franchise owner was. They had already owned their own business and achieved some measure of success. They had already risked their money. They had already lived life as a small business owner. And, most important, they didn't have someone looking over their shoulders checking to see if they were following The Plan. The Plan was all theirs. They owned it. Transitioning from a position of absolute control as an independent small business owner to a franchise business owner, with a lot less control over the business, can be difficult. I really put these people through the paces to see if they would really be able to relinquish lots of the control that they were used to having.

A Phone Call

Pretend for a moment that you had a pretty successful business for the past 15 years or so. You were able to expand it and were making a nice living. You had built some equity and could actually sell it one day. But then something happened. Let's say that some type of economic downturn affected your business in a way that you never thought possible and from which you couldn't recover. You ended up being forced to sell your company for a lot less than you wanted to, but at least you got out. You can't really retire yet, so you start looking at some options.

You *could* just go and get a regular, nine-to-five job. However, after 15 years of running the show, you just can't bear the thought of working for someone else or taking orders from a boss. In fact, the mere thought brings a wave of nausea, the likes of which you've never experienced before.

You could also become some type of consultant and figure out a way to sell your business knowledge by the hour. Of course, you'd have to go out and pound the pavement a bit to find some clients who were ready and willing to pay you for all of your amazing knowledge. It's a possibility, but one about which you're just not sure.

Maybe you can buy an existing independent business. But you know that finding just the right one, at the right price, may take a lot longer than you're willing to wait. Again, you're not really sure what to do.

You've thought of buying a franchise. You knew a little about them; heck, you may have competed with them in your business. You figure it's worth a look. And once you did so, you found me. You made a phone call and left a message on my cutting-edge voice mail system, and here's how our conversation went:

Me: Hi, Jack! I'm returning your phone call from yesterday. The message you left on my voice mail said that you were referred to me because you were thinking of looking into a few franchises, and you heard that I was the guy to go to for this kind of thing.

You: Yes, Joel. An attorney friend of mine knows of you, and he said that you wouldn't BS me around.

Me: Well, he's right! So why now? Why are you thinking about investing your money in a franchise?

You: I had a pretty successful auto-related business for about 10 years, and I just, well . . . lost it. My CFO was not as good as I thought he was. He screwed up the books, big time, and I had to liquidate. I owned five stores. So now I'm at a crossroads. Maybe you can help me.

Me: I'm sorry to hear that you lost your business. That must have . . . well, it must have really sucked, to put it bluntly.

You: It did, Joel. I was doing pretty well. I put my two boys through college and enjoyed the fruits of my labor. I still want to have a business of my own, so I was thinking about a franchise.

Me: Well Jack, I'd be happy to work with you, but here's my fear: You've been a small business owner already. You've been the guy running the show. You were the rule maker, right?

You: Correct. I was the boss, and I made the rules. I think that it would be really hard for me to take orders from someone else at this point in my life. I really can't see working for someone else . . . you know, getting a regular job.

Me: I totally understand. I would have to *really* be up against the wall before I would ever work for someone else again! So I can completely see where you're coming from.

You: Yes. No "job" for me, thank you very much.

Me: All right. Well, what about money?

You: I'm pretty good there. I can invest about $75,000 to $100,000 of my own, and I have access to more if I need it.

Me: Fantastic! One more question, and this is the most important one I'll be asking. Do you feel confident that you'll be able to follow *someone else's* system? I mean, you've had your own system of sorts for many years. You thought it out. You made it happen. You do realize that if you end up buying a franchise, you'll have to follow a 200-page operations manual—right? You'll have to abide by their rules. Are you going to be okay with that?

You: Joel, let me tell you something. I'm 55 years old. I'm probably not going to be able to find a good job, for what I'd need to be paid. It's just not realistic. I don't want to buy someone else's business and someone else's problems. I really would have no choice but to follow their system. I could do it, Joel.

Me: You know what, Jack. I think you could, too. But I know of a way that we can be sure. I've created a test of sorts—a quiz for you to take that will help me determine if you'd be a good fit for franchising. Now keep in mind that it's a totally unscientific quiz. I'm not a psychologist, and I don't fantasize about becoming one. I designed it around the thousands of conversations that I've had with clients, current and former franchise owners, and franchise company executives over the years. It's free, and it works.

You: That's fine. I'd be happy to take it. Where can I find it, Joel?

Me: I have a website set up just for the quiz. Go to. . . .

That was *mostly* a real conversation I had with a gentleman who had found himself in a similar situation. I don't want to reveal everything about him nor the conversation we had. I just want you to get a feel for someone who was willing to seriously adapt to a much different way of doing things just so that he could be in business for himself again.

Is that something that *you'd* be able to do? That's only something that you can decide.

Now I really did create a totally unscientific quiz for prospective franchise owners to take. It *is* free, and it *does* work. Hundreds of people have taken it—and I want you to take it now, too. In fact, I need you to take it. You *need* to take it before you go on to the next chapter.

So go to www.takethefranchisequiz.com. The entire thing only takes 10 minutes. There's a place on the quiz to put in your e-mail address, so I'll even personally score it for you and then send you the results.

In Chapter 4, I'm going to teach you about the business model of franchising. You need to know how it works because once you understand the model, you'll be in a much better position to decide if becoming the owner of a franchise type of business is really the way for you to go.

4

Explained: The Franchise Business Model with Benefits

"To succeed in business, to reach the top, an individual must know all it is possible to know about that business."

—J. Paul Getty

So you've taken 10 minutes out of your day to visit www.takethe franchisequiz.com. Hopefully, the results you received didn't disappoint. While it's important to remember that the quiz is totally unscientific, I do feel that it's a helpful tool because it allows you to easily take a look inside your head. At the end of the day, you're the only one who really knows if you may be right for franchise ownership. I hope that you are because if you've taken your efforts this far, you likely have quite a bit invested in this option, not to mention that it sure beats working for someone else.

Now what should you do if your www.takethefranchisequiz.com score was low? Well, just keep reading this book because there *are* other options that exist for you. Maybe you could partner with someone who is better suited for franchise ownership. Maybe you have an idea for a product or a service that you can turn into a franchise type of business. Or maybe my book will move you *away* from the idea that you had of investing in a franchise and *into* something else that turns out to be even better for you. As famed children's book author Dr. Seuss aptly advised, "Think left and think right and think low and think high. Oh, the thinks you can think up if only you try!" (Dr. Suess, *Oh, the Thinks You Can Think!* Random House Books for Young Readers; 1st edition, August 1975.)

You should never feel as though you've exhausted your options because there will always be more alternatives out there for you.

What Franchising *Is,* Exactly

It's now time for me to define precisely what a franchise is and what the franchising model consists of so that you know what you may be getting yourself into (and I mean that in the best way possible, of course!).

The following is my nonlegal definition of the franchise model: the entrepreneur (the franchisor) has invented a business—and its model—and is looking to replicate it by partnering with people that would like an opportunity to own their own business while building equity for themselves and their families. The franchisor invests his or her own money up front, while leveraging company growth by using other people's (specifically, the franchisees') money.

Now here's a textbook-style definition: a franchise typically involves the granting by one party (the *franchisor*) to another party (the *franchisee*) the right to carry on a particular name or trademark, according to an identified system. Franchises are usually located within a territory or at one specific location for an agreed-upon amount of time. The franchisee receives a franchise license to use the franchise company's trademarks, systems, signage, software, and other proprietary tools and systems in accordance with the guidelines set forth in the franchise contract.

Doesn't that sound exciting? Are you feeling a sense of unbridled enthusiasm like you've never felt before? I'll just bet that you're ready to take your checkbook out *right now* and go out and find a franchise business to buy.

Here's the real deal: a franchise company (the *franchisor*) came up with the idea for the service or product (or both) and is essentially granting you the right to market it for them. Because it is *their* idea, they require you to market it in a specific way. It is their system, so they write the rule book, and, in this case, the rule book includes parameters like their operations manual and the franchise agreement. Not only are you required to do things their way; you must pay them an upfront franchisee fee (a license) as well as ongoing royalties. The royalties are usually in the form of a percentage of your gross sales although there is occasionally a flat monthly fee. In addition, there is almost always an advertising or marketing fee paid monthly along with the royalties.

The Benefits

The business model of franchising brings several benefits to the table—maybe, someday, even to *your* table. These include the following:

An operating system. This is what franchising is all about. These companies follow a proven business formula; it's what allows the business to be duplicated again and again.

A formal training program. Franchise training programs are generally top-notch and include just about everything that franchisees need to know about opening and operating a successful branch.

Technology. Access to a powerful suite of tools designed to provide things like sales and lead tracking, point of sale systems, and Internet or social media marketing can set a franchise business apart from an independent one.

Group purchasing power. Medium to large franchise systems can almost always purchase products and services that are sold by the franchisees cheaply. This is a serious advantage of the franchise model.

Brand recognition. A franchise system that has attained brand status is a powerful thing; it's what allows these franchises to charge premium prices to consumers and clients that are willing to pay them.

It also makes it that much harder for an independent business to compete with a well-known brand.

Marketing/public relations (PR)/advertising plan. Franchise systems have proven marketing and advertising plans that can attract customers and clients on both national and local levels, providing a steady stream of interested prospective customers and clients.

Support. Franchisors provide support to their franchisees in several different ways during various times in the business cycle. Some examples include the following:

Prelaunch

Grand opening

Local marketing

Technology

Phone and e-mail support lines 24/7

Franchisee network. Franchise systems have a built-in network of owners that are located all across the country and who communicate with each other freely. They frequently share best practices and ideas amongst themselves and sometimes present them to the executives at franchise headquarters for the betterment of the entire franchise system.

As you can see, the franchise business model does have lots of powerful benefits, all of which you should be able to use to your advantage—as long as you're operating according to a well-honed franchise concept.

What Franchising *Isn't*

In the last chapter, I wrote about The Rules. Now that you know some of the numerous advantages of the franchise business model, the question to ask yourself is are you willing to follow The Rules in order to receive the many benefits that come from being part of a franchise system?

I'm going to assume that you're okay with The Rules for now. Keep in mind that rules are a necessity for the franchise model to work. None of the benefits of the franchise business model would be a reality if franchising was a free-for-all. Things need to be incredibly consistent in a franchise system in order for it to be successful.

There's another really important thing that you need to really understand about the franchise business model, and that's *what it isn't*. It isn't really a very entrepreneurial model.

Are you disappointed? Have you been telling your friends that you're thinking about becoming an entrepreneur? Whoops.

There are a couple of reasons that I'm bringing this up.

1. I'm trying to ~~pound it into your head~~ make it clear to you that becoming a franchise owner means that you're investing in *someone else's* entrepreneurial vision.
2. If you're going to become a franchise owner, you really need to live and breathe the concept of franchising. You also need to be aware of some of the debates that have been taking place concerning franchising, especially the one about franchise owners not really being true entrepreneurs.

You must always keep the following fact in mind: *the person who came up with the concept for this franchise, who invented and established its system, is the true entrepreneur.* It is *not* the individual franchisee, which means that *it's not you.* If you fully understand that, you'll be that much closer to being a successful money-making franchise owner.

There *is* quite a debate going on about franchises and entrepreneurship. From my perspective, which has to do with me trying to protect would-be franchise owners from making a mistake, it's wrong for franchisors to use the word *entrepreneur* in their print or online advertisements. Here's an example:

Own a Billy-Willy's Frozen Yogurt Shop!

(*Not* a real franchise. I *think*.)

Indulge That Entrepreneurial Spirit!

Franchise Opportunities Available in Your Area

Call 1-000-Bily-Wil to Request Information!

In the following, you'll see specifically the type of entrepreneurial spirit that the marketing department of Billy-Willy's Frozen Yogurt is referring to:

(It would be included *here*. But it's not.)

Exactly.

Now, do you *really* think that owning and operating a frozen yogurt franchise will involve some real entrepreneurial trailblazing? (Before you start thinking too much here, I am aware that there is a real possibility of one or more franchisees coming up with a wonderful new flavor of frozen yogurt that the folks at headquarters deem worthy. So I guess that's entrepreneurial.) But what else might this entail? Does there really seem to be room for that much creativity?

Now I don't want you to feel that I'm slamming the frozen yogurt sector of franchising (although it sure sounds like it.) There's absolutely nothing wrong with investing in a frozen yogurt franchise—as long as it matches what *you* want in a business. What *is* wrong is how this particular franchise opportunity is being peddled. The marketing department for this company knows that prospective franchise owners are attracted to the E word—*Entrepreneur*. This is no doubt a powerful term—one that evokes visions of multimillion dollar homes overlooking Malibu Beach, 100 foot yachts, and indoor swimming pools.

Now what Billy-Willy's Frozen Yogurt Shop *should* provide is a terrific franchise operating system that's easy to follow and to duplicate again and again.

I'm one who tends to see things in black and white, which is why I'm sticking to my guns on this issue; franchisees *are not* true entrepreneurs. However, there are some other business experts who disagree with this point. One of them is my friend Rieva Lesonsky (who also happens to be the person that wrote the foreword for the book you're now holding.) She shared her views in a blog post on the AllBusiness.com website. She stated that "there are no absolutes in entrepreneurship—and that includes franchising." I agree with her there. For example, as a potential franchise owner, don't allow yourself to be sucked into the franchise industry hype that sometimes seems to suggest that it's less risky to buy a franchise. My feeling is that *sometimes* it's less risky to buy a franchise. It just depends on the situation. There are lots of variables in a business— whether it's a franchise business or a non-franchise business. Rieva feels that those variables make franchise owners entrepreneurs.

Rieva also points out that "many franchisors (and not just the new ones) are very open to franchisee input." She reminds her readers that "it was a McDonald's franchisee who famously created The Big Mac (and another came up with the McFlurry), and a Subway franchisee brought Jared Fogle to the attention of headquarters." Rieva's correct; sometimes a franchisor is very open to new ideas from the franchisees in the system. But it would be a huge mistake for you to invest in a franchise hoping to come up with amazing new product or service ideas of your own that the folks at franchise headquarters would approve and adopt systemwide. Buy a franchise because you already believe that the franchisor has a great product or service, and you want to capitalize on their system.

Rieva brings up a couple of great points, for sure. Mine are better. (I'm kidding, Rieva.)

A Manual

All franchisors have a pretty detailed operations manual; it's kind of like a Bible for their business.

Everything from A to Z is there. *Everything.* It's meant to be followed under all circumstances. So think about it in those terms: how entrepreneurial is it to follow someone else's operations manual? I have that answer for you in the following.

Typically, an operations manual is divided into several sections:

Section 5: Unit Operations

1. Pricing structure
2. Quality control

3. Inventory
4. Customer service policies
5. Hours of operation
6. Brand policies

How much potential for entrepreneurial activity do you see there? For example, let's say you run a sandwich shop. You're likely going to face the following issues.

1. Do you think that you'll be able to establish some "buy two subs, get-two subs free days" without there being some type of national or regional marketing program going on? (Maybe you can; it all depends on what it says in your franchise contract. However, this probably isn't the case—so much for getting creative with your business's offers.)

2. Do you think that you'll be able to flex your entrepreneurial muscle around the franchisor's quality control rules? For example, if one of your more stellar employees baked an entire day's supply of foot-long sandwich buns a little too long, and they were all rather crispy (as opposed to soft and fluffy like they're supposed to be), would you take a risk and come up with some type of new name for what are basically burnt buns and try to sell them to your lunch customers as is?

3. Keep in mind that you'll be required to keep a certain amount of inventory on hand and that there may also be rules on how long you can keep it. After all, if you're managing a food franchise, you probably won't want to think too much out of the box when it comes to reading the expiration dates on your perishables. It's not like you can suggest to the operations department at your franchise's headquarters that all the other franchisees should really look into *not* throwing their perishables out on the date of their expiration but would benefit instead by waiting three days and using it as an inventory cost-cutting measure.

4. The information on great customer service—as well as exactly how you and your employees must achieve it—is all spelled out. Lots

of companies are stressing the importance of the entire *customer service experience*. In other words, you alone will not be dictating (on the corporate level) just how that customer experience is supposed to look and feel. Don't expect to get creative in this area; it's already been well thought out by someone else, long before you came along.

5. For the most part, the franchisor dictates the business's hours of operation. I have seen some exceptions—like the time I matched a franchise candidate to Wisconsin-based Batteries Plus, a retail and commercial chain of battery stores. Opening on Sundays was optional at the time my candidate purchased it, but it was something he decided to do; he felt would help his location gain more customer share. But even considering this example—just how much entrepreneurial savvy is needed to make a yes or no decision about opening your franchise up on Sundays? It's either yes or no. If you open on Sundays, you may be able to bring in enough revenue to cover your operating expenses for that day. Or maybe you won't. The point here is that you will rarely get to make a decision about something like opening your franchise operation on a Sunday. It will most likely be spelled out in your franchise contract.

6. This last one should be pretty easy to figure out. There's only *one* brand upon which you have to focus, and that's the one in which the franchisor has invested. It's your job to represent it exactly as it's been laid out. This includes the need to *always* use things like the franchisor's color scheme, signage, slogans, and whatever else the franchisor's brand represents. There's no wiggle room here; if the franchisor's colors are orange and black, you can't go out and buy green and purple signs to use as your first entrepreneurial experiment.

Now let's return to my friend Rieva's post on AllBusiness.com for a moment. As mentioned earlier, she pointed out that there is *some* entrepreneurial-related activity in which you'll be involved in should you opt to manage a franchisee. Just be aware that *most* of your workday will probably consist of sticking to the directions in the operations manual.

You'll be following The Plan; and come to think of it, isn't that why you invested in a franchise in the first place? Because *they* have The Plan—and you don't have to worry about implementing one?

There are, of course, some minor entrepreneurial activities worth mentioning—strategizing on how you're going to integrate local networking activities into your monthly business activities, developing creative customer or client acquisition ideas or implementations, and devising an employee recruitment plan. You can usually get as creative as you want in those instances as long as you don't break the rules and regulations outlined in your 25-page franchise agreement (read: *contract*)

Here's the bottom line; if you want to be in business for yourself and feel that the best way to do it is by following someone else's *plan*, then the franchise business model is definitely worth some serious consideration. However, if you want to show the world your amazing entrepreneurial prowess, then you should opt to launch a company on your own or buy someone else's existing business. You'll save yourself a lot of money—and a lot of headaches.

Other People's Money (OPM)

The franchise business model is a fabulous way for companies that sell products and services to get to market. It's the classic OPM—Other People's Money—model. Instead of building company-owned stores and hiring employees for each one, the company that invents the product or service can turn the operation into a franchise. It's a smart strategy for the company because they can use OPM to grow instead of taking out a loan from the bank every time they want to add another location. The company lowers their financial outlay, and everyday people get to take a shot at business ownership.

As a future franchise owner, it's important to know that franchisors still have taken quite a risk in putting their franchise business concepts together. They still have to invest a lot of money up front to put all their systems in place, and there's no guarantee that their franchise concept will even turn out to be a successful one into which people will actually invest their hard-earned money. And, unfortunately, in some cases, the companies that decided to franchise their businesses never should have. That's because not all businesses are really right for franchising.

I asked Mark Siebert—CEO of franchise advice and consulting organization iFranchise Group, Inc.—to share what some of these types of companies are. He cited the following:

Complex Businesses. The more multifaceted a business is, the harder it is to franchise. Of course, some people can franchise complex businesses by focusing on a candidate that has existing experience in the industry or by doing a *conversion franchise*. An example of this is a fancy French restaurant requiring a Cordon Bleu chef. Another example would be a real estate franchise requiring specific licensing; but real estate has been franchised very successfully by targeting real estate professionals. More complex restaurants or higher-end restaurants have succeeded in franchising by selling franchises to established restaurant operators. Medical franchisors might target medical practitioners. Insurance franchises such as Fiesta target licensed insurance agents (or will help them to get licensing).

When a medical-related franchise is sold to a medical practitioner (not all are, by the way), they do *not* teach the franchisee medicine. Instead, they teach the business systems surrounding the practice.

Businesses in Which the Product Being Sold Is Thought of as a Commodity. Branding is an important part of any franchise, and, in order for a franchise to ultimately be successful, the franchisor needs to make the brand stand for something. If the consumer does not believe they will get better quality, better pricing, or better *something* from an operation, they will not be inclined to purchase at a commodity type location. Some examples of this are a farmer's market or fruit stand because these types of businesses aren't selling anything that is especially unique.

Low-Margin Businesses. While there are exceptions to this rule, low-margin businesses are more difficult to franchise because the franchisor needs to take their royalty, thereby further reducing the margin. So while

Piggly Wiggly grocery stores work as a franchisor, grocery stores in general would ordinarily not be the best candidate for a franchise.

High-Investment Retail Businesses. Franchises are generally sold to individuals, so the higher the investment, the more difficult it is to franchise. Combined with a retail environment (which reduces margins), franchising becomes impossible. An example of this are stores like IKEA, K-Mart, and so on because the inventory needs are so tremendous. There aren't many would-be franchise owners who would be comfortable keeping millions of dollars worth of merchandise on hand 365 days a year. The higher the investment, the smaller the pool of qualified candidates there are. In franchising it's all about volume; the more franchise units there are that are producing revenue, the better the franchisor does financially. There's no such thing as a successful franchisor that has three franchise units.

Businesses in Which the Franchisor Is Not Committed to Franchisee Success. Though we all know who they are, I will take the fifth on getting specific.

■ ■ ■

Entrepreneurial companies that are considering turning their business concept into a franchise need to ask themselves about several things, some of which include the following:

1. Do we have a time-tested, proven business model?
2. Have we duplicated our concept at least once?
3. Do we have a strong management team?
4. Do we have the basis for a detailed start-up operations manual?
5. Do we have the desire and energy to expand our concept?
6. Is our concept truly unique? Does it fill an unmet need?
7. Are our profit margins large enough to attract franchisees?
8. Can we design a great formal training program?
9. Do we have strong enough relationships with lenders to obtain investment and growth capital?

10. Do we have technology in place to help with system efficiency?
11. Are we prepared for the complex legalities involved with franchising?
12. Are we willing to invest substantially in marketing our concept to potential franchisees?
13. Do we have the ability to change our current management roles into ones that are focused on new franchise development and new franchise marketing?

It's not cheap to franchise a business. If a company feels that they *are* ready to franchise, they'll have to commit $100,000+ to do it properly.

There are several firms that offer complete franchise development services by providing services like the following:

Strategic planning

Operations and training manual writing

Legal services

Branding

Marketing

Technology, including web development

Franchisee recruitment

Franchise development or sales

Of course, not all franchise development firms are created equal; some are better than others. There are even a few that belong in a class all by themselves; these are what I like to call *pond scum* franchise development firms. These firms will tell practically *anyone* who approaches them—and who happens to have a little money—to franchise their business. They will claim that their business concept is *fantastic* and should, of course, be franchised—the sooner, the better.

Lots of franchise concepts don't make it. Some end up selling two or three franchises and then go under.

As is the case with any business on which one is considering spending money, it's always wise to get the names of others that have used their services. It's too easy to get caught up in the moment, when egos are getting rubbed in quite the pleasant way. For example, "WOW! You have an amazing business going! This one is definitely ripe for franchising. As a matter of fact, we'll even help you sell your first few franchises. This is going to be awesome! You've done a brilliant job."

The franchise development firms that I like to refer folks are the ones that don't just take *anybody* on as a client. My feeling is that if a company has the courage to turn away potentially $100,000 in revenue, it's one about which I want to learn more and one with whom I probably want to work.

My dad used to tell me that lots of the franchises that never made it did it on the cheap; instead of using a franchise development firm, they got a lawyer to draw up the necessary legal paperwork and thought that they would just be able to sell franchises because they were legal. This reminds us to be aware that some franchises simply don't make it. Some concepts never see the light of day because they didn't have well-thought-out concepts, and they didn't do things right in the beginning.

There's an example of this that comes to mind for me right away, one that involved meal preparation or meal assembly. The following is the idea:

A harried housewife would visit her local meal assembly franchise on a Saturday morning and choose from a menu of offerings that they offered to assemble. She would then follow a prepared recipe with a set of ingredients that have already been chopped, sliced, diced, peeled, and cut. After that, she slid them into plastic bags and took the meals home where she could refrigerate or freeze them until needed. The process itself ends up taking about two hours or so, depending on how many meals this woman wanted to prepare.

Unfortunately, the concept didn't turn out too well. And it's easy to figure out why because I'm part of the "dual income so we have no time to do anything crowd" that the geniuses who came up with this idea in the first place were hoping to attract.

Here were the first two questions that popped into my head immediately after I had initially heard about this idea—right after these franchises first started appearing on the scene a few years ago:

1. If truly busy people can barely find the time to cook on weeknights, how would they find the time to spend two hours (or more) putting meals together on a Saturday morning?
2. What if the people using this service didn't have enough freezer space? Would these customers be forced to go out and buy an extra freezer just because a franchise that offered meal preparation or meal assembly opened a few miles away?

Those two reasons—as well as a slew of others, like a high cost of entry for franchisees—caused most of these locations to either go out of business or to change their business models and not offer franchises anymore. There have been a couple of lawsuits, too.

I remember several spirited conversations that I had with some fellow franchise professionals about these goofy franchises. We all wondered why the people who came up with this idea didn't think it all the way through. Heck—why didn't they talk to *us*?

I remember participating in several online forums when the meal preparation franchise fad was going on, one of which took place on Sean Kelly's Unhappy Franchisee website (www.unhappyfranchisee.com). A franchise marketing expert and friend, Sean, reminded me of a couple more franchise flops that have come along in recent years:

eBay Drop-Off Stores Franchises. Hundreds of individuals invested in franchises with names like iSoldIt, Snappy Auctions, and QuikDrop. They gambled $250 or more on the chance that consumers would pay *them* to sell unwanted items on eBay from their storefront franchises. But these franchisees bet wrong, and these chains have all but disappeared—along with their savings and credit ratings.

Men's 30-Minute Fitness. In the mid-1990s, Curves for Women—a woman-only, limited circuit training program—became the fastest selling franchise in history. Cuts Fitness for Men thought it could quickly capitalize on Curves' success by creating a *men-only* 30-minute workout club. However, the attributes that made Curves attractive to women (single sex membership, group exercise, no free weights) were, in fact, *negatives* to men. Because of this, most Cuts locations failed, and the chain imploded. Some survived as independents, but only by changing the concept and making the gyms coed.

■ ■ ■

Another reason that some franchise concepts never get very far is this one: Occasionally, companies that turn their business concept into a franchise awards or, rather, *sells* their franchises to the wrong people. Unfortunately, this happens all too frequently. Sometimes, in their zeal to grow their franchise, franchisors get a bit too aggressive, and they start to sell locations to practically anyone with money and a heartbeat. So instead of lowering his or her financial risk, the franchisor has increased it—substantially.

Franchisors with lots of underperforming (read: *failing*) franchises can get in trouble quickly. Their monthly income (from franchise royalties) drops, precipitously. Word starts to get out that their franchisees are failing, which leads them to run into additional difficulties as they try to sell new franchises. Expensive legal problems begin to set in as the franchisors start to go after franchisees that may be late with their royalty payments or who aren't bothering to pay their royalties at all.

This kind of scenario happens more than you may think in the world of franchising, and I try to prevent it from happening every day. So it follows that this would be a great time for me to share the elements of My Mission:

- To make franchising more transparent by aggressively informing all who wish to become franchise owners that there's definite risk involved and then teaching these individuals how to *lower* that risk by providing articles, books, podcasts, and personal advisory services.
- To gently (sometimes a bit more firmly) encourage franchisors to only choose the *best-of-the-best* franchise candidates, thereby helping to increase their chances of mutual success while lowering the failure rates in franchising.

Franchising has provided opportunities for hundreds of thousands of people to live their dreams and go into business for themselves. It's a great business model that works really, really well, for the most part. It's just not for everybody. But then again, what is?

Some Professional Opinions

Here's what some hand-picked franchise industry professionals think about the business model of franchising and why they feel that it works so well. Read them carefully; there are a lot of gems in here.

According to Don Hay, President of Maid Brigade, a large residential cleaning franchise with over 300 franchise units in North America:

> Clearly, the more obvious advantages to franchising lay in an opportunity seeker's ability to get an incredible amount of information about the business including revenues, profits (from existing locations), advertising methods, staffing relations, and much more. This person removes all risk of not knowing anything about the concept, including how it works and just how successful it is. Of course, it doesn't hurt that they get the experience factors, developed technology, training, and continuous support—none of which is available to individuals who open their doors on their own. What could be better?

As Paul Segreto, CEO and founder of franchisEssentials—a firm that provides integrated franchise marketing, media, and development—claims:

> It can certainly take a lot of time to start a new business concept to the point of being successful. Investing in a franchise sure can speed up the start-up process. The model comes with well-documented systems, processes, and procedures in sales, customer service, operations, and marketing that should minimize both the learning curve and risk. [What's] often overlooked is the potential of increasing each

unit's value as the brand continues to develop and as the franchisor protects the integrity of the brand name and trademark. On their own, independent business owners may control their own destiny with little or no outside interference, whereas a franchisee controls their own destiny by following the system—and improves the probability of success with franchisor assistance and franchise collaboration. Taken together, these factors contribute to unit economics that makes franchising a more viable option, especially in the minds of lenders who are now looking at the franchisor and the franchise system as key factors in approving loans.

James Young, president of Spring Green Lawn Care, a 35-year old Chicago-area lawn care service franchise with locations all across the United States adds:

My favorite part of the business model is [the ability it provides] to harness the collective knowledge of the organization—including the franchisees' experience, customer information and business intelligence. The trick is to share this information with franchise owners in meaningful and relevant terms to help drive revenue and profitability locally.

Franchise consultant/broker Barney Greenbaum explains:

Franchising as a business model creates a safety net to the end goal of working for yourself and building equity. Most people want to work for themselves; yet when they're asked why they don't, they usually respond by claiming that "it's way too risky." The franchise model [eliminates some of this risk by providing] proven systems and territory protection (created by trial and error and then re-engineering), that can lead to predictable results. You're investing in yourself and have someone there to go to [at all times who's "been where you are"]. Many franchises come with a brand name they have built (where you share some of the risk) for advice, strategy, systems, marketing, etc.—all of which are areas [in which you must excel in order] to run a successful business.

Elza Gennicks of franchise consulting firm Powerhouse Franchising offers his thoughts as well:

I like franchising because it takes the pseudo-entrepreneurial characteristics of an individual, and implements them in a proven [easy to duplicate] business model designed to make a profit. [When] done correctly, [this approach provides] freedom in all facets of life; that is, assuming one makes an appropriate choice of franchise after—and *only* after—they TRULY know what it is for which they are looking and best suited.

Sean McGarry, CEO of Franchise Direct, states:

What I like about the franchise model is its resilience in the face of economic adversity. We have just experienced one of the greatest recessions of our time and once again the franchise model has not only survived but is bouncing back, offering people who have been made redundant in other sectors the opportunity to build a new future using its tried and tested system.

Here's one more opinion, and it's my own: My favorite part of the franchise model is speed, that is, speed to market. A franchisor with a solid system can help new franchisees gain local market share rapidly and possibly even dominate their markets in a very short amount of time.

The franchise business model is an amazing one. It can work really well when designed for an appropriate concept. Of course, the right people have to buy into it. And by right, I'm talking about the necessary mind-set and basic personality traits like discipline, commitment, perseverance, and the ability to follow rules that others have set.

In Chapter 5, you'll learn the meaning of your score from the quiz you took online at www.takethefranchisequiz.com. This will allow you to decide if franchise ownership is for you. Of course, you'll only be able to find that out *if* you've taken the franchise quiz. If you haven't taken it by now, either you didn't see where I asked you to take it earlier in the book, or you chose not to. If you missed it, just chalk it up to human error, and take it now. If you chose not to take it, what was your reason?

You don't have a problem following directions, do you? And I'm sure it's not because you want to do this *your way*.

Gosh. I *hope* it's not because you don't like rules.

5

Are You Right or Wrong for Franchise Ownership? Reviewing the Quiz's Results

"It's much better to prepare and not have the opportunity than to have the opportunity and not be prepared."

—Anonymous

HOPEFULLY, YOU NOW have a good understanding of the business model of franchising. You understand that it's an enterprise based on someone else's business idea—an idea that you're going to execute. You've learned that while there may be *some* entrepreneurial aspects to franchise ownership, in general, it's about following The Plan.

Now that you grasp the basic concepts underlying franchising, it's important to understand what it's going to take to become a *successful* franchise owner. In my experience, I've found that profitable franchise owners do the following:

- Act according to the procedures that are stated in the operations manual
- Follow the rules and regulations stated in their franchise agreements

71

- Take the suggestions given to them by their field reps and remain coachable participants
- Use all the technology tools made available to them by the franchisor
- Follow the franchisor's marketing plans
- Are obsessive about their numbers
- Create close relationships with other franchisees in the system
- Are involved in the local community
- Are always making an effort to network
- Are amazingly enthusiastic and positive
- Consistently want to win

To these franchise owners, winning means being profitable. It may also mean that they will do the following:

- Enjoy more freedom than a *regular* job offers
- Have more control than a regular job might provide
- Possibly build equity in something
- Establish a legacy to pass on to their children

In order to have a shot at those four things, these folks have had to take a hard look at themselves. They had to figure out whether they truly had the right personality traits for franchise ownership. As I've stated several times already throughout this book, this franchise thing is not for everybody. As a matter of fact, it's probably *not* for most people.

I don't mean that to sound negative, in a "you just aren't right for franchising" kind of way. I mean it in a realistic way. In its simplest terms, the franchise business model is a system, and not everybody wants to work within a system. You're going to have to decide if you're really going to be okay working within a system for the entire term of your franchise contract (which averages about 10 years).

■ ■ ■

If you completed my www.takethefranchisequiz.com quiz, you should have received an e-mail with the following information:

1. The following is a reminder that my franchise quiz *is totally unscientific:* "Please look at this quiz as one of many tools that can help you decide if a franchise—or any type of business ownership option—is for you. This is not a scientific quiz! Consult with those who know you best, and then go with your gut instincts. If you decide to go down the road of business ownership, use professional resources including legal representation, accounting professionals, and other business advisors that can help protect your interests."

2. The following information concerns the scoring system used and the actual score key: "The higher the total score, the more likely you are to be suited for franchise ownership, that is, working within someone else's system. The lower the score, the more you may want to consider including other options, such as launching a nonfranchised business, launching a start-up idea of your own, or embracing more traditional employment."

   Score Key:

   50–55: High

   Looks like franchise ownership is in alignment with your personality traits; however, keep in mind that this isn't necessarily a *guarantee* that you'll be successful if you decide to become a franchise owner. The specific franchise you choose—and how well you do your research—will go a long way toward predicting your success—combined with factors such as market conditions, supply and demand, and current business trends.

   44–49: Pretty High

   Franchise ownership *could* work for you, but you'll want to find out how rigid the system really is before jumping in. Remember, this business is *someone else's* idea. It's their baby. Make sure that you'll really be comfortable following the rules—*their* rules.

   39–43: In the Middle

   Franchise ownership is one option to consider; however, it might not be the best one for you. Think instead about launching a start-up of your own or perhaps taking over an existing nonfranchise business. However, you may well find a franchise business that you feel is perfect for you. While it may be a little higher risk in your case, it could work if you can move your ego off to the side and commit to following the system's rules.

30–38: Low

Franchise ownership may not be right for you; a nonfranchise type of business is probably the direction you should take. Chances are that you most likely won't follow the franchise's rules anyway, and you'll probably be fighting the system within six months of becoming a franchisee. A traditional job could be the way to go or maybe buying someone else's business; this would allow *you* to be the one calling all the shots.

Under 30: Not

Franchise ownership is not for you—no way, no how. Forget about it. A job in a great company is likely your best option. Don't even go to a franchise website. Monster.com is where you may want to hang out. Of course, a nice, already-existing business could be worth a look.

3. My disclaimer:
   Please remember that this is only a test. The *real* test is one of deep self-discovery that you must undertake yourself by asking those who know you really well their opinion on whether they'd consider you to be a good fit for a franchise-type business.

■ ■ ■

I hope that I've succeeded in reminding you that my franchise quiz is *an unscientific tool*. You may find this hard to fathom, but I'm really not very scholarly; I don't have a degree in psychology. I don't have a degree in business, either.

Actually, I don't have *any* college degrees.

Everything I've learned (that I'm now sharing with you) has come from an on the job training sort of approach. I observe. I ask lots of questions. I watch the best of the best in action. Then I try it out myself. I observe some more, and I do it some more. I practice over and over again until I feel that I'm getting there. Then I observe some more, and so it goes. This process works for me.

In addition to relying on these kinds of firsthand experiences to keep me moving in a forward direction, I use my innate ability to quickly size up everyday situations and people. I also rely heavily on my intuition, which I believe is supersized in my case. *That's* what's behind some of the questions you answered on www.takethefranchisequiz.com. Of course, some of the questions that I use are ones that I've asked numerous prospective franchise owners in the past. Most of these have been proven to be crucial in flushing things out, with regard to how they react to elements such as rules, money, and commitment. I also include a few surprise questions that I've inserted in the quiz for very specific reasons. These involve things like business philosophy and personal confidence.

Scoring

I've had my franchise quiz online for about three years now, and during that time, I've had quite a few people complain about it. They've said things like, "It's not a very scientific quiz," or "You're not qualified to score a test like this," or "It's not like you're a psychologist," and so on.

And they're correct. Well, kind of. That's because although I'm not a psychologist, *I am* qualified to determine if someone is a possible fit for franchise ownership. My quiz works amazingly well for what I've wanted it to do: force prospective franchise owners to take a hard look at themselves and what they may be about to do, while allowing me to see for myself what they're bringing to the franchise table.

I'd like you to take one more look at your score; then read my more-detailed, no-holds-barred scoring key that follows. No more guesswork for you, okay?

50–55: People Who Score Really High on the Quiz Are Perfect Candidates for Franchise Ownership. Of course, that only applies if they were totally forthright in their answers. I've consulted with franchise candidates that scored really high on my quizzes because they said all the right things; however, they turned out to be someone totally different than how they portrayed themselves.

For example, I remember meeting with someone who had a score of 50 but who then roared into our first meeting like a steroid-induced baseball player! This gentleman interrupted me constantly and didn't want to participate in my fairly methodical franchise consultation. He just wanted me to give him some specific franchises to look at so that he could be on his way. I responded to his demands by letting him know that I couldn't help him. I then granted him his wish; he was on his way. Out.

What the heck happened? After all, he scored really high on the quiz, and he sounded great during my follow-up phone call. At that point, I started to question myself: was *I* doing something wrong? Was my franchise quiz useless? Was I a lousy consultant?

I looked over the answers to his franchise quiz again. Nothing unusual stood out. I looked at the notes I took during our meeting. Still nothing. Then it hit me; *he had lied.* This franchise candidate came to me for one reason; he wanted names. He wanted to know which franchisors I was working with, so he could start looking at them. Maybe he figured that the "franchisors" a franchise consultant was working with were probably the good ones. So, when he took the quiz, he gave answers that he thought would portray him as a perfect candidate for franchising—just to get a meeting with me. Nice.

I never heard from him again and have no idea what his real score would have been if he would have been honest. I'd be willing to wager that it would be on the low side, though, and that if he *did* end up going into franchising, it's probably not working out all that well for him.

I've worked with plenty of people—both in person and on the phone—who've tried to take control of my consultations. It's *usually* a bad sign. Granted, some people try to take control early on because they have large bank accounts, and their egos are leading the way; they want to prove to me that they're super-business savvy, and different from the other would-be franchisors I encounter. They usually try to monopolize the conversation, and they try to get me to rush through my process.

I've found that if I can't slow them down enough to explain how the franchise selection and research process works, they may not be franchise owner material. After all, if they aren't willing to follow *my* system, how much success are they going to have following one that may have a 300-page operations manual?

44–49: People Who Score in This Range Should Seriously Think about Becoming a Franchise Owner. Of course, this score—and every other one—is based on the assumption that the quiz-taker is answering honestly. There's a reason that people who are "interested" in becoming franchise owners tend to score slightly lower than those who are perfect for franchise ownership, and this has to do with having a little bit of self-doubt. I'm not talking confidence in ability; I'm referring to self-doubt as in being completely comfortable with the business model of franchising. The people who score 44–49 may have given negative answers to one or two of the questions that ask how comfortable they are with following their bosses or supervisors directives. Or perhaps they failed to answer one of the questions that require writing a short sentence or two very seriously. Chances are that they left something or, possibly, a couple of things blank, which is likely what triggered their lower score.

In almost every case, I've chosen to work with people who have scored in the 44–49 range and have then contacted me for guidance on choosing and researching franchises. My conversations with them allowed me to dig a little deeper with them and figure out why they answered a couple of the questions in a negative way. In some cases, it was something as simple as misunderstanding the questions or maybe even a bad experience with a boss in which there was a valid reason for not sticking to the plan. Generally, people that have scored in this range can make great franchise owners.

39–43: A Score That's in the Middle Range of My Franchise Quiz Is Very Telling. It tells me that this may not work out too well for these people!

But, in all seriousness, the people that score in this range are usually better off going out and getting a new job or looking into investing in a nonfranchise type of business. They've likely answered several of the questions about following systems in a negative way, and these answers have shown that they really don't like following rules. That's perfectly okay; it's just not okay for franchising!

My franchise quiz also includes a couple of questions about general business philosophy, which I slipped in to prompt some consideration and responses from quiz takers. Believe it or not, there are some folks who love the idea of investing in a franchise business but don't feel like they should have to pay things like monthly royalties or marketing fees to the franchisor. Unsurprisingly, that kind of outlook doesn't usually bode well for positive and fruitful franchisor-franchisee relationships.

This type of score doesn't mean that it's over for these people; it just means that they could be really good business owners as long as *they* are the ones that are in control. They may want to look at companies for sale in their geographic area; while they usually cost more than a start-up franchise, they tend to be a much better long-term fit for people that have scores in the middle. Or they can just forego the idea of business ownership and find a new job that allows them to be the boss.

30–38: Franchise Ownership Is Most Likely a Nonstarter, with Scores Like This. Now there *is* a slight possibility that the people who scored this low didn't really understand the quiz, or maybe they overanalyzed things a bit, but probably not.

If someone came to me for guidance after scoring this low on my franchise quiz, here's the advice they would receive: "Don't waste your time looking into franchise ownership. Get a job. Or find a business to buy that's already up and running."

I'll be telling them that because they'll probably end up losing their money in any franchise in which they are stupid enough to invest *as the person who'd be running the business*. Their 10-year franchise agreement will feel more like 30 years because they'll be absolutely miserable having to follow *all those rules*.

Wait. Forget that last statement; they won't have to worry about a 10-year franchise agreement; they won't make it past year one.

The only game-changer in a situation that has the potential to be this bad is if this person found a partner that is the exact *opposite* of them. This partner would have to be the face of the franchise and heavily involved in its daily operations. This person would have to score between 44 and 55 and commit to absolutely following the system. Also, if a partnership ended up being formed with these two people, the partner with the really low score would have to find something else to do. No franchisor is going to want this partner around the business for fear of a mutiny!

Under 30: Really? If you'd really like me to analyze a score that's unprecedented in the history of www.takethefranchisequiz.com, just send me an e-mail at: thefranchiseking@sbcglobal.net. I'll get to it eventually.

You now have some decisions to make. If your score is 44 or higher, you're probably feeling pretty darn good about things right now. You're *certainly* glad that you bought my book and are feeling confident that you're likely to be a good fit for owning a franchise. You're ready for the next step. Congratulations!

If your score is 43 or less, you may be feeling less than positive about your future. You may even be mad that you bought my book and might be thinking *refund*. But wait! There are some other options available to you such as:

- Partner with someone who is a much better fit for a franchise type of business.
- Start looking around for an existing independent business to purchase.
- Research some nonfranchise business opportunities.
- Get a new job.

See? Maybe it's not over! There *really* are alternatives. However, if you truly had your heart set on opening up your own franchise business and now know that it may not be the best idea, you may actually be angry that you bought this book. I understand—and I want you to know that you still have some choices:

- You can keep reading it and learn about *business*.
- You can give it to someone you know who's been talking about going into business for themselves.
- You can donate it to a local high school or university.

Are you still angry? Are you depressed about it? Well, if you are, consider the following: would it have been better to go into franchise ownership not knowing what it really involved? You very well might have joined hundreds—maybe even *thousands*—of others who failed miserably as franchise owners because *they had no idea what they were getting into*. Maybe these failed franchise owners thought that they didn't really have to follow the system that was laid out by the franchisor. Maybe they thought that they could kind of reinvent things a little and make it all their own. Maybe they thought that all they had to do was buy a turnkey operation and then simply turn the key. Maybe they thought that buying a franchise would almost *guarantee* them success.

Failed franchise owners all have something in common; they lost their money. And I'll bet it was a lot more than what you paid for this book.

> *"Money is better than poverty, if only for financial reasons."*
> —Woody Allen

If you're one of the people that scored on the higher end of the spectrum, you're probably excited to get going. Don't worry; we're almost there.

I'll assume that you've invested in this book to learn *the right way* to find a franchise business *that's right for you*. There *are* a couple of different ways to find one: (1) the right way and (2) the wrong way. Most people do it the wrong way, as you'll see in the next chapter.

But, because you bought this book (and you're making a commitment right now to follow my suggestions), your story shouldn't turn out anything like James Pennington's.

6

Search for a Franchise without Searching for a Franchise

"Do not learn from your mistakes; learn from the mistakes of others so that you do not make any."

—Sean Karsten

LET'S REVISIT JAMES, from Chapter 1, who is still busy trying to unwind the personal and financial nightmare he created. That's because James didn't have a clue. He thought that by starting his search for a franchise with the franchises themselves, he would find a winner. Unfortunately, this approach is completely normal and common. In fact, that's where most people start their searches. Heck, that's where I would start my search, too, if I didn't know any better.

It's also the entirely *wrong* way to commence a franchise search.

You need to resist the temptation to start looking around to see "what's out there" if you want to become a successful franchise owner and make money.

If you don't want your franchise ownership experience to be like James's was, you're going to have to start searching in a completely different place and in a completely different way. You're going to have to start with *you*, or you'll end up *being James*. Not being James is a commitment you need to make (or have made already) to *not* follow in the footsteps of so many failed franchise owners: the ones who *thought* they knew what they were doing, but didn't. This means that you'll have to follow the plan that I'm laying out for you in this book. It means that you'll have to trust me.

I've helped countless people find, explore, and research franchises over the years; I know what works. I've also seen too many times what *hasn't*. For example, check out this comment that was left on my main blog by someone named Joe (www.thefranchiseking.com/blog):

> I was a guy with a net worth in 2006 of over $500k, perfect credit, a good job in the medical field, a good passive income from some rental property. I lived on my 80+ acres farm in my own home. I was also engaged to get married. I was taken in by a [well-known] franchises' lies about the wonders of being your own boss and how much success I could have. How stupid I feel now. This settlement is just a drop in the bucket to me. I understand that I will get a check in the mail for seventeen hundred dollars. . . . [And] it will be delivered to my mom's house, because that is where I now live. My home, farm, rental property, credit rating and fiancé are all gone after my bankruptcy last year. Fortunately I was able to go back to my job and I'm getting back on my feet and doing well at repairing the damage, but it will take a long time.
>
> I know how they got me. I was a dreamer with no business experience and I played right into the hands of these liars. Some of my fellow owners in my area were experienced at business and they fell for it too, so [this company] was really slick. I hope one day they put these people in jail.

Of course, I feel terrible for Joe. But I wonder if he used a methodical way to go about his search for a franchise to own. I'm also curious about his franchise research techniques.

Now, here's what I *can* verify:

The franchise was sued for millions by a group of franchise owners. They ended up reaching a settlement. They didn't admit to any wrongdoing.

I also don't know much about Joe's circumstances. I don't know how he went about buying a franchise. For example, did he have any experience in that specific service industry? Did he talk to any franchisees before he bought his franchise? Did he have a formal business plan? Did he know how to deal with employees? Was Joe a guy who had failed in business several times before? Did he really *have* to declare bankruptcy? Did he have a farm? Was he really engaged? I just don't know.

There's one more thing I wonder about: whether Joe's expectations concerning franchise ownership were realistic.

Here's what I *do* know: investing in a franchise is *not* a sure thing. And far too many people launch franchise businesses of their own with extremely unrealistic expectations. It's partially the franchise industry's fault. (I'm trying to change that.)

Lots of prospective franchise owners have a few false impressions about how things work in the franchise industry. They might think the following:

1. If I ever have a problem, all I have to do is pick up the phone, and it will be fixed.
2. Because the franchisor has a marketing or advertising plan in place, I won't have to go out and find lots of clients or customers.
3. I am lowering my risk a lot by investing in a franchise business, as opposed to a pure start-up.
4. I'll make my investment back quickly.
5. Getting a small business loan won't be difficult because, after all, a franchise business is a proven successful business model.

Are those five things part of the reason that *you're* considering franchise ownership? Think back to James's situation. Were those five things in the back of his mind when he wrote his check for the 23-Topping Pizza franchise fee? Do you think they're factual?

Let's find out:

1. **Constant franchisee support.** Well, there is one thing that's 100 percent correct about this expectation. There certainly *will* be problems! But as pleasant as that sounds, picking up the phone to call the franchise company's headquarters and assuming that you'll receive an immediate solution to your problems probably won't happen. You are probably *not* the only franchisee that has called that day with a problem, so chances are, you'll have to wait your turn. You also have to gauge what kind of problem it is; in other words, how important might it be compared to other issues? Are you suffering from a lack of business? Is there a problem with the software that came installed on the personal computer (PC) that was part of your franchise package? Is your advertising not getting the job done? You must realize that the franchisor *cannot* and *will not* be able to solve every problem that you have. As a small business owner—of a franchise or anything else—you are now an official problem solver. You'll have to find solutions for some things—in fact, most things—yourself.

2. **Franchise marketing or advertising plan.** In most cases, your franchisor *will* have a formal marketing plan. But is it a good one? For example, have you invested in a fairly new franchise? If so, the franchisor may be still trying to figure out the marketing part of the business. If that's the case, you may have to get really creative and figure out a way to get to market yourself. In situations where the franchisor is more seasoned, the marketing plan might be a stellar one. If that's the case, then you have one less problem to deal with and can concentrate on some of the other ones that will surely exist.

3. **Statistics.** Franchise success and failure statistics have been bandied around for decades. I do believe in my heart that investing in a franchise that's right for you—and that you have researched correctly and thoroughly—*does* lower your risk compared to a pure "I have an idea for a business" type of start-up; however, you must always remember that there are no guarantees. Investing in a franchise of your own is not a magic bullet, though it does sometimes give you

a better shot of making it as a small business owner, that is, as long as it's truly the right fit for your skills, personality traits, investment comfort area, geography, and timing.

4. **Speed of your ROI.** Just in case you don't know, ROI stands for "return on investment." If you're used to working for someone else, you're used to getting a steady paycheck or, if you're in sales, a fairly steady paycheck. The most difficult part of transitioning from being an employee to a small business owner is that you won't be getting a steady paycheck for a while. As a matter of fact, the first year in your franchise business may not yield you a paycheck at all. This is why I always recommend that you have some funds set aside for your household expenses. Building a small business start-up means that you are starting at zero and hopefully making your way uphill from there.

   I remember getting a really nice thank you note from a gentleman that used my franchise advisory services in which he wrote, "I really appreciate how you changed my thinking concerning franchise ownership from a short-term view into a long-term one."

   If you're thinking about becoming a franchise owner because you're looking for a short-term fix to a career-related problem, you better think long and hard about your decision because your franchise business is probably not going to turn into an overnight success.

5. **Small business loans.** I've found that, during normal market conditions, lenders tend to be more enthusiastic about loaning money to a franchise business as opposed to a pure start-up. However, during *not* so normal times, lenders look at making small business loans on a strict case-by-case basis. In other words: your franchise loan won't be approved automatically. But one way to improve your chances that it does is to have a powerful, formal business plan. A strong business plan will go a long way in helping you secure that franchise loan. (Go to www.franchisebizplans.com, one of my franchise-related websites, for some suggestions.)

In summation, make sure that you're going into franchise ownership with realistic expectations. When the right person finds the right franchise, it can be a wonderful thing.

Let's Do This

This book is all about *you*, your dreams, your aspirations, and your future. It's also about lowering your risk to an acceptable level, making enough money to do what you want to do, and then finally getting to the point in your life where you can (and *will*) own what you do.

Ready?

Grab a spiral bound notebook and a pen or pencil. Kick off your shoes. Eliminate any distractions. Your search for a great franchise begins *right now*.

You're invited to a party!

Welcome to your first-ever list-making party! Aren't you excited? Are you ready for some fun? You're going to be making a bunch of cool lists! I'll bet that the enthusiasm emanating from your being is overpowering your entire neighborhood!

Now before you start thinking that my crown may be on a little too tight, I want you to think back to James for a minute. How did he start *his* search for a franchise business to buy? Did he start off by sitting down and writing some lists? (Go ahead and check. I'll wait.)

You didn't read *anything* about lists, did you?

But wait . . . wait . . . I think I see something here.

Amazing: James *did* actually sit down and write some lists, but they were written *after* he had to close his pizza franchise down. The lists included the following:

- A list of local lawyers who specialized in business closings
- A list of U.S. Government agencies to whom he owed money
- A list of creditors to whom he owed money
- A list of job-related connections
- A list of companies to whom he may want to submit applications to

I'll assume that you don't want to end up making *those* types of lists. Good choice.

List #1

Now let's start with your first list. We'll call this "List #1" (a creative name, I know). Open your notebook, and write down the following words:

Strategy

Sales

Marketing

Operations

Hiring/human resources

Management

Bookkeeping

Accounting

Problem solving

Logistics

Technical know-how

Customer service

The next thing I want you to do is to rank yourself on those business functions/professional skills and really take your time. On a scale of 1 to 5, with 5 being the best, determine how good you are you at each function. Base your rankings on facts, not on how much you may like or not like each one of them. Maybe others in your life have given you compliments about some of them. Essentially, you're trying to figure out what your core competencies are.

Now circle the business functions/professional skills at which you feel you perform at a 4 or 5 level. These are the only skills on which you're going to need to focus. Write those on a separate sheet of paper. Put that list off to the side. Let's start the second list.

List #2

On another sheet of notebook paper, I want you to do the exact same thing—but with the following list of personal and character traits. Rank each one 1 to 5, with 5 being the one that best describes you, and 1 being least like you. Now I know that it would save you time to just put the numbers 1 to 5 right in the book; however, I don't want you to do this. I want you to write down each word. It will force you to think about each word as you're writing them down, one by one, line by line. Please take your time; this list is incredibly important!

Engaging	Introverted	Creative
Outgoing	Aloof	Artsy
Sales-y	Belonger	Different
Determined	Congenial	Handy
Competitive	Dependable	Leader
Focused	Educated	Innovative
Enthusiastic	Efficient	Refined
Energetic	Honest	Personable
Candid	Principled	Versatile
Detail-oriented	Socially conscious	

Now I'd like you to take *another* look at the personal/character trait list you just wrote, along with the rankings you assigned to each one. Look at each one carefully. Are you absolutely *sure* about the rank you gave yourself on these particular qualities or tendencies? If you're not completely certain, another thing you can do is think of a couple of examples of yourself in action using the personal trait in question. Try to think of some situations you've faced in the past and whether you had to call on any of these abilities to get yourself through them. Write those examples down next to or below the number rank. Now look at the entire list of personal/character traits again.

Are the numbers correct? If you're satisfied with them, I want you to circle the personal/character traits that are 4s and 5s. Unless you can convince yourself otherwise, the 4s and the 5s are going to be your focus as we move on toward selecting some franchises that may make sense for you. Write them down on a separate sheet of paper and put it off to the side. You'll need it later, along with the list of your top core competencies that you put aside earlier.

We all have different core competencies and personal traits. Mine are probably different from yours; and that's okay. In fact, that's what makes our world go around. Just think how things would be if we were *all* outgoing and sales-y; the behind-the-scenes operational work would never get done. The trick here is to match your unique abilities and characteristics with franchise opportunities that could be a great fit for your particular talents and interests. It's actually the franchise opportunities—combined with what your specific role would be as the owner— to which you're looking to match yourself.

Unfortunately, most franchise buyers don't choose franchises like this. James *definitely* didn't do it this way. But *you're* going to. You're worth it. (And you're really interested in lowering your risk, making money, and owning what you do!)

Looking

I'm going to assume that you've already spent some time looking for franchises in the months or even years before you bought this book. Did you find one or two that really aroused your interest? If so, I want you to take a look at them again. See if you can remember what attracted you to them in the first place.

If, by chance, you never found any franchises that really piqued your interest, just go to any of the major franchise opportunity websites. (You'll find a list of them in the resource section at the end of this book.) Determine which ones you're most attracted to; spend at least an hour or two looking around.

As you go through this exercise, you're probably going to start mentally referring back to the two lists you just put together. If you do find yourself doing that, give yourself a pat on the back. You're starting to get it. You're learning exactly how to choose a franchise that fits.

Are you able to start disqualifying some franchises as you look at different ones? Good! That's what you *should* be doing. The more franchise opportunities that you're able to eliminate because your professional skills and your personal/character traits don't match, the closer you're going to be to finding ones that *do* match, so keep disqualifying!

Now that you're starting to look at the franchise exploration process a bit differently, I want to make sure that you're not looking at just the franchise *concepts* themselves. Make no mistake: the concepts *are* important because *you do* have to be able to visualize yourself as the owner of the concept. But you need to make sure that you're not just looking at the franchise business concept itself as you're looking around but that you're looking at the role of the franchise owner. Are your top skills—your strongest personal/character traits—a good match for an owner of that particular franchise? A better question is this one: do you even know what the role of the franchise owner is for the businesses you're considering?

Let's say that you were really interested in a couple of specific franchises before you bought this book. Did you know what your role would be as the *franchise owner?* Really? Are you sure? Did you have a call with the franchise development director or franchise salesperson at the company's headquarters? Or, as I suspect you might have, did you base your information on what you saw on the franchise website or in a brochure? I don't want you to think that I'm being a royal jerk here, but could you possibly be making some assumptions with regards to those opportunities in which you were (or still are) interested? If, by any chance, you *did* have a call or two with someone from the franchise development team of the business you were considering and found out what your role would be as the owner, kudos to you, my friend! But if you didn't—keep reading.

Let me give you a specific example of how our assumptions can sometimes bite us in the you-know-what.

Are you familiar with FastSigns or SIGNARAMA? They're two pretty well-known franchises in the sign industry. I happen to know a bit about the sign business—companies that produce signage for things like sporting events, retail store windows, and even automobiles. I've actually helped a few people get into this industry.

Do you happen to know where the nearest sign business is in your area? I do. Most likely, it's located in a strip center. Right next to it, you may find a fast food franchise, a hair salon, or maybe even a pet supply store. Now, based just on where I told you a franchise of this type is located (make sure that you can easily visualize this business), what do you think your role would be as the owner? Go ahead and think about it for a minute or two.

What did you come up with?

Do you see this as a retail-type of business, in which your role would be the guy (or gal) behind the counter, waiting on customers (with the help of some employees) as they come through the door, looking for the right products or services to purchase? Good! Now, keep in mind that you're also in charge of your store's inventory, payroll, and advertising. You'd certainly be working lots of hours as the owner of this retail business because your store is open at least 12 hours a day, six to seven days a week. That's just how it is in retail these days.

Retail businesses can be excellent companies to own because they're great for involving entire families as employees. They also usually have high visibility in the community, so almost everybody knows who you are and where your store is located. And if the people in your area have a strong *buy local* mentality, that's even better!

There *are* some negatives when it comes to owning a retail franchise business. They include extremely long hours, which can burn out owners; issues with theft; potentially high inventory costs; and the rent tends to be pretty expensive as well, especially if your business is located in a high-traffic, prime area. Also, current economic conditions can impact your store in a big way. Consumers tend to pull back their spending during periods of elevated inflation. If the stock market has a bad run, people get scared. The opposite is true, too, of course; if things are good, then consumers spend! It's great to have information like that if you're thinking about getting into a retail franchise business, like the sign business.

Except the sign business *isn't* a retail business. It's not even a first cousin to a retail business. It's a business-to-business (B2B) franchise. It only *looks* like a retail business.

The owner of a sign business franchise doesn't sit behind the counter, waiting for customers to come to him or her. This owner can't afford to *wait* for things to happen. Sign franchise owners are people who *make* things happen; they're salespeople. That's because walk-in traffic to a sign shop is minimal. Therefore, the owner's role is one of business development—in other words, sales. The owner must be out and about practically all day trying to drum up business. The owner has to call on country clubs, golf courses, malls, retail stores, restaurants, manufacturers, expo halls, and even schools because all of these places buy signs. So it's really a sales business and a manufacturing business because the owner's employees are actually making the signs and fulfilling the orders that the owner is bringing in.

A sign franchise is only open five days a week, from 9 to 5. The owner has the weekends off, unless the shop is really backed up and they need an extra day to catch up with incoming orders. Not bad, huh? (And you thought this was a retail business.)

Guess what? Before I learned about franchising, I thought that a sign business was a retail business, too. I had no idea that it was an outbound type of company—one for which the customers have to be found. A company owner has to go out and gather any potential customers.

Assumptions like these can get us into big trouble. Can you think of a particular case in which your assumptions about someone—or something—got you in trouble?

As you're searching for a franchise opportunity, make sure that you don't start assuming that you know exactly what the business does or what the franchise owner's role is. Sometimes, you won't find out a lot of things about the business until you have a real, live conversation with a member of the franchise development team.

> *"Begin challenging your own assumptions . . . [they] are your windows on the world. Scrub them off every once in awhile, or the light won't come in."*
> —Alan Alda

Not Yet

I'm not sure that you're ready for the next chapter of my book yet. I'm not feeling it because I haven't done justice to this really, *really*, important topic.

This book isn't about spending a paltry $25,000 on a new car. It's about investing anywhere from *$100,000 or more* (easily) in a business of your own. This is the big time. Most people who make a mistake here—like choosing the absolute wrong franchise or doing insufficient research on one—are likely to endure pain that will last a long time. (Think about what James is going through now.)

My late father and I helped haircutting chain Great Clips enter the Northeast Ohio market. As a matter of fact, we were instrumental in helping the folks at Great Clips corporate in Minneapolis sell out the entire area. We found great franchisees for them, but it wasn't easy. You see, we had to teach people to not make assumptions.

For example, whenever we presented the Great Clips franchise opportunity to a candidate of ours, one or more of the following sentences would emanate for their lips:

"I don't know anything about cutting hair."

"Why the heck would I want to own a *hair salon?*"

"I really don't want to mange a bunch of chattering 20-year-olds."

"What? You're nuts."

"What else can you show me?"

I think you get the drift.

Now I need to tell you that the folks to whom we were presenting the Great Clips franchise opportunity were pretty high-level people. They had to be; the financial requirements were pretty serious.

Most of the candidates to whom we introduced this idea weren't interested. They didn't want to hear about the specifics. They obviously had a certain preconceived notion of what their life would be like as the owner of a hair salon franchise. They probably pictured themselves learning how to cut hair, or maybe they thought that they'd be sitting at the front desk greeting customers and answering the phone. They obviously *assumed* a lot about the business, but they had no *facts*. Once again, this is all too common in the franchise industry. Folks that are looking at different franchises, especially online, presuppose that they know about the franchise businesses they find—*without bothering to get the facts*. I wonder how many people over the years have passed up opportunities that could have been perfect for them, their professional skills or their personal/character traits, simply because they thought they knew something about a franchise that they really didn't.

Let's go back to Great Clips, which is a perfect example of just what I mean. The folks who made the assumptions about what their lives would be like as a franchisee of Great Clips couldn't have been more wrong. Here's why:

- Great Clips franchisees don't cut hair
- They aren't greeters.
- They aren't receptionists
- They don't need hair care industry knowledge

Here's another interesting thing about most Great Clips franchisees: they're hardly ever in their stores. If you don't believe me, try the following experiment for yourself. Go visit a Great Clips salon—or any of the other large franchise hair salon chains—and go to the front desk. Ask for the owner, and check out the look you get from the receptionist; it will be followed by something like this: "The owner isn't in; as a matter fact, he's hardly *ever* here. I can get a message to him if you'd like."

Do you think any of the candidates to whom we presented this opportunity would've been interested to know that Great Clips was a semi-absentee opportunity? And that it's a multi-unit opportunity as well? There are several more cool things about this franchise, but I'll leave it to you to learn more, that is, if you're interested. Like any franchise that's mentioned in this book, it's not for everybody, and I'm not making a recommendation. I'm just sharing what I know.

The bottom line is this: please don't make assumptions with regard to any franchises you're considering. If you do so, you may be passing up one or two that just might be a perfect fit for you. Got it?

As you continue to start looking around for some franchise opportunities that *could* make sense for you (based on your dominant professional skills and personal/character traits), think about the sign business and hair salon franchise examples. Make sure that you're not discounting opportunities before you know what your role would be as the owner. I *still* want you to disqualify as many opportunities as possible; I just want you to do it methodically and sensibly.

There's no pressure on you to blow through this part of the process quickly. As a matter of fact, take as long as you need, a few hours, heck, a few days. See what's really out there. Don't worry if you don't find The One, yet. I'll reveal more information in the next chapter. I'm going to teach you how to drill down even further so that you'll be able to really customize your search for the right franchise—for *you*.

"It ain't over till it's over."

—Yogi Berra

7

Do We Have a Match?

"A #2 pencil and a dream can take you anywhere."

—Joyce A. Myers

ARE YOU READY to find some franchise opportunities that could really make sense for you? Is *this* the part of the book that you've been waiting for? Are a few butterflies starting to visit your abdominal cavity?

First off, if you're *not* yet nervous, you're going to be soon enough. It's one thing to read about things like *the history* of franchising and learn about the business model. Visiting www.takethefranchisequiz.com was probably pretty revealing, and gave you a better feel for what you can bring to the table. Because the unique professional skills and personal/character traits that define you are really an important part of the franchise buying process, I'm glad you put in the time needed to take a hard look at *you*. And beginning all of this by reading how James Pennington went about his search for a franchise and was forced to face its ultimate demise hopefully served as a wake-up call on how *not* to do it. Those butterflies may have actually first made their debut during the end of James's story. I hope so. I really want you to think long and hard about this huge decision that you're going to eventually have to make; it's going to have to be a yes or a no, if and when you find an opportunity at which you feel you can be reasonably successful. So prepare yourself. I used to tell my franchise candidates that "many a franchise contract has arrived in a franchise headquarters mail room, wet" (from the sweaty palms of the new franchisees that just signed it!) Gross, I know, but most certainly true.

Let's Drill Down

Are you starting to get a better idea of the kind of franchise opportunities you should be considering? Are the pieces of the puzzle starting to come together a little? If so—great!

Of course, I wouldn't fault you if you were feeling somewhat overwhelmed by all the choices that are available in franchising today, so don't worry about that. Looking for franchises that may turn out to be right for you is a huge undertaking if done right. Anyone can Google the word *franchise* and start looking around; but you're not just anyone, anymore. You're someone who has made a commitment (I know you did) to do this right. You're becoming an educated franchise buyer, and that alone will go a long way toward helping you **lower your risk, make money**, and **own what you do**.

In the following, you'll find several specific examples of skill and personal/character trait combinations, along with suggestions of franchise types that could be a *possible* fit for them. Now I'm not even remotely suggesting that the examples I'm providing will perfectly or accurately describe *your* specific skills and personal/character traits. If they *do* happen to exactly match you, then that's fine. However, I don't recommend that you stop everything and just go out and locate the franchise types that I've provided as possible matches to those specific skill sets and personal/character traits. Again, they are only examples (and darn good ones at that!). So begin by taking some deep breaths. Go to that happy place. Be patient. You'll be on your way to finding some great franchises soon. All in good time . . . all in good time. (You're welcome to use your best Wicked Witch of the West voice from *The Wizard of Oz* while saying the preceding sentence aloud.)

Before you start considering the following fine examples of possible franchise matches—and thinking about how you'll be able to use them in your own franchise search—you need to learn what the basic franchise categories are, along with their approximate investment amounts* so that you have a baseline for comparison.

Franchise Categories

Food and Restaurants

From Auntie Anne's Pretzels to McDonald's, this sector is the largest and most visible in franchising today. Food franchises are best for those that aren't afraid of long hours and high employee turnover. Investment amounts range from $150,000 to $1 million-plus. This sector features a lot of multi-unit opportunities.

Retail

Some of these location-based stores (that, of course, need prime locations) include names like Ace Hardware, vitamin and supplement retailer GNC, and salon chain Great Clips. These can be great family-type businesses because of the staffing hours. Like the food franchise sector, the hours in retail tend to be long and almost always include working six to seven days a week. Investment amounts for

---

*Please keep in mind that whenever I discuss *investment amounts*, two things are true: (1) they're always merely *estimates*, so you need to get the exact information from your franchise sales representative; and (2) they are estimates of *total* investment amounts—a figure that usually includes the up-front franchise fee, plus things like equipment, inventory, travel to headquarters for training, leasehold improvements, state and local fees, and some working capital. *You're* part of the total investment will vary, depending on loan terms (if you need one).

some of the smaller retail franchises begin around $120,000 and can easily top $500,000.

Lodging

Hotel and motel franchises are the most expensive types of franchises in which to invest. For example, if you're thinking of becoming the owner of a Courtyard by Marriot hotel, you have to have a real estate net worth of at least $5,000,000 according to their franchise website. And what about managing a Hilton? The total investment necessary to begin operation of a typical 300-room Hilton hotel is from $53,486,500 to $90,169,000. Obviously, these are long-term investments.

Home Services

Owners of home service franchises provide more than services; they help families free up their time to do other things. Some businesses in this sector include cleaning franchises like Maid Brigade, lawn care companies like Spring-Green Lawn Care, and home maintenance services like Mr. Handyman. Owners of service franchises generally don't *do* the actual work, although it depends on the specific franchise concept chosen. You should figure you'll need about $100,000 to $250,000 to buy one of these types of franchises.

Business to Business (B2B)

If you can sell (and you enjoy it), a B2B franchise could be just the thing. Franchise opportunities in this sector include things like Sandler Sales Training, in which franchisees provide sales training to small businesses and advertising and marketing sales companies like Valpak and Money Mailer. Staffing franchises like Express Services provide both temporary and permanent employees to small businesses in their geographic areas. You can purchase some franchises in the B2B category for under $100,000 and can some even be home-based.

Children's Related

This sector of franchising encompasses lots of different types of business models, including almost-part-time ones. Opportunities include tutoring, like those provided by Huntington Learning Centers. If you're interested in child care (and have deep pockets), Goddard Schools and Primrose are two franchises that offer these kinds of opportunities. Young Rembrandt's and Abrakadoodle are franchises that offer enrichment programs for children. There's quite a wide range of investment amounts in this category. If you're thinking of investing in a children's-related franchise, you could spend anywhere from $80,000 to $750,000-plus.

Health and Fitness

This growing category includes everything from senior-care franchises like Brightstar Healthcare and Synergy Healthcare, to fitness franchises like Snap Fitness and Gold's Gym. Even franchises that offer therapeutic massages like Massage Envy and Massage Heights are included in this franchising sector where the required investment ranges from $150,000 to $900,000 or more. There are lots of multi-unit owners in this sector of franchising.

Green Franchises

This relatively new category of franchising features mostly young franchise concepts like solar panel design and installation company Solar Universe, residential energy auditing franchise Dr. Energy Saver, and LED Source, a distributor of professional and high quality LED lighting products. You can expect investment amounts to range from $75,000 to $300,000.

Now that you know the basic franchise categories, it's time to see how people's specific skills and personal/character traits match up to opportunities in the world of franchising. I'm going to provide several examples of exactly how all of this comes together. Hopefully, this will help you start thinking about specific franchising sectors toward which you may want to put your energy and begin investigating.

Examples of Possible Franchise Matches

Example #1

Skill Sets: Operations, Management, Problem Solving

Personal/Character Traits: Efficient, Dependable, Versatile, a Belonger

Possible Franchise Matches:

Food/Restaurant: Casual Food, Ice Cream-Frozen Yogurt

Automotive: Oil Change Services, Transmission or General Auto Repairs, Automobile Rentals, Tire Stores

Lodging: Hotels or Motels

Why do these match up? Most people don't usually consider the businesses described above to be ground-breaking types of franchises. They are what I call *everyday* organizations that need a steady hand to run efficiently. Franchise owners need to be dependable, partially because their employees may not be. Therefore, they also need to be versatile enough to be able jump in and do what's needed to keep things moving along. The more efficiently these businesses run, the better the bottom line looks.

Example #2

Skill Sets: Sales, Marketing

Personal/Character Traits: Energetic, Sales-y, Competitive

Possible Franchise Matches:

Business to Business (B2B): Advertising or Direct Mail, Sign Businesses, Staffing Franchises, Business Coaching-Consulting

Why do these match up? These types of franchise businesses are suited for people that have a type A personality; high-energy, competitive types do well in these B2B franchises. Franchise owners must have a strong sales and marketing aptitude and also need to be pretty fearless. They must also be self-motivated as their sales duties are usually of the solo variety; they're out and about making sales calls on their own, with no supervision.

Example #3

Skill Sets: Hiring/Human Resources, Bookkeeping, Accounting, Management

Personal/Character Traits: Introverted, Principled, Educated, Congenial, Efficient

Possible Franchise Matches:

Retail Optical Stores, Tax Services, Hardware Stores, Picture Framing Stores, Check-Cashing Services

Why do these match up? The franchise business types that I've named here are possible matches for people that consider themselves to be a bit more on the introverted side. These franchises are all location-based, and that's where the franchisees are most comfortable: *inside* their stores. Although I included accounting in the preferred skill sets that I laid out, franchisees need not have a degree in accounting per se. They just have to be comfortable dealing with details because all of these franchise types have this kind of work as part of their business models.

Example #4

Skill Sets: Strategy, Logistics, Management, Sales

Personal/Character Traits: Dependable, Principled, Determined, Detail-Oriented

Possible Franchise Matches:

Home Services: Kitchen Remodeling Franchises, Residential Cleaning Services, Pest/Critter Control Services

Retail: Packing or Shipping Stores, Gas Stations, Convenience Stores

Why do these match up? You'll notice once again that the word *detail* appears here. That's because the franchise types that are listed *do* require franchisees to be good with details. Though there's a sales aspect to these franchises as well, it's more of a consultative type of sales. Franchisees need to be good at logistics, scheduling, and management. The franchise types mentioned have lots of competitors, and the more determined franchisees are to win, they more they'll excel as owners.

Example #5

Skill Sets: Management, Problem Solving, Operations, Customer Service

Personal/Character Traits: Different, Energetic, Educated, Socially Conscious, Engaging

Possible Franchise Matches:

Green Franchises: Solar Energy Stores, Residential or Commercial Energy Audit Franchises, Junk Removal

Retail: Tutoring Centers

Food/Restaurants: Smoothie Bars, Healthy Food Restaurants

Why do they match up? Some people are attracted to franchises that they believe can help change the world. Part of a franchisee's role in an organization that focuses on change involves providing genuinely positive customer interactions, followed by great customer service. Although selling is part of the franchisee's role in these businesses, I didn't include it as a skill set. The reason for this is because people that are focused on change rarely need *formal* sales training because they're naturally energetic and engaging and because it's so easy for them to sell their products and services because they believe so strongly in them. Outstanding operations and management skills are especially helpful in businesses like these.

Example #6

Skill Sets: Technical Know-How, Marketing, Problem Solving, Management

Personal/Character Traits: Focused, Detail-Oriented, Handy, Creative

Possible Franchise Matches:

Home Services: Computer Repair, Building or Remodeling Services, Home Inspection Services

Retail: Hobby Stores, Hardware Stores

Why do they match up? These franchise business types are best for people that aren't afraid to work with their hands. Although technical know-how should be part of the franchisees' makeup, the franchisees will have employees doing a lot of the hands-on work in most cases. Therefore, except in the retail franchises, the franchisees themselves really need to be out and about, marketing and promoting their products and services to their local communities. However, being handy can definitely be a plus—especially when employees are stuck. Once again, people that are interested in utilizing the skills mentioned in the preceding also need to be good managers of both people and time.

Example #7

Skill Sets: Operations, Strategy, Management, Problem Solving

Personal/Character Traits: Determined, Competitive, Enthusiastic, Leader

Possible Franchise Matches:

Lodging: Hotels and Motels

Food/Restaurant: Multi-unit Restaurants

Retail: Multi-unit Hair Salons, Dry Cleaners

Health/Fitness: Multi-unit Fitness Centers, Tanning Salons, Massage Centers

Why do they match up? Franchises that operate in a highly competitive arena need highly competitive and determined franchisees. Think, for instance, about how many membership-style fitness- or health-related franchises—and even nonfranchise businesses—are around nowadays. These types of franchises need to have franchisees that are always on the lookout for new ways to recruit new members for their clubs, while continuously strategizing on how to keep their current members. Strong leadership qualities are a must here in order for owners to keep their teams highly motivated—in both membership and nonmembership style fitness- and health-related franchises. Many franchisees in this sector are multi-unit owners.

Example #8

    Skill Sets: Management, Sales, Customer Service, Operations

    Personal/Character Traits: Sales-y, Personable, Socially Conscious, Leader

    Possible Franchise Matches:

    Health/Fitness: Senior Care Services, Weight-Loss Clinics

    Green Franchises: Solar Franchises

Why do they match up? These franchise types require franchisees to have a pretty unique combination of skill sets and personal/character traits in order to thrive. For example, not only do franchisees need to be socially conscious to manage these types of franchises, but they also need to have strong sales skills. It's one thing to be interested in helping people; it's quite another thing to actually be able to *sell* the products and services that can do the most good. In addition, franchisees must have the ability to manage a staff and a good understanding of the operational aspects of the business to keep things moving smoothly.

Your Actual Mileage May Vary

When I worked in the car business, we always had to make sure to add the phrase "your actual mileage may vary" in the small print just below the advertisement that we submitted to the local newspaper. In car speak, that phrase means that there are lots of variables that can affect how many miles per gallon (MPG) your vehicle will actually get. Factors such as using the vehicle's air conditioning, driving in heavy traffic (which usually leads to lots of stop-and-go driving), or driving in extreme conditions (say, desert heat or an Alaskan winter) all play a role in the amount of gas mileage a car actually gets. Gas mileage isn't set in stone and never can be. So what does all this have to do with becoming a franchise owner? Well, nothing, actually. (I'm kidding. I'll show you exactly what it has to do with becoming a franchise owner.)

But before I do, I need to give credit to my friend, Chris Brogan, for popularizing the phrase "your actual mileage may vary" in his writing. Chris is not only a social media marketing rock star, he's a prolific author who's written two books already, with more to come, I'm sure. His uber-popular blog www.chrisbrogan.com provides thousands of posts. Chris uses this phrase in several of them and does so to make the point that we're all different, and all of our circumstances and situations are different, too. So not all of Chris's readers can use the tips and suggestions he provides in their own specific situations—something he makes clear by his intelligent use of the phrase "your actual mileage may vary". (Thanks for the inspiration, Chris.)

I introduce Chris's phrase here because I'm using it in much the same way. In the previous section, I gave you eight pretty specific examples of how certain skill sets and personal/character traits can be matched up with certain franchise types. The important word here is *examples*. You may have a totally different combination of skill sets and personal/character traits than the ones I presented, and that's fine! Just mix and match to find the option that suits you best. You're probably *not* going to know the exact skills and traits that you'll need for the specific franchises that interest you at first. That's okay; the point is that you're going to be in a much better position to identify the specific things you'll need in order to succeed with the franchises you're considering. Just remember: your actual mileage may vary.

The combinations of skill sets and personal/character traits combined with the several possible franchise business type matches I provided aren't etched in stone; they can't be. Just like the example I gave you of how gas mileage can (and *does*) vary among different vehicles that are driven under diverse conditions, so it is with trying to match specific franchises to specific skills and traits. There are lots of variables; one size doesn't fit all.

Start thinking about the types of businesses that could be a fit for all—or at least most—of the skills and traits in which you scored particularly high. I don't expect you to be able to jump right in and figure this all out right away. But you will get better at it as you start looking at the different franchise websites and blogs in your quest to find some franchises that may work for you. You can use the resource section toward the end of the book to find out where you should look.

However, before you flip the pages of this book to begin reading that section, I have something that's really important to share with you. It's a tool.

I'm Throwing in a Wrench

I need to share a true story with you. The names have been changed because I don't remember the real ones.

I'll kick this off by saying that I really love public speaking. It's one of the reasons that I said "yes" to my Dad's offer to join his franchise consulting firm after he told me that a big part of the business was speaking at seminars and events. I actually think that this was one of his main reasons for asking me to join him; he knew how much I loved presenting to live audiences. Most people who've heard me speak tell me that they really felt that I spoke from my heart; they enjoyed my sense of humor and were able to tolerate my somewhat intense style because I'm just so darn straightforward.

As I was setting up for a franchise ownership seminar a couple of years ago, a rather attractive lady entered the room. I could tell by the determined look in her eyes that she was there to see me before the other members of the audience started to trickle in.

"Are you Joel Libava?" she asked.

"Yes, I am." I said. "I'm actually speaking in a few minutes; how may I help?"

"Well, my name is Beth, and I wanted to catch you before you spoke to see if you could help me with something. You see, my husband and I bought this franchise last year, and we don't really like it."

"Interesting," I replied (looking perplexed, I'm sure.) "Why don't you like it?"

"Well, we really thought we would. It fit our backgrounds, and I really thought that we could make it work."

"What type of franchise business is it?" I asked.

"It's an advertising type of business. Direct Mail."

"Ok." I then asked her, "What don't you like about it?"

Her answer—*and this is a classic*—"the selling part."

This is probably a good time to share a couple of things about me:

1. I don't do a real good job with two important (to society, I guess) things. I've always missed having one piece of optional equipment included in the Joel Libava chromosomal package. It's the "wait five seconds before you respond to someone" option. I guess it wasn't being offered when I was conceived.

2. I can't seem to be able to *not* say what's on my mind, even if it may offend someone a bit. I seem to lack what is commonly called a *filter*. In other words, you probably won't see me running for political office anytime soon (although I feel that I could probably get some stuff done).

It's weird; I thought that most folks are supposed to start mellowing out a bit as they grow older. But I guess that I'm not like most folks because I'm actually getting more passionate and more vocal than ever about certain topics. (Dr. Phil, where are you when I need you, man?) For instance, I've become an advocate for franchise buyers (like you) on the topic of franchise ownership.

So, back to Beth, who is sharing her pain with me. I proceeded to ask her the next logical question:

"Beth, didn't you guys *know* that you'd have to do sales?" (I told you it is hard for me to *not* say what's on my mind.)

"Well, yes, we knew that, but we just didn't think that it would be as hard as it is," she said.

(I think that my blood pressure was starting to rise a wee bit at this point in our conversation.)

"Not as hard? Can you explain a little more about what you mean?" I asked.

"Well, almost everybody we try to sell our direct mail advertising program to says 'no' to it."

"Well that's probably not that unusual. In sales, sometimes you have to go through lots of no's before you start getting some yeses."

"We know that; both of our backgrounds are in sales and marketing. But we're still hardly selling anything!"

"Have you brought this up with the franchisor?"

"No . . . not really. We just don't want to do it anymore. We just want to get out of it. How can we do that?"

"Well, you'd have to try to sell it, Beth."

"Can you help us do that, Joel?"

Because I had to start getting ready for the seminar attendees (who were starting to file in by this point), I told Beth to leave me her contact information and that I'd follow up with her. Before she took her seat, she told me that she "was serious about wanting to get out of her franchise" and that she *really* wanted my help.

I have a little confession to make; I knew that there was actually no way that I could help Beth, unless I decided to write her a check out of my own pocket for the $130,000 that she invested in her franchise business. And it's a darn good thing that I was about to start my seminar on franchise ownership; I didn't have time to grab my checkbook as she took her seat.

My speaking engagements always include a portion where I emphasize *just how important it is* to carefully match your skills and personal/character traits with the franchises that you're interested in pursuing. This one was going to be no different, except for one thing: Beth, a lady who supposedly had a sales and marketing background, along with her husband, had invested in a sales and marketing-related franchise that was failing, and I knew that she was going to be focused on my every word.

I remember looking at Beth during my presentation, particularly as I spoke about the importance of ensuring that attendees *carefully investigate* the opportunities they planned to consider—and that they knew exactly what their roles were going to be as franchise owners of those franchises. It was weird—really weird—because I know that I was probably revealing some of the errors that she and her husband made during their franchise research. First of all, if they didn't work with me, they didn't do their research right. (I'm not being pompous; I just know that they had to have missed a few really important things that I may have been able to help them flush out well before they got their bank loan and wrote a check for their franchise fee.)

Now, just for the heck of it, let's say that I'm wrong. I'll give them the benefit of the doubt and assume that they didn't miss a thing and actually did a fantastic job with their research. Let's also say that they *really* did feel that they were looking at the right type of franchise business. After all, Beth told me that they *both* had a sales and marketing background.

It's worth it to note that I've actually met lots of people who've told me that they've come from a sales and marketing background. However, I've found over the years that sometimes *their* definition of sales and *my* definition of sales are quite different. For example, maybe they *managed* a sales call center at a telecommunications company. Or maybe they were in retail sales, a situation in which the customers were coming to them. I've even had folks tell me that they have a sales background, only to find out that they were actually sales *support* representatives that did no actual selling.

Let's assume in the case of Beth and her husband that they both actually *did* come from a sales background and that it was pretty similar to the type of sales (business to business) that would be required for an advertising sales franchise. This sure sounds like a good franchise fit, right?

So what the heck could have happened? Well, I have 10 ideas:

1. They didn't talk to enough existing or former franchisees as part of their research.
2. They didn't write a formal business plan.
3. They didn't have enough money in reserve to get them through the first year of a start-up franchise business.

4. They had very unrealistic expectations of exactly what was involved in being a small business owner.
5. They weren't very good salespeople. (Hey, it's possible.)
6. They started listening to their prospective customers a little too much and becoming negative about the product *themselves*, because so many people that they were calling on were saying "no."
7. They didn't ask for help from the franchisor, but, more important, they never asked for help from the *other* franchisees in the system.
8. The franchisor's product was lousy.
9. The franchisor's system was lousy.
10. They just didn't like it.

Can you think of any more things that could have forced their hand? Obviously, *something* went wrong; otherwise, they wouldn't have wanted out of their franchise after less than a year of being in business.

I wonder what Beth was hoping I could do for her as she approached the podium where I was setting up for my franchise ownership presentation. Now that I think back on it, I do remember her asking me if "she could just give her franchise back" or something of that nature. I'm also pretty sure that she asked me if I thought she would be able to "just get her money back" from the folks at franchise headquarters. (You know, just walk away from her franchise business and get a full refund.) Now, because that probably wasn't going to happen, Beth really only had two choices:

1. Walk away.

    Beth and her husband would obviously lose their entire $130,000 investment if they simply walked away from their franchise business. In addition, they would still have to pay back their small business loan and would have to try to break the lease if they had rented office space. Of course, if the landlord wouldn't let them do so, they would owe the remainder of their monthly lease payments. (Is this starting to sound familiar? Didn't our old friend James have to go through something similar?) Additionally, the franchisor could go after Beth and her husband for royalties and try to sue them for failing to honor their other contractual obligations. (For example, this franchisor's franchise contract may have been a 10-year one, which would leave nine more years of obligations—an ugly possibility.) The advertisements that Beth and her husband sold would still have to be published. But for how long? Sometimes, direct mail advertising contracts are yearly. These advertisers may have signed up to be included in four mailings a year. So what happens to their ads if there is no active franchisee in their area anymore? And what happens to the thousands of dollars that they paid up-front for a 12-month deal? Do the folks at franchise headquarters jump in and make sure everything is mailed out as promised?

2. Sell their business.

Beth and her husband's other option is to try to sell their business, which seemed to be what Beth wanted *me* to do for her. However, it would've been a tough sell. I mean, what would they be selling? Here are their current business assets:

Leased office space

Sales and marketing materials

A miniscule book of customers

A prospect list

A business that's a franchise

Barely any revenue

If *you* were looking to buy an *existing* franchise business like Beth's, what would *you* pay for it? It's not exactly a thriving, wildly successful business. Plus, this franchise business model is one of *outbound* lead generation; there's no one coming into your office, offering to give you their money. Customers—lots of them—have to be found. Then you must convince those same customers that they should *renew* their advertising contracts. You're not managing a highly visible retail store or restaurant; there's no inventory or valuable employees that can be included as part of the sale (or the sales price.)

I'm not saying that Beth's business doesn't have potential. It actually does. Lots of companies use direct mail. It can be a great way to attract new customers, and it makes tracking where these new customers came from much easier. It's really a viable business model for the right person. It's just that owners of direct mail advertising franchises have to do the following:

A. *Be* tigers

   Or

B. *Hire* tigers

(Tigers in this case are very aggressive, extremely hungry, fearless salespeople that tend to get the job done—no matter what.)

On a positive note, if Beth and her husband were able to sell their business, the new franchise owner wouldn't have to find office space or order a lot of marketing materials. They may have already set up a local website, and there would probably be a list of all the businesses in the area that needed to be called on—all of which would save the new franchisee some time.

I just didn't feel that *I* was the right person to try to help Beth and her husband sell their business. I really wasn't up for the challenge. And this *would* have been a challenge. Imagine trying to find a buyer for a brand-new but totally unprofitable franchise business. I just didn't see it as a valuable use of my time.

When I was in the car business, there was an old saying that was passed down from some of the older car guys that could apply to this situation; "There's an ass for every seat." In other words, every car for sale on a car lot had a buyer, somewhere. This soon-to-be-for-sale direct mail franchise probably had a buyer, too. It just wasn't going to be up to me to find one.

There's actually one more thing that I need to share with you concerning my lack of motivation to take on a franchise sale like this one: *I wasn't sure that I'd get paid.* I'm dead serious. I wouldn't have gotten paid a dime until the sale was actually completed (if it even sold.) I felt that Beth and her husband were kind of up against the wall, here, and I didn't think that their money situation was very liquid. In my mind, it was entirely possible for them to forget about little old me if and when they got a check for their business.

Now it's important to know that there *are* safeguards that can be put in place in situations like this. Beth and her husband could establish an escrow account in which all the proceeds from the sale would be deposited; then the escrow agent would pay me directly. However, I've heard stories about those types of set-ups, and I wasn't willing to risk losing what would have been due to me. Besides, how confident would *you* feel if you were asked to sell an almost ready to close franchise business? Do you think that you'd be able to spin a powerful enough story to sell this bad boy to someone that's really been eager to get their hands on a losing business just like this?

I can just picture Beth and her husband reading the paragraph you just read. I can almost hear them say something like this:

What a jerk! Of course we would pay Joel if he helped us sell our business. We just wanted out! We're very honorable people. How dare him! Why does he think we wouldn't pay? He doesn't even know us!

And maybe they would have. I just don't know. I guess that I didn't like the following obstacles:

A. Being able to actually *sell* a franchise that was close to closing its doors and that didn't have much to offer a prospective buyer

B. Actually getting paid

I don't know how Beth and her husband fared; maybe they got lucky and were able to find a buyer. I hope so because the alternative wasn't very attractive.

About the Wrench

It's really important for you to understand that, even if you've taken the time to do a thorough self-analysis, you could still miss something—either concerning your franchise choice or during your franchise research—that might cause you to lose your money in a franchise that you've purchased. Even with all the tips, techniques, and tools that I'm providing you in this book, there's no guarantee that you'll make the right decision. Look what happened to Beth and her husband. They obviously took their sales and marketing backgrounds into account and proceeded to match themselves up to a franchise business that (they thought) aligned with their skills. However, they didn't seem to account for or prepare themselves for the normal, day-to-day rejection that all salespeople experience. It also doesn't appear that they did their franchise research properly; I don't think they talked to many franchisees. Even if they did, I doubt very much if they asked them the right questions. I don't think that they really dug in deep enough. How do I know this? Because if they *did* do their research properly, they would've found out that it wasn't necessarily as *easy* as they assumed to sell direct mail advertising. Just because direct mail is a viable way for lots of organizations to advertise, it doesn't mean that *every* small business owner will be receptive to writing the franchisee of a direct mail franchise a check for $2,500 just because the franchisee believes in the product. "If it was easy, everyone would be doing it" is a saying that I've heard many times in my life, and it is one that definitely applies to owning your own business. Saying that "I know that I'm going to have to work really hard" and then actually doing it are two *very* different things. Add to it that you'll be working really hard—for nothing—at first, and maybe you now have an idea on why so many people fail at business ownership. But it doesn't have to be that way for you. That's why I wrote this book; I'm trying to help you avoid losing your money in a franchise.

Speaking of money, would you like to find out how much you can afford to invest in a franchise? I mean, wouldn't it be rather silly to start looking at all the different franchises available now (especially with all of your newfound knowledge) if you didn't really know the ones in which you could actually *afford* to invest? Talk about a major bummer; you find one or two franchises that you *just know* are a good fit, only to find out that you're not financially qualified to even be taken seriously by the franchise development team. Let's avoid that, okay? We will in the next chapter; it's about the money.

8

Show Me Your Money

"I made my money the old fashioned way. I was very nice to a wealthy relative right before he died."

—Malcolm Forbes

IF YOU USE the techniques that I'm teaching you in this book, you're going to save a lot of time searching for a franchise opportunity that's right for you. In addition to learning about the history of the franchise business model and about James Pennington's story (and, therefore, hopefully what *not* to do when buying a franchise), you went to www .takethefranchisequiz.com, received your score, and started on the path of self-analysis. This analysis included discerning your top business skills while identifying your dominant personal and character traits. Armed with these insights, you are well prepared to go out and find some franchises that just may be a great fit for you. But there's still one thing missing that you need in order to focus like a laser beam on the franchise opportunities that may be right for you. And that, of course, is. . . .

The Money Part

You've learned so much about how to go about your franchise search. Your new *franchise brain* has retained a lot more than you think, and I'm supremely confident in the newfound abilities you've developed that will enable you to find opportunities that are truly right for you. Remember: the more time you spend looking around now, the better you're going to get at identifying franchises that align with your skills and personal/ character traits. Repetition is the key here.

As I've mentioned previously, matching your talents and traits with appropriate opportunities puts you in a much better position to lower your risk, make money, and allow you to *own what you do*. Remember, most franchise buyers don't have a specific, step-by-step plan to help them get where they want to go; but *you* do.

However, there's still a missing piece to The Plan, and it's a fairly big one.

Let's say that you *were* able to find a franchise that ended up matching *all* of your skills—and even *all* of your personal/character traits— perfectly. Wouldn't that be great? Of course it would! That's what you wanted, right? Well, maybe you didn't know that's what you wanted until you read this book, but now that you *do* know, it's a great feeling, right? So, you've found a franchise that's right for you. Congratulations! Enjoy the moment. Be at one with nature. Feel your bliss.

Now come on back. *Slowly* open your eyes. Wasn't that enjoyable? Great! We're all allowed to dream, for a little while at least. And, in your case, finding that one franchise that's perfect for you *was* only a dream. It *is* a total fantasy. It *can't* happen for you, but not for the reasons that you might think. It can't happen for you because the franchise development representative of the franchise, that you felt you matched up perfectly to, informed you that you didn't qualify.

That's right; you didn't meet the minimum financial qualifications to become a franchisee. Boo! What a waste of time and energy that was! So much for your dream!

If you'd like to avoid a scenario like that one and actually be able to have a *real* shot at realizing all of your dreams, then please follow along with me.

Your Financial Picture

Unless your last name happens to be Rockefeller, Buffett, or Gates, you're going to have to figure out exactly how much you can invest in your venture. There's no way around it. Well, actually there is; you *can* just wing it. After all, we're only talking about an investment of around $200,000 or so. No big deal. I'm sure that you took a similar approach and just *guessed* how much you'd be able to put down on your house or condo when you purchased it. I'm also almost positive that you and your spouse, partner, significant other, or your best buddy Fido didn't sit down and figure out precisely what you had to work with. And I'm doubly sure that the banker who approved your home loan didn't really need to know the exact amount of money that you were going to put down. No biggie. Your banker probably just said something like, "Don't worry about how much you're going to be able to put down toward a house. Just go out and find a few. We'll worry about your down payment when you find one or two that you like." Right.

(The preceding sarcastic paragraph was brought to you by all the ex-franchisees who didn't feel setting a budget was all that important, and who—because they lost everything—are currently living in a double-wide.)

My point is this: you've come this far. Why start *rushing* into an opportunity now? If you plan on being a successful franchise owner someday, you're going to have to do a lot more things right than you do wrong. Finding out what you have to work with moneywise is something that you *have* to do right, so let's figure it out.

When you're interested enough in a specific franchise that you take the time to fill out the request for information form for, you may face some basic financial questions that you *must* answer before you can even submit the form. It's fairly common to confront questions about your approximate net worth or about the amount you're able to invest, so it would behoove you to know the answers to those questions before diving in. The best alternative is to have your entire financial picture right at your fingertips. After all, if you don't know where you *are* financially, how can you know where you want *to go*?

Now, if you don't feel that you're currently in a good financial position, *please* don't ignore this part of the process. You still need to know *exactly* where you're at, even if that happens to be a pretty ugly place. Remember: nothing stays the same. There are times in our lives when we've been up, and there are times when we've been down. The ability to accept *that* fact can go a long way in keeping one's sanity during those down times. I mean, do you really think that you're the only person that's experienced highs and lows?

If you're requesting information from a franchisor that *doesn't* ask you for any financial information up-front, don't assume that they're letting you off the hook. They're still going to want to know where things

---

Did you know that Donald Trump's companies have filed for bankruptcy *four* times?*

While Mr. Trump has certainly made a lot of money, he's lost a lot of money, too. Even this guy's had his share of ups and downs.

I've provided Mr. Trump as an example here for a couple of reasons:

1. He always seems to come out on top. Trump is a winner, financially. Do *you* have a 100-story building with *your* name on it?
2. I want to make sure that you're able to separate feelings from facts. Some people really like Trump, and some people just can't stand him. In either case, people are sharing their *feelings* about the man. Facts are facts, though; Donald Trump is a wildly successful businessman, and that *is* a fact.

"I like thinking big. If you're going to be thinking anything, you might as well think big."

—Donald Trump

*Source: http://abcnews.go.com/Politics/donald-trump-filed-bankruptcy-times/story?id=13419250

stand for you in terms of money. It can (understandably) be intimidating for some people to disclose very personal information like one's household finances. I know this from experience as I ask some basic questions about finances when I'm working with franchise buyers in an advisory role.

Over the years, I've actually been involved in a few mild *arguments* with prospective franchise buyers who didn't feel that it was important *for me* to know about their financial situation. Admittedly, I'm not the most patient person when people who have requested my guidance refuse, for some strange reason, to give me the information I need to do my job properly. I do completely get how some people may be a little leery about disclosing their financial information. After all, we do frequently hear about incidents in which people have been scammed by con artists— either in person, or more commonly, online. Heck, I don't really derive a lot of pleasure from having to give up my own financial information to a stranger, either. It's a bit uncomfortable, but it's part of life, and if we want to buy things on credit, make investments, or even send our children to college, we have to relinquish that information. The reality is no different for people looking to invest in a franchise business; the franchise company needs the information. Now, if you want to spend your time and energy fighting the fact that you're going to have to disclose everything about your finances when you decide to seriously look at specific franchise opportunities, then that's certainly your choice, but you'll never end up buying a franchise. Franchise development representatives aren't going to chase you around or beg you for your financial information. They'll just move on to the next prospective franchise owner. Personally, I'd rather you spend your energy on the things that you *can* control—like deciding how much you're going to budget for a franchise business.

Before I show you how to put your budget together, it's important that you understand exactly where the franchisors stand in terms of their need to know your personal financial information. Try putting yourself in the franchisors' shoes for a moment. Most of them have invested hundreds of thousands of dollars into the creation and development of their concept. They know that in order for it to continue to grow, they must sell new franchises—and doing so isn't easy. Franchisors have to talk to many candidates before they can find one that says yes and becomes a franchisee.

There are a lot of steps that have to take place before these individuals can sell a franchise. For example, it's important for the franchisor's sales team to *only* spend time with franchise candidates that have enough money to invest in their concept. It's just good business. If members of the franchise sales team spend an inordinate amount of time talking with anybody and everybody that's inquiring about the concept—whether they're qualified or not—they won't be able to sell any franchises. Franchisors who've invested their money into developing their concepts won't be too happy about that. Initially, new franchise sales are primarily what drive the machine. As the former president of IBM famously said, "Nothing happens until a sale is made." This claim certainly rings true in franchising as well. When a new franchise is sold, not only does the franchisor receive a nice-sized check (from the franchise fee), but they also, all of a sudden, have the potential to collect hundreds of thousands of dollars in future royalties from this single, new franchisee. And if you're the CEO of a franchise company, you'd obviously like to see royalties coming in from more than one franchisee.

Alright—let's do some math now. (I invite you to take out your calculator.)

Let's say that you're the CEO of Light on the Starch Dry Cleaning Franchising, Inc. You've invested $300,000-plus in your franchise concept and currently have 25 franchisees who each have one location up and running. You're fairly happy with how your franchise has grown in the five years that you've been in business. Your franchisees pay you 7 percent of their gross revenue every month. On average, each franchisee's store does $625,000 a year in gross revenue.

The math works as follows:

$625,000 yearly gross revenue × 7 percent royalty = $43,750 from each franchisee

$43,750 in royalties × 25 franchisees = $1,093,750 a year

Therefore, you—as the franchisor—are receiving over $1 million a year in royalties. Not bad. But you want more. So you decide that you want to sell 75 new franchises over the next 24 months, which would give you a total of 100 franchise units. (Some of your franchisees would probably have more than one by that time, but let's keep this simple.)

The *new* math:

$43,750 in royalties × 100 franchisees = $4,375,000 a year

As the franchisor, you are now receiving checks from your franchisees every year that total well over $4 million dollars.

Now do you see where the franchisors are coming from? There's a lot of money on the line—that which the franchisor has invested to get the franchise concept up and running, and as you saw in the preceding, the future royalty stream.

Hopefully, you now have a much better understanding as to why you need to provide all of your personal financial information. If you *are* qualified for the franchises in which you're interested, you need to make sure that the franchise development representatives *know* that you are. Be prepared to provide the information that they're undoubtedly going to request so that you can start things off on the right foot with them—*qualified*.

So do you know where you are financially at this very moment? If you know *exactly* where you are, you are more than welcome to skip this section. If not, I'm going to help you find out just where you are. (I wonder if James Pennington knew exactly where he was financially before he invested in his food franchise. Something tells me he didn't.)

For this next part, you're going to need a calculator, and some scratch paper, along with all of your financial information.

This is all about your assets and liabilities. That's it. It can't get much simpler than that. Even if you *don't* end up investing in a franchise business, the data that you'll have amassed and figured out at the end of this little exercise will provide you with some great information that you can save and update as needed. Having your net worth statement filled out and readily available will save you lots of time when other financial matters come up—like college, your retirement plans, and more.

Fill out the following form to the best of your ability. It's fine if you don't have the exact figures for things like the payoff amounts on your vehicles or credit cards. Same goes for the balance (if you have one) of your mortgage (although a phone call to the bank holding your mortgage to get the exact amount wouldn't hurt). Typically, a good deal of your net worth will come from the equity in your home, so it's worth it to spend the extra time needed to determine its precise amount.

If you have a whole life insurance plan, there's a cash value to it right now. You will, therefore, want to get that information and put it over on the asset side of the form that I've provided. Your household items have a cash value, too; your appliances, furniture, electronics, and pretty much

Assets		Liabilities	
Cash in Banks, etc.	_____	Notes Payable, Banks	_____
Miscellaneous Cash	_____	Notes Payable, Other	_____
Stocks and Bonds	_____	Charge Accounts	_____
IRA	_____	Credit Cards	_____
401K	_____	Finance Companies	_____
Cash Surrender Value, Life Insurance	_____	Due on Life Insurance	_____
		Mortgage, Residence	_____
Real Estate, Residence	_____	Mortgage, Other	_____
Real Estate, Other	_____	Due on Automobiles	_____
		Due on Other Vehicles	_____
Automobiles	_____	Taxes Payable	_____
Other Vehicles	_____	Other Liabilities	_____
Collectibles	_____	Total Liabilities	_____
Other Assets	_____		
Total Assets	_____		

Net Worth (Assets Minus Liabilities) $_____   Liquid Capital: $_____

anything that's not physically tied down in your home are considered assets, so make sure that you include them. Everything else on the form is pretty self-explanatory, but if you need help putting everything down, you can consult an accountant or a financial planner.

Once you've gathered all of your information and have filled in both sides of the form, all you have to do is subtract your liabilities from your assets to get your current net worth. You can write this figure down in the space provided on the form.

The next thing that you need to do is figure out your liquid capital, which is what you have that can be readily (i.e., quickly) turned into cash. Savings accounts, individual stocks, and nonretirement types of mutual funds are considered liquid capital. Once you have that figured out, put that amount down on the form provided, and you're done!

Now you know *exactly* where you are at. There's no need to guess. So the next step is figuring out just what you can afford.

Some Averages

A few years ago, I thought that it would be interesting to know how much money the people to whom I was providing franchise guidance had ended up investing in the franchises that they had researched and chosen. I also wanted to average out their collective net worth. I really had no specific reason for doing so; I was just curious. And here are the two things I learned:

1. The average total investment of the franchises these individuals bought was around $175,000. (I defined the *total investment* as the amount that the franchisors stated in their documents.)
2. The average net worth of these individuals was about $450,000.

I'm pleased that I spent the time needed to come up with this data a few years ago. I've been able to use it and discuss it at my seminars, and I'm obviously using it now for this book.

Because the averages I figured out are a few years old (I did this in 2006), I think that it would be wise to raise the figures a little bit for inflation. Therefore, I'm going to go with $200,000 as the average investment and $500,000 for the average net worth.

Now don't close this book yet if *you* don't happen to have net worth of $500,000. Maybe you need to go into another room to yell into a pillow. Take it easy. Go back to your happy place for a couple of moments. Inhale. Exxxxhale. Feel your blissssss.

It's really important that you know who I was working with back in 2005 to 2006—some pretty high-level people. Most of them were downsized middle managers such as executive VPs and the like. Some of them were even ex-CEOs. They had severance packages, and most had money in the bank. Some of them even had working spouses. They had equity in their homes. I'd say that 80 percent of the people I met back then were in pretty good financial shape.

There's another really important thing to know about these people (and, therefore, the averages that I worked out.) It has to do with geography. I was working *locally*. I was meeting with people that lived in *my* general area: Cleveland, Ohio.

Cleveland is basically an old manufacturing city that used to be known for making things. John D. Rockefeller (who would end up being the richest man in the world) got his start in Cleveland. Rockefeller started a little company by the name of Standard Oil, which would eventually end up refining 90 percent of all the oil used in the United States. In addition, Cleveland used to be a major business center and was the seventh largest city in the United States in 1950. But not anymore.

When I compiled the preceding averages in 2005 to 2006, Cleveland wasn't exactly a mecca for Fortune 500 companies and the like. It wasn't known as a major business hub, and there just wasn't a lot going on. Cleveland wasn't (nor is it now) a destination for those looking for high-paying corporate jobs. People just don't move here unless there's a really strong reason to do so. Now some may feel that I'm being negative about my home town, but I'm not; I'm merely being honest.

However, one of the positive things about Cleveland is that it's not a very expensive place to live. Our housing markets have always been pretty stable; we don't go through the crazy up and down cycles like, say, some areas of California do. So we have pretty affordable real estate as well as some nice suburbs. Commercial office space is pretty reasonably priced, too, as are our utility costs such as electricity and natural gas.

"So, Joel, why did you share that stuff about Cleveland?"

I'm glad you asked that question. There are two reasons:

First, when you receive information from a franchisor, you'll notice that the *total investment* is never exact because *it really can't be*. You're given a range for a reason. When it comes to launching a new franchise business, *your geography* will dictate which end of the total investment range in which you'll end up. For example, starting a franchise in Boston or San Francisco will cost someone a lot more than starting a franchise in Cleveland, especially if one needs to rent out a commercial space of some kind.

Second, if your area of the country has a high cost of living, then you need to have more money to live on. (Of course, you need to *make* more money, too.) It's simple math. A net worth of $500,000 in a city like Cleveland or, let's say, Tulsa, Oklahoma, will go a lot farther than in a city like San Francisco. That $500,000 average net worth probably translates to more like $750,000 to $800,000 in the more expensive areas of the United States. So, if you live in a really expensive place, and your net worth *is* less than $500,000, go yell in that pillow. (I'm kidding!)

When you start looking for some franchises to further investigate, make sure that you consider *the total investment* ranges given, and figure out which end of the spectrum you're likely to fall based on your geography. It's incredibly important to adjust those numbers to fit your locale.

Let's make sure you know what's included in the total investment required to launch a franchise. A franchise *start-up* is a *new* franchise unit. In other words, the franchise buyer is starting a brand new business, very different from a franchise *resale*. A franchise resale is a unit that's *already been up and running*—except now, it's for sale. And it may be so for lots of different reasons:

- The franchise contract has been completed, and the existing franchisee is choosing to not renew it.
- The franchisee is retiring.
- The franchisee is in trouble and wants out.
- The franchisee owns multiple units and wants to sell one of them.
- There may be personal issues or even health issues that are forcing the sale.

Buying an existing business (franchise or not), can get pretty complicated, so it would be wise to consult an experienced business broker and a competent business attorney to assist you in the process. But because the focus of this book is on start-up franchises, here are some typical costs associated with them:

- Franchise fee
- Travel/living expenses during training
- Store build-out/design fees
- Inventory
- Furniture/fixtures
- Computers/business equipment
- Deposits for utilities, etc.
- Business insurance/licenses
- Legal and accounting costs
- Grand opening marketing
- Loan fees and interest
- Employee retirement plan fees
- Working capital

Let's go back to the averages that I had figured out and shared earlier. There are just *way* too many variables in franchise concepts and franchise models for me to properly give you a clear-cut answer to the question of "what's the average franchise investment?" That's why I chose to share *my own* experiences as they relate to average total investment needed to buy a franchise. For example, a typical retail franchise that requires inventory and a leased space may be in the $250,000 to $350,000 total investment range, whereas a home-based B2B type of franchise may have a total investment that's in the $60,000 to $80,000 range. These are totally different endeavors, though, and chances are that you'd either be a fit for one or the other, not both, so the averages really don't come into play.

The reason that these franchises would likely be a fit for two different people has to do with the self-analysis you conducted in the preceding chapters. My experience tells me that franchise buyers who are skilled in sales—and who have personal/character traits that include being energetic, outgoing, and candid, for instance—would be more suited to a B2B type of franchise, which would typically require those talents. Folks like that, who have lots of energy, and who are what I call *tigers*, don't do particularly well in a behind-the-counter retail environment. They really need to be out and about, networking and shaking hands. These folks don't need to have a net worth as high as some of the folks whose skills and personal/character traits are better suited for a franchise that needs a physical space in which customers and clients would be *coming into to see them*. So, in a way, you don't really need to know what the average investment is across the board in franchising. Your investment is going to depend on several things, like the types of opportunities for which you're a fit, your geographical location, and, of course, your budget.

What Can *You* Afford?

Can you afford to invest in a franchise? I mean, is this really the right time in your life to be doing this, or are you just dreaming? A better question might be *should* you be doing this?

Let's find out.

First off, full disclosure: I'm not a financial expert. I don't know enough about investments to advise anyone on theirs. That's why I pay someone to do it for me. Whatever your financial situation is, it's totally unique to you. Therefore, I recommend that you sit down with someone who is an expert on all things financial before you make any type of major investment like a franchise.

One of the greatest things about investing in a franchise is that you don't necessarily have to invest a lot of money to *make* a lot of money. Yes, you read that right. Now read it again.

Investing in a franchise is not like investing in the stock market. Let's say that you buy an individual stock. You know that the more shares you purchase up-front, the bigger *the potential* payoff is. Of course, the more shares you purchase, the more money you stand to *lose*, too.

When you buy a start-up franchise (in every case except one, which we'll cover in a moment), the amount you invest does not have a direct bearing on what your potential income will be. Most of the folks with whom I've shared this bit of information had no idea about that.

The single case in which what you invest up-front *does have* a direct bearing on your income potential is if you were to invest in a Master Franchise. This scenario typically involves control of the franchise rights for an entire geographical region, such as an entire metropolitan area, rather than just one local location. *The Master Franchise model is like owning your own franchise company inside of a franchise.* Master Franchisees share in the franchise fees and royalty income from the subfranchises that they sell in their area. The up-front franchise fee may be $150,000 or more for a Master Franchise. It's based on population, and the fee is usually calculated on a per-person basis.

Let's use the city of San Jose, California, as an example, which has a population of around 900,000 people. The franchisor charges .23 per person for the franchise fee. 900,000 × .23 = $207,000. The franchise buyer would have to come up with $207,000 up-front, just for the franchise fee! Of course, the franchisee fee doesn't include the other start-up expenses needed to launch the franchise. Those expenses could easily take the total investment to the $300,000 range or more. But the potential is huge because the Master Franchisee is actually selling *franchises*, instead of products or services that would be sold in a typical franchise. The Master Franchisee receives a portion of the up-front franchise fee and can also offer financing, which enables the Master Franchisee to make money from the interest. So, in the case of the Master Franchise model, the more one invests (because it's based on the size of the territory), the more one can make because of how the franchise model is structured. (That is, if things work out like they're supposed to!)

Very few people are interested in becoming a Master Franchisee, mostly due to the high cost of entry. One also needs to make a major commitment; it's really for people that want to grow something big and are hyper-focused on making a lot of money in the long term. Being a Master Franchisee is akin to being like one of the following:

1. The franchisor
2. A CEO

It's really for those that have a type A personality and thrive in a high-pressure, take-no-prisoners environment.

So . . . How Much Do I *Really Need,* Joel?

I personally feel that you shouldn't invest more than 15 percent of *your own money* in a start-up franchise. What I mean by *your own money* is the amount for which you'll be writing a check before a business loan. Here is an example:

Let's say that your net worth statement shows that you have a net worth of $400,000, $80,000 of which is liquid. Because fifteen percent of $400,000 is $60,000, that amount is the most that I feel you should invest in a franchise. The rest of the money with which you'll need to fund your franchise will come from a small business loan of some type or maybe even from your friends or relatives. Plus, you'll still have $20,000 available that's liquid for whatever other situations—business or personal—may arise.

In a normal lending environment, most lenders want to see franchise buyers come up with 20 to 25 percent of the total investment in the franchise they're trying to buy. So, using the figure of $60,000 that I just gave, this means that you shouldn't be buying a franchise that has a total investment of any more than about $240,000.

Here's the math:

$60,000 = 25 percent of $240,000

Now, the rule to use only 15 percent of your own money for a franchise investment is not based on anything other than my own risk tolerance. I didn't use any historical financial data, nor did I find an amazing piece of software that I was able to use to calculate my own risk tolerance versus an investment in a franchise business. While there may actually *be* a software program like that out there, I didn't look for one, nor do I care to. (Perhaps this is an opportunity for someone to create something like that?)

I let you know that I'm not a financial advisor and that I wouldn't be offering any specific financial advice. This is precisely why everyone needs to figure out their own risk tolerance. Maybe you feel that using 15 percent of your money to invest in a franchise of your own is way too much and just too risky. That's fine; maybe you need to dial it back a bit. Or perhaps you're on the other side of the spectrum and feel that only investing 15 percent of your own money in a franchise business is *not* enough. Do you feel that you should dial it *up*? It's totally up to you. It might also be that you're just not sure *what* percentage of your own money you should be investing in a franchise. That's okay; it's perfectly fine to get some help with it. Investing in a business of your own is a *big deal*—certainly big enough to pay a financial expert to help you figure it out.

I remember when I received a referral from a counselor from one of my local Small Business Development Centers (SBDC). Small Business Development Centers are funded by the Small Business Administration (SBA), and they have counselors who provide free help for those looking to get into business. Anyway, I contacted this would-be business owner and asked what he wanted my help with. It turns out that he was very interested in buying a food franchise. The total investment was around $175,000 if I remember correctly. He wanted to know if I felt that he was on the right track. Fair enough. I had him fill out some information, which included a net worth statement.

His net worth was around $200,000, with around $40,000 being liquid. He was currently employed and making about $50,000 a year. He was married, but I'm not sure if his wife worked. Here's what I do remember; I told him that investing $175,000 in a start-up food franchise having a net worth of only $200,000 was crazy. The bank would want him to use $40,000 of his own money before the loan, which would leave him with no extra liquid cash available for the business or for anything of a personal nature that he might need. *Not good.* Let me add that he had absolutely no experience in the food industry. If you remember, James Pennington didn't have any experience in the food industry, either, but at least *he* had more money!

This gentleman wasn't very happy with my analysis, but I wasn't backing off. I pretty much told him that his idea for the franchise he should be buying was not ready for prime time. A $175,000 franchise investment was way too rich for his blood. Plus, he had no food service background—*none*. In short, he had no idea what he was about to get into.

Luckily, he didn't end up investing in that franchise. It's a good thing, too, because it would have been ugly. My hope is that anyone else out there who's about to do something stupid like that reads this book first. (If you know someone who may be about to make a poor decision in a franchise, then please pass this book onto them!)

Once you have *the money part* figured out, make sure that you stick to your budget. I also firmly believe that you shouldn't invest one dollar more than that with which you're completely comfortable in a franchise of your own. The amount you invest probably shouldn't be an amount that is so high that it keeps you up at night. That's not me giving you financial advice; it's just common sense.

Please write this next thing down somewhere. As a matter of fact, write it down in more than one place, so you'll be reminded of the statement that you are about to read:

Stash some living expenses! *One more time*: Stash some living expenses. You're going to need money to live on during the start-up phase of your new business. You're still going to have to meet your monthly obligations, some of these which may include the following:

- Mortgage payment
- Utility bills
- Car payments
- Kid's braces
- Car/house/life insurance
- Countless other items that I cannot possibly imagine for your personal situation

I wrote a blog post about this very subject that's been really popular over the years. It's called "Buying a Franchise? Stash Some Money in Your Favorite Sock Drawer!" Please read it (http://thefranchiseking.com/stash-some-money).

You're Not Going to Make Money

You're not going to make money at first, that is. Did you really think that you would? Really? How? Did you think that the Franchise Fairy Godmother was going to sprinkle some magic dust over your new franchise business, enabling it to bring you a steady fat paycheck starting the moment you opened for business?

Perhaps you forgot to consider the following things:

- The transition from an employee to a small business owner is a drastic one.
- There's no starting salary.
- There's no year-end salary reviews from your superior.
- There's no two-week paid vacations.
- There's no sick leave.
- There's no maternity leave.

Owning a small business is an entirely different game. *You're* the one with the employee headaches. (Even if you've supervised employees in past positions, nothing beats being the supervisor *and* the owner of the business at the same time.)

Not only that, but you can pretty much forget about getting a paycheck for a while if you invest in a start-up franchise. If you *do* get a paycheck early on, it's because you've arranged to have some of your working capital set aside for one. But, in general, forget about it. When you open a franchise business, you first have to break even before you can even think about making any profit.

Here's what break even means in the context of a franchise business: it's when the revenue generated by producing, marketing, and selling your goods or services can sufficiently cover all of your expenses. These expenses include the cost of materials, equipment, labor, advertising, rent, and so on, plus any other miscellaneous expenses that you as the owner put out.

The transition from *employee* to possibly an *employer* can be extremely psychologically challenging as well. You're going to be working your tail off for a long time and for no immediate rewards. True, it will be quite rewarding to be in more control of your own destiny; it really *is* empowering to own what you do. It's a great feeling to be the one unlocking the door to the office, the restaurant, or the storefront, *as the owner* of the business. It's quite gratifying, and you'll definitely have a spring to your step. It's all good.

The pressure can get to you, though, along with the fact that you won't have anything to show for your efforts moneywise, for a while. That can be (and is) pretty tough on your emotional state.

I remember when I started working with my dad in his franchise consulting business. My wife was working, so we were basically meeting our household expenses. But I was new, so I was learning the business and not making any money. There was no paycheck. It was rough, especially because I had come from a position in automobile franchise management in which I was getting paid twice a month and had a company car. Even though I hated the job (and it would prove to be my last *job*), the steady income was delightful, compared to *no* income.

So please make sure that you are ready to *not make money* for a while. If you're not ready to not make money, then please don't invest in a start-up franchise. You'll hate it. Remember, once you write a $35,000 check to the franchisor and sign your franchise contract, you own it! There's no turning back. It's not like getting a new job that you don't end up liking, quitting, and looking for another one. If you invest in a franchise, there's not going to be an opportunity to say to yourself, "I'll just quit this franchise, and find another one." (Well, if you're a multimillionaire, I guess you can do that, but I'm assuming that you're not!) Think through what I just wrote. Visualize going into *your* new business every day, working crazy-long hours, and then not getting paid for your efforts. Reading about how difficult this can be it is one thing; *living it* is an entirely different story. I'm trying to make it a story that has a happy ending for you.

Go Ahead! Start Your Search!

If you're convinced that you have enough money to invest in a franchise (as well as some money set aside to live on), are right for the business model of franchising, and have done a thorough self-analysis, then it's time for you to find your franchise.

The most common way to find a franchise is to go online and enter *franchise opportunities* in the search box of your favorite search engine. That's one way, and it could work for you. You'll find 10,000,000 options, and it could take a few days (maybe even weeks) to go through all of the opportunities listed.

You could also go online and hone in on any number of franchise opportunity websites. These feature hundreds of franchise business choices, and some of the better ones do a good job categorizing them for you using criteria like investment amounts, industries, new opportunities, and even types: home-based opportunities, part-time businesses, and so on. I've listed several in the resource section of the book, or you can see the list of the Top 10 Franchise Opportunity Sites by visiting http://thefranchiseking.com/the-top-10-franchise-opportunity-websites.

Franchise buyers find franchises that interest them in many other ways that they discover beyond conducting an online search. Some folks who've purchased franchises were actually customers of the franchise that they bought. They liked the products or the services so much that they just had to buy one themselves. Some people have invested in a specific franchise because a friend or relative told them about it. Some folks found the franchises that they now own from an advertisement they saw in a magazine or a newspaper. There are even some people who've read interesting articles or blog posts about certain franchises and ended up liking them enough to become owners. My point is there are several ways to find franchises that may end up being The One . . . for you.

Even though it can get a little overwhelming at times, for the purposes of this book, I'm recommending that you do your initial search online. Remember, you really have a leg up on the people who haven't purchased this book.

You've taken www.takethefranchisequiz.com; you know if you're franchise material. You've done self-analysis; you know what your strengths are, and you are only focused on opportunities that are a fit *for you*. You've done your net worth statement; you know what you can afford to invest. You have a resource section at your fingertips and will, therefore, be saving lots of time.

Believe me—the people that haven't read this book are at a huge disadvantage. Most of them have no idea what they're doing. You *do*. So take advantage of all of your newfound knowledge about yourself, your finances, and the greatest business model ever invented: the Franchise Business Model. Go ahead; find your franchise!

Secret Internet Agents

One more thing to keep in mind as you begin your online search for your franchise: you're going to be putting yourself out there, so to speak. You're going to start to receive e-mails out of nowhere from people that I call *secret Internet agents*. These e-mails will contain eye-catching phrases like the following:

"This is the opportunity you've been searching for!"

"You owe it to your family to check this out."

"There's never been a better time to invest in our franchise."

"Here's an extraordinary opportunity."

"Check out our award-winning opportunity!"

"An executive opportunity."

"Hot New Franchise!"

So how did these agents find you? Well, some of them have purchased your information. When you search for things online, you're probably visiting many more websites that you think. For example, you can visit 20 to 30 different websites while spending just one hour online. If you're online only two hours a day, six days a week, that means that you've probably visited 200 to 250 different websites in only a week's time. There's no way that you're going to remember all of the places you visited. You may have gone to some nonfranchise websites, too. Maybe you stopped by a job-seeking type of website and responded to an ad like this:

"If you're interested in building significant income, wealth, and you want to have the lifestyle you've always desired, you may want to consider becoming a business coach with ____ ___."

If you filled out their request more information form, you'd be contacted not by a company looking to *hire* a business coach, but by a company looking to sell you a business coaching franchise. Pretty sneaky, huh? It's manipulative, and it's wrong. But it's also one way that these secret Internet agents get your information.

Anyone who has used one of the major search engines has probably noticed that the ads on the right-hand side closely match the topic of item you're searching for. The technology that's available today is amazing, and it's getting better all the time. Advertisers magically appear whenever you search for something. It's no different in franchising. You may have responded to the ad and given the franchisor your information. Then they contacted you, seemingly out of the blue, but in reality, based on the information you provided.

Some franchise opportunity websites allow a specific type of secret Internet agent to pay them for access to your information. I was unknowingly one of them for awhile. Several years ago, the franchise brokerage with which I was a franchisee charged me for *leads* (the names of people who have shown interest in buying a franchise.) I would pay for them, hoping that they would turn out to be people that I could match with the franchises I represented so that I would get paid a commission. But there was a problem.

For a while, the leads would frequently have absolutely no idea why I was calling when I contacted them. These people would (understandably) get pretty pissed off. Here's an example of what a typical phone conversation was like when I was a franchisee of this brokerage:

"Hi, this is Joel Libava from _____. I received a request from you asking for assistance in finding the right franchise. I'd love to see if I can be of any assistance."

"WHO is this? I was interested in a Krispy Kreme franchise. Do you work for them?"

"No, I'm a franchise consultant. I help match people like you to franchises that could be right for you." *My service is free!*

"Can you help me with a Krispy Kreme franchise in Toledo, Ohio?"

"I don't represent them, but maybe there's something else I can show you."

"Nope. I'm only interested in a Krispy Kreme. Bye."

Boy did those phone calls get old in a hurry. I certainly don't blame the folks who I was calling. They wanted information on specific franchises, but instead were receiving unsolicited calls from franchise consultants like myself who never should have been calling them in the first place. I place the blame on the owners of the franchise opportunity websites who were selling us these leads.

I'm not sure if these things continue to happen anymore, but they certainly used to. I still get aggravated thinking about how much time I wasted and how much money I spent on those leads. But that's the life of a franchise consultant, and I'm glad that I'm not one anymore.

As you can see, looking for a franchise online, that is, putting yourself out there, is going to open you up to possibly receiving numerous e-mails and maybe even a phone call or two from all sorts of people who operate in the world of franchising. It's kind of hard to avoid, but just knowing that it's going to happen is half the battle. Make a commitment right now to only stick with opportunities that are a great match for you, no matter how you find them—or in this case, how these *opportunities* seem to find *you*.

Finally, if you decide to go online in an effort to find different franchise opportunities, you're going to run across lots of offers by a totally different breed of secret Internet agents that offer things like "Free Help Finding a Franchise" or "Get a Free Consultation." It's true; you *can* get free help finding a franchise.

I'll explain just what *free help* means in the next chapter. You're going to learn *the real deal* about the people and the companies that are offering some of these free services that offer to help you find that perfect franchise. Should you use them to find the franchise business of your dreams? Or will using them to help you find your dream franchise turn out to be a totally different type of dream then you had planned? Perhaps even a nightmare?

9

Should You Have One of Those *Free Franchise Consultations?*

"When it's a question of money, everybody is of the same religion."

—Voltaire

I'VE NEVER MET anybody who doesn't like the idea of getting something for free. Come to think of it, I know a few people who get pretty excited just considering *the possibility* of getting something for free!

In this chapter, I'm going to share the real deal about some of the *free services* that franchise consultants and brokers offer—services that you'll undoubtedly run across as you intensify your search for some great franchises. After reading this chapter, you'll be able to make an intelligent decision on whether you want to get some free help finding the right franchise from a franchise consultants or brokers. I'm also going to share some very personal things about myself that may help explain why I'm wired the way I am and how this benefits you as a franchise buyer.

First of all, let me get a confession out of the way: *I myself* am a recovering franchise consultant/broker. That's right; I used to provide these free services myself. If you remember, I began my career in this field by joining my dad's franchise consulting firm and becoming a consultant/ broker. My dad and I offered free services for those looking to get into a franchise business. We were franchise matchmakers, and when we made a successful match, we would get paid handsomely by the franchisors with whom we had contracts.

Before I share how the business model for franchise consultants and franchise brokers works, you need to know one very important thing: a franchise consultant and a franchise broker are pretty much the same thing in the context of providing a free service to prospective franchise buyers. Some of them call themselves franchise *consultants* (as I did), while others refer to themselves as franchise *brokers*. I suppose that using the title of franchise consultant sounds a little better, but there's really no difference; if someone is paid a finder's fee or a commission for finding a new franchisee for a franchisor, he or she is brokering a deal. Therefore, that person is a broker; so I'm going to use the word *broker* from now on, okay?

A franchise broker essentially facilitates a match between prospective franchise buyers and franchisors who are looking to add new franchisees. The franchisor pays the franchise broker a significant finder's fee (commission) for a successful match, which occurs when the prospective franchise owner signs a franchise contract and pays the franchise fee.

Now keep in mind that franchise brokers don't work with *all* of the approximately 3,000 franchise concepts that are currently registered in the United States. (Other countries like Canada, the United Kingdom, and Spain have franchise brokers, too.) They only work with the ones with whom they're contracted. This, of course, means that not every franchisor works with franchise brokers, and that's because not all franchise executives believe in using them. (Only a small percentage of franchisors consistently use brokers to help them sell new franchise units.) The ones that do use them are generally happy as long as the brokers are bringing high quality candidates to the table, and some of these candidates actually end up buying a franchise. The franchisors that I call *antifranchise brokers* are usually the ones who don't want to pay 40 to 50 percent of the up-front franchisee fee to a franchise broker for providing a qualified franchise candidate that ends up buying a franchise. That's right;

with franchise fees averaging around $30,000 currently, this means that today's franchise brokers are making a $12,000 to $15,000 commission each time one of their candidate's buys a franchise. Not a bad payday!

My Life as a Franchise Broker

Although I had some experience managing franchise operations, I didn't know about *this* area of the franchise business when I initially got into it, so I had a lot to learn. Luckily, my dad provided some great training and support, so I got up to speed pretty quickly. I also had flown out to California for three days of intensive training by the president of the franchise brokerage where my dad was a franchisee. Two other guys from other parts of the country were there, too, and we received first class training and became franchisees, and, after we completed it, I flew back home and started working closely with my dad.

I started finding people who were interested in exploring franchises. I learned how to do presentations on franchise ownership and spoke at local libraries and outplacement offices. I was meeting with prospective franchise owners and becoming more comfortable with the process of franchise matchmaking.

It took a little longer than I thought it would to close my first deal. (That's what they were called.) I received my first nice-sized commission check in the mail about four months after I became a franchise broker. I'd be lying if I told you that I wasn't totally ecstatic to receive it, and I definitely wanted a lot more of them.

I started seeing more and more candidates and was making more deals and more money. (In brokering, we call the folks we tried to match up to franchises, our *candidates* because calling them our *clients* wouldn't be right.) We represented the franchisors; *they* were the ones paying us. In my head, though, I was working for the candidates, and that was important to me.

For the most part, I enjoyed doing franchise brokering. It gave me the chance to do lots of public speaking (which I love), I was able to make a pretty good living (for a while), and it was a great fit for an outgoing guy like myself.

I was even starting to develop a reputation around town as "a guy to connect with if you were interested in a franchise." Admittedly, being hooked up with my dad—who already had made a name for himself locally—helped me open more than a few doors.

Now, I have two reasons for going into this highly detailed explanation of my life as a franchise broker:

1. If you're looking for a low-investment, sales, or consulting type of franchise business, you may end up looking at a franchise brokerage opportunity yourself. Therefore, I wanted to provide a snapshot of what it's really like to be a franchise broker.
2. I want you to know where I'm coming from as you read this chapter.

As I said, I really enjoyed what I was doing. It was strange, though, because I really wasn't interested when my dad first approached me to join him in his firm. And it wasn't like I had anything else going on. I had just been fired from a management position at an automobile franchise operation. I was in a funk and was looking at things through some pretty dark glasses. But my dad kept on me despite my initial refusal. I guess he saw something that I didn't, and so he kept on me some more. He wouldn't stop! (It's a Libava trait; we're kind of like bulldogs sometimes.)

Things at home were a bit intense, to say the least, for several reasons: (1) I wasn't working. (2) I wasn't working. My wife Jeannine and I had been having some high level (actually, more like high VOLUME) discussions about my dad's offer, but we couldn't seem to agree on whether I should join him or just go out and find a new job.

Joining my dad would be a little risky because it wasn't like he could pay me. If I was going to become a franchise broker, we would have to throw some money into the pot and hope for the best. When I finally did make the mental choice to join him, I knew that I would have to do some serious selling to get Jeannine on board.

I had been an observer in my dad's office for a couple of weeks and had watched him work with some candidates. I realized that my dad was right; my skills and character traits would probably be an excellent match for brokering. I was comfortable in a consultative role, and I knew that as soon as I learned how to do actual presentations on franchising for groups, I would rock at it.

Needless to say, I pulled out all the stops during my sales presentation to Jeannine. And after I managed to convince her, I started on my journey.

Some Issues

In my decade as a franchise broker, I was able to pull together a few pretty strong years, financially. Though I could have made more money, I didn't for a couple of reasons:

1. The franchise model of the franchise brokerage with which I worked was a *local* model. That meant that I was only supposed to work with folks that were interested in exploring franchise ownership that lived in my area: Cleveland/Northern Ohio. Earlier in the book, I shared that Cleveland isn't exactly a business or financial mecca like it had been in the last century. In short, it's been tough here.
2. I was really careful about the individuals with whom I worked. I wouldn't work with *anyone* who I felt would be taking on too much risk. Instead, I told them to "go get a job."

The franchise brokerage I was with wanted us to position ourselves as *local* franchise brokers. We were to meet with our candidates, face to face when possible. We were supposed to get involved in local networking events and arrange speaking engagements at area venues. I was fine with these requirements, and I believed in that way of doing business. After all, who better than someone local to help another local resident figure out what franchises could work in the area?

Then the World Wide Web showed up.

When I started as a franchise broker, I didn't really know what e-mail was. I really hadn't used a computer too much. It was all so new in 2001. But my dad had a computer in the office, so I just dug in. I learned about things like memory and floppy disks. I learned about the Internet and how to find stuff. I e-mailed people. They e-mailed me back. WOW!

However, the computer in my dad's office was kind of slow. As a matter of fact, it took 10 minutes just to connect to the Internet! It was dial-up, and I remember hearing lots of weird noises as it tried to connect . . . over and over again.

Obviously, I wasn't the only person learning how to use a computer, e-mail, and the Internet; others were learning how to use this newfound tool, and some of them were doing so faster than others.

The Day It Changed

"Never innovate to compete; innovate to change the rules of the game."
—David O. Adeife

Our franchise brokerage organization got caught napping; that's really the gentlest way to say it. While our leaders were trying to figure out a way to use the Internet to find gobs of prospective franchise buyers, a rather aggressive competitor appeared one day and created a seat at the table. As a matter of fact, this brand new competitor *brought his own table*.

I don't want to give you the impression that this new competitor appeared out of nowhere because nothing like what he managed to do can really happen overnight. He had most likely been planning something like this for a year or so. I'm not going to bore you with the details; however, this individual had supposedly been in negotiations with the president of our brokerage to join us in some fashion two years earlier. But things must not have worked out too well because from what I've been told, this gentleman launched this new franchise brokerage *two years to the day* after his noncompete agreement with the president of our franchise brokerage ran out! I'm sure it was "just business, nothing personal," but it was still a blow to our company.

There's always the threat of new competitors entering a market in the business world. Some of them stay, and some of them go. *This* competitor was different, however, because he discovered a way to leverage technology and combine it with the nationwide reach of the Internet—and in doing so was able find a huge quantity of prospective franchise buyers. *His* franchise brokers were going to be getting *all* of their leads directly from the Internet. They had no territorial restrictions like we had; *their territory was all of North America!* His franchise brokers didn't need to lease office space like we had; rather, they could work from their couches and make follow-up calls while sitting by the pool, while on vacation—wherever. It didn't matter. Our new competitor created a portable industry, one that, although he probably didn't know it at the time, would impact the way franchise brokers nationwide would conduct business in the future.

Now it's not like the franchise brokerage industry was the only business to be impacted by technology and the growth of the Internet. I'll bet that the industry in which you currently work—or in which you *used to* work—has changed dramatically from what it looked like 10 years ago as well.

I could go on and on concerning my feelings that our organization didn't adapt quickly enough to our changing world, but there's really no point for me to do that. The bottom line is this: both I and other members of our brokerage were starting to lose prospective local franchise candidates to this new competitor, and that was making me angry. Some of us were starting to show our frustration with this new competitor, which caused our national meetings to become a little heated. We instituted *some* changes and, with them, lots of new rules. Yet some of these rules were starting to cost *me* money, and I became increasingly frustrated. I really didn't want to follow these new rules; there were too many of them. As a matter of fact, I didn't want to follow *any* rules, *anymore*. I was becoming a lousy franchisee. After all, if one doesn't want to follow the rules, he or she shouldn't be a franchise owner, right? The upshot was that the way we were doing business wasn't working as well anymore, and I knew it. And it was during this time that I found out a couple of things about myself:

1. I came to the realization that I hated rules and always had. It was becoming abundantly clear that I was becoming a lousy franchisee.
2. I was growing braver and more outspoken by the day.

In short, I became very vocal about a lot of the things that were going on inside our organization. I made it absolutely clear that I was sick of being screwed over. It's almost as if a switch was all of a sudden turned on inside my head, and, for the first time in my life, I decided that I wasn't going to take any more crap from anyone. I was sick of all the games and manipulations that I felt were taking place in our group. I stood up for what was right, and—with the help of some other members of the group—I was able to make a few minor changes in the way we were doing business. But it wasn't enough. I learned about power and who *really* had it. (Hint: it wasn't the franchisees from the small and low-revenue producing markets like mine!) But there was something else going on during this time, and it was a lot more important than the squabbles that were taking place in our organization.

My dad had been disappointed with the organization for a long time; he saw what was happening, and his enthusiasm for the business was starting to dim. *I* became the face of our local franchise. While I was busy doing most of the day-to-day stuff, my dad was starting to get worried about his health. He kept getting bronchitis, and his doctor decided to do some tests. It turned out that his bronchitis wasn't bronchitis at all; *it was lung cancer*. My dad had quit smoking 25 years earlier, so this really came as a surprise to all of us—mostly him. The only other time he had been sick (really sick) was the year that I was born; he had contracted a bizarre type of pneumonia and was hospitalized for over a month. Though his cancer may have had something to do with scar tissue that may have formed during that period, the doctors were never able to determine that for sure.

My father had to have surgery to remove a cancerous lung, and he was really never the same after that. He also went through chemotherapy while he was recovering from the surgery and had to constantly carry around an oxygen tank to help him breathe, which was really tough to watch. My dad had always been a guy who had a seemingly endless amount of energy. He was always flying around . . . but not anymore. He pushed himself really hard to stay as active as he could, though. I vividly remember him accompanying us to my daughter Grace's basketball games during this time; he loved to watch her literally rip the ball from the always larger opposing player's hands and run like lightning down the court with it.

The chemo actually seemed to be working, but only for awhile. The doctors informed my dad that the cancer was now in his other lung and that he didn't have a lot of time left.

I remember talking with my dad toward the end of his life about lots of things, one of them being where I wanted our business to go. I told him that I was thinking of leaving the franchise brokerage group we were with, and he basically told me that I should go for it and that I didn't need them anymore. He said that I was doing a great job on my own and that he liked my marketing techniques. He was really proud of how far I had come.

In June of 2007, we lost him. Man, my dad knew lots of people. People who paid their respects in person, with sympathy cards, or online described my dad, Jerry Libava, as "enthusiastic, ethical, honest, a lover of children, a great salesman, authentic, and energetic." He was all those and more. I'll always be grateful that he encouraged (essentially forced) me to join his firm. And I *really* wish that he was around now, holding this book. He would have been incredibly proud of me.

A couple of months after my dad died, I left the franchise brokerage group with whom we had worked and became an independent entrepreneur. I had lots of ideas, and I still do. And, as you know, I'm not a franchise broker anymore; I'm an advisor. I don't receive commissions from franchisors. This time around, my clients are the folks who are interested in becoming *franchise owners*—not the franchisors. And this is where I shine.

Not only am I able to teach prospective franchise owners *exactly* how to select and research franchises (as I'm doing in this book), but I've also really become an advocate for them. I had always been very protective of the candidates with whom I worked, though it was the franchisors I was paid by, even when I received commissions. I remember several instances in which I got on the phone with franchise salespeople and told them in no uncertain terms that they needed to change the way that they were doing things (i.e., being too aggressive, not disclosing information quickly enough, etc.) or I would take my franchise candidates elsewhere. I didn't care about my commission at that point; I only cared about my candidate, and I didn't want anyone to take advantage of them. That's how I ran my business, and it's how I run things now. It's just how I roll.

Working with Franchise Brokers

There are tons of franchise brokers around. There didn't used to be, and I'll share some of the reasons for the increase at the end of this chapter. However, you'll recall that I started out the chapter by talking about the fact that all of us like things that are free. Most franchise brokers provide free services, which is one the main reasons that some franchise buyers are attracted to the idea of working with them. Yet it's crucial to keep in mind that these services are free because brokers can potentially make large commissions if their candidates buy a franchise with which the broker has a contract.

Most franchise brokerage groups offer hundreds of choices, and, typically, they *do* have contracts with a couple hundred different franchise concepts. In addition, some brokerage groups loudly proclaim that they prescreen the hundreds of franchise concepts with whom they work. Now what's the first thing that comes to your mind when *you* hear (or read) the phrase *prescreen*? I'll tell you what my first thought is when I hear that a franchise concept is prescreened—that it is somehow safer. Did you have a similar impression?

Now I'm not saying that a prescreened franchise actually *is* safer than one that hasn't been prescreened. What I *am* saying is that carefully crafted wording and marketing messages* can have a huge impact on how we, as consumers of goods and services, perceive things. If you're thinking about working with a franchise broker who claims that their franchise offerings *are* prescreened, you need to ask them what that *really*

---

*If you'd like to learn a little more about just how much a carefully crafted marketing message can really impact you, I highly recommend that you check out Copyblogger (www .copyblogger.com). I've been able to learn from and have met hundreds of very savvy small business people over the years, but very few are in the same league as Brian Clark. Brian has built himself an empire of sorts, and he's done so by using words. From his website, Copyblogger.com: "Brian seeks to empower online writers and content producers to command attention, create engagement, and influence people." There are hundreds of amazingly written posts on his site if you want to engage in some learning. Brian and his team of writers have certainly helped *me* a lot.

means. For example, I felt the brokerage group with which I worked actually had a pretty good screening process. The franchisors that wanted to contract with us had to undergo and pass this test. I won't go into detail about it here, but in the few instances that my candidates asked me what *prescreened* meant, I gladly shared what I could with them.

Finally, know that you have lots of choices if you're going to work with a franchise broker. There are about a dozen different franchise brokerage groups around, plus some independent operators. There are also business brokers who specialize in selling existing businesses but who occasionally try their hand at franchise brokerage as well. Some of these franchise brokerages are actually franchises themselves. It can get a little confusing, but don't worry; I've provided a list of must-ask questions to pose to any franchise broker before you decide to use their free services:

1. How long have you been a franchise broker? What did you do before?
2. What is your *franchise* experience?
3. Have you written any articles on franchising?
4. Do local reporters call on you as a resource?
5. Can I have a list of 10 current franchise owners with whom you've worked?
6. Which franchise attorneys do you recommend? Will they vouch for you?
7. Do you work with all types of franchises? If not, why not?
8. Can you help me with a business plan?
9. Can you help me get a franchise loan?
10. Are you part of a franchise yourself?

As I was writing this chapter, I was thinking that maybe our old friend James could have used the services of a good franchise broker. First of all, most franchise brokers don't work with food-related franchises. Therefore, there's a chance that James wouldn't have bought a restaurant franchise because he never would have seen one. Remember, James had absolutely no experience in the food business. He just seemed

to like the idea of owning a bustling restaurant—from the outside looking in. A franchise broker would have offered him several different types
of franchise choices. (Actually, *three* different franchise choices would
have been presented to James. While I'm not sure who came up with
that number, most franchise brokers usually present three franchises to
prospective franchise owners.)

Good franchise brokers do more than just match their candidates
to suitable franchise opportunities; they help their candidates find the
proper small business resources they'll need to start a business. Franchise
buyers need help with business plans, loans, and, of course, they need an
attorney who is familiar with franchise contracts.

When I was a franchise broker, I had a list of accountants, attorneys,
and bankers who I knew, liked, and trusted. My candidates benefitted tre-
mendously from my relationships with these professional service providers;
it was part of my protect-the-franchise-buyer philosophy and still is today.

I wonder if the situation in which James found himself could have
been prevented with some simple advice and counsel from a certified
public accountant (CPA) or franchise attorney. Unfortunately, we'll
never know, and, even more unfortunately, neither will James.

Would You Like to Make a Six-Figure Income?

"A little inaccuracy sometimes saves a lot of explanations."

—Saki

If you're pretty outgoing and have strong sales and presentation skills,
you're bound to run into a couple of pretty tempting offers to become
a franchise consultant or franchise broker as you start exploring different
franchises that may be a match for you. Franchise brokerage companies
spend lots of money advertising their opportunities, and it's easy to see
why. They tend to have a really low cost of entry, which is an element in
itself that opens the doors to lots of prospective franchise owners. Some
of these opportunities are themselves franchises; others are licensing or
business opportunities that aren't as rigid in their structure and don't
have many rules.

If you read the advertisements about becoming a franchise broker enough times, you may actually start to believe them. Here are some of the advertising headlines that I've read:

Become a Franchise Broker!

Make Executive-Level Income!

Verifiable Six-Figure Income

Become an Entrepreneur!

Small One-Time Up-Front Fee

No Experience Required!

Professional Training Available

No Cold Calling/Leads Provided

No Inventory

No Employees

Work Part Time or Full Time

Starting in a niche industry like franchise brokering with no prior franchise industry-related experience could prove to be quite challenging. First off, there's a long learning curve, which is something that those trying to sell you the opportunity may forget to tell you. It can take years to earn a steady income from franchise brokering. Economic cycles, geography, and the plethora of choices that prospective franchise owners have nowadays all contribute to this rather long learning curve. You really won't know what you're doing for at least six to nine months.

As I said, there's a pretty low cost of entry; I've seen up-front investments as low as $20,000. What do you get for your investment? About three days of training. The ads claim that you get leads, and you do, but the brokerages *charge* you for them. *That's* never mentioned in the ads. All the leads are from the Internet. And, as I found out the hard way, they're usually not *exclusive* leads; sometimes, other brokers get the same ones. Interestingly enough, there are usually no territories to speak of in today's franchise brokerages; it's a freaking free-for-all! Somebody who's looking for a franchise opportunity and who just so happens to live right down the street from your house in Nantucket may get called by a franchise broker from your own brokerage group who lives in Phoenix because it was his or her turn to get a lead from the corporate office. How would you feel if you saw a brand new Dunkin' Donuts open up right down the street from you with an owner who learned of the opportunity from a franchise broker *from your organization* who happens to live 2,500 miles away? I know how I'd feel!

I'm almost done throttling the franchise brokerage industry (really) because there actually *are* some genuinely first-class brokers out there who care about their candidates and who truly want to make sure that you have a good shot at success as a franchise owner. I know several, and, if you'd like a referral, just contact me. (I'm serious.)

The problem is that the industry is really, *really* crowded—and the main reason for this is because it's way too easy to get in. If you're *breathing,* look and talk like a businessperson (including speaking pretty good English), and can write a check for around $20,000, you're pretty much guaranteed a seat at the table. It's a cheap way to get into business! I mean, if you're in a fairly good financial position, it doesn't really matter how well you actually *do* in the business, right? After all, it's only $20,000; if you lose it, you lose it (or so you say to yourself.) Not surprisingly, there's lots of turnover in franchise brokering, and you just found out some of the reasons why.

Using a franchise broker is one way of finding franchise opportunities that could prove to be right for you. If you decide to use one, make sure that you refer back to this chapter, ask (all of) the questions that I've provided, and talk to people that worked with the franchise broker with whom you're thinking of working. Who knows; he or she could help you find your franchise.

There are two *incredibly* important things that you must do if you're going to become a successful franchise owner. And here they are:

1. Select the right franchise.
2. Do proper franchise research.

So far, I've been focusing on how to *select* a franchise that makes sense for you. I've taught you how important it is to match up your skills and personal/character traits to the types of franchises that are available. I've also shown you how to decide on a budget for a start-up franchise. Additionally, you just learned about franchise brokers and how they may be able to help you find some franchises that could make sense for you. You even learned a little about what it's like to *be* a franchise broker, just in case you go that route yourself. Hopefully, you've already contacted a few franchisors and are getting ready to learn more about them. If so, the next chapter is especially important for you.

10

It All Comes Down to Your
Franchise Research

"There is no such thing as an unreasonable question, or a silly question, or a frivolous question, or a waste-of-time question. It's your life, and you've got to get these answers."

—Marcia Wallace

By now, you've likely found a franchise opportunity or two that really interests you. Hopefully, they're a fit for your top skills as well as your unique personal/character traits. Maybe you've already reached out to these franchisors and have in turn received some general information about the opportunities there. You may have even had a conversation or two with the franchise development representatives and are starting to dig in a bit. Great!

Then again, maybe you're not *quite* there yet. Maybe you *haven't* found an opportunity or two that you're interested in yet. But considering the fact that there are 3,000-plus different franchises from which to choose, you'd think, based on numbers alone, that there must be one or

157

two franchises that could work. I mean, if you've decided that you're truly franchise material—and have been following my suggestions on how to go about selecting a franchise that's right for you—then there must be *something else* going on. After all, it's not like you're actually *investing* in a franchise yet. All you're supposed to be doing now is *learning* a little more about a few of them and deciding if there are enough appealing things about the opportunities to warrant further investigation.

I'm thinking that if you're really having that hard of a time choosing a couple of franchises to start investigating, you may be experiencing a condition called Mystical Franchise Experience Syndrome (MFES), which isn't all that uncommon. Mystical Franchise Experience Syndrome has prevented more people from becoming franchise owners than almost anything else. It can eat away at the psyche of a franchise buyer in no time flat, and it can be a little scary to endure. As a matter of fact, in some of the more serious cases, franchise buyers have reported *hearing voices* in their heads saying things like, "you're a loser," or "what is it with you? You can't find *one* franchise out of the 3,000 that are available?"

Franchise buyers who are affected by MFES usually show symptoms of this syndrome during the early stages of their franchise searches. The following are some of the more common ones:

Lack of enthusiasm

Lack of desire

Nonclinical depression

Cold extremities (usually the feet)

Extreme tiredness (usually taking place in front of a computer screen)

Job hunt relapses

I've found MFES to be pretty widespread among the franchise buyers with whom I've worked over the years, so, if you think you have it, don't despair. I'm here to help you silence those wretched voices. *I have the power.* I can cure MFES. (I *am* a King, you know.) First, let me share what I know about the syndrome.

Mystical Franchise Experience Syndrome affects one's sense of reality and usually rears its head during Internet searches for franchise opportunities. Once it appears, it's difficult to ignore. It's not a *physical* syndrome, mind you; it's purely mental. (If it *was* a physical malady, it would be akin to a blood-sucking parasite that attaches itself to one's intestinal wall and doesn't let go.) Like many mental illnesses, though, Mystical Franchise Experience Syndrome starts out gradually and then progresses over time.

I first started noticing MFES back in the days when I met with local franchise candidates *in person*. I could usually tell almost immediately when someone had it because there was a look of total boredom etched onto their faces. That was usually followed by this very telling question:

"Joel, are there any *other* franchises you can show me?"

So far, the cause of MFES can only be traced to one thing: unrealistic expectations (UEs). I'm not really sure if these UEs are self-imposed or if they have to do with something more sinister like the way that movies and reality television shows portray things these days. However, I'm actually more interested in *the cure* than the cause, and, as I said, *I have the power to cure* MFES.

Most of the seminars that I lead on becoming a franchise owner do include a brief discussion of MFES. I jokingly tell the audience that I really think that some of the prospective franchise buyers that I've met over the years really expected to have some kind of mystical experience from working with me. (Hey, I'm good, but not *that* good.)

In the warped minds of these franchise candidates (Okay, not warped. These fine folks obviously had MFES. Sorry about that rather mean and totally unfeeling reference), this mystical experience might involve dreamy music playing in the background, combined with a spectacular light show (both taking place inside my 150-square-foot office), immediately after I presented an idea for a franchise business that could turn out to be an absolutely *ideal* match for them. In other words, these candidates were really expecting something magical to happen during a single consultation with yours truly.

Now I'll admit that once in a while (maybe once a year) I'd meet with someone and immediately just *know* which opportunity was for him or her. If the person liked it and proceeded to follow my franchise research steps, he or she would feel great about the decision and be very happy to have met with me. But the lights never flickered on and off, and no music played in the background. (I can only vouch for my own experience; *I* never heard any dreamy music playing after presenting franchise opportunities to my candidates. I can't tell you what *they* heard.)

The closest I feel that I came to having a mystical experience occured during a franchise consultation with Mike Burzminski. Mike was a direct referral from a highly regarded career outplacement counselor. He was a former corporate executive who was looking to go another direction (that is, a direction besides holding a corporate job). He let me know during our meeting that he was looking for an opportunity that would allow him to "bridge technical with commercial."

The second he told me that, I knew exactly what franchise would probably be a fit for him: Batteries Plus. This was a franchise that did exactly what Mike had just described in his one sentence. Batteries Plus is a retail operation with a heavy commercial component that was seeking new franchisees that were comfortable with technology. Mike also confessed that he didn't want to sit behind a counter all day, and, if he invested in this franchise, a lot of the activities required of him would actually take place outside of the store. He'd be calling on commercial accounts to try to get their battery replacement business. And just so you know, we're not talking about the kind of double A or C batteries that go in your remote control. Rather, the batteries that Mike would be selling were commercial grade batteries—in short, very specialized stuff.

Now just because I felt that Batteries Plus was a great fit for Mike didn't mean that it necessarily *was*. Mike had to do the legwork to find this out for himself—and he did a phenomenal job. He talked to lots of franchisees. He even visited a couple and spent a day or two in their stores. He got his spouse involved in the process at the appropriate time. He dug into the numbers a *lot*. He went through the process at his own pace. He worked with a franchise attorney. Sound overwhelming? Don't despair. You'll soon learn how to do phenomenal franchise research just like Mike did. (By the way, Mike now owns three Batteries Plus stores.)

That was the short version of just one of my own experiences with a franchise candidate. But remember, as my friend Chris Brogan (www.chrisbrogan.com/author-social-media/) says, your mileage may vary. Don't think that just because you too have an interest in "all things commercial and technical" that you should immediately run out and invest in a Batteries Plus franchise. There are all sorts of factors about Mike's business background that contributed to the fact that he was a good fit for Batteries Plus. There are also pages and pages of information on the Batteries Plus franchise opportunity itself that I didn't share with you here because I'm not trying to sell you a Batteries Plus franchise. It's just the franchise business that ended up being the one for *Mike*.

By the way, I never asked Mike if he experienced something mystical, magical, or an otherwise out-of-body experience during the part of his meeting with me when I suggested that a Batteries Plus franchise merited his attention. But, knowing Mike, he would have told me.

It's totally unrealistic to think that you'll experience something supernatural or anything else of that nature while searching for (and maybe even finding) what you think to be that perfect franchise. It's probably not going to happen. (If it does, please share your experience with me. That way I can document it for future MFES research.)

I'm serious; things don't happen that way in franchising, so lower your expectations right now. I'm not going to back off on this, either, so if you don't want to find yourself hanging out in Franchise Fantasyland for weeks on end, make a commitment to yourself *right now* to operate solely in reality. Doing so will allow you to focus on getting the facts you'll need to make your decision.

I almost forgot to share one last critical tidbit about MFES; there's only one cure, and it involves an injection of a specific dose of medicine. You'll administer it yourself, and the level of discomfort you'll experience depends wholly on how quickly you take it. The name of the medicine is a long one, so I've abbreviated it here: ACDOR.

It's a little hard to remember. Maybe if I share its formal name, you'll have an easier time remembering it. The name is:

A Certain Dose of Reality

That's right; franchise buyers that have MFES need an injection of a certain dose of reality to cure their syndrome. There's no other way around it, unless, of course, they don't want to get the help they need. In that case, they'll end up in what I call *search limbo*—a state in which they are continuously searching for a nonexistent franchise opportunity, for months—maybe even years—on end. They'll never end up actually *investing* in one because none of the businesses they start to consider ever seem to pan out. And they never will . . . unless there's a sound and light show included during one of the sales presentations.

Are You Ready?

This chapter may change your life. I'm serious. Don't let its cold, somewhat emotionless title fool you into thinking that it won't. In fact, you might as well throw all the things you've learned about franchising (and about yourself) in the preceding chapters of this book out the window if you don't follow along here and do *exactly* what I suggest.

It won't matter if you've had some really powerful revelations about yourself and about what you really *do* bring to the table. The great things you've discovered about your own abilities—talents that you believe you can use in your franchise business—won't be worth *anything* if you're out of business because you shortchanged yourself when it came to your franchise research.

The story about James Pennington's *horrible experience* as a franchise owner may have taught you some important lessons about what *not* to do when buying a franchise. However, those lessons aren't going to matter if you do everything right up to this point but then screw up your franchise research.

If you were thinking of working with a franchise broker, you now know what to ask *before* you decide to work with one. If you're *already* working with one, then start asking your broker some of the questions I provided in the last chapter. Doing so will allow *you* to be in control; it'll slow the process down a little and may even provide the broker with a needed push to present some alternatives that he or she hadn't thought of. However, even if your broker *does* find you an opportunity that seems to be a great fit (and may very well *be* a great fit), it won't matter much if you skip any steps that I teach in this section.

Have I mentioned just how important it is for you to do a superb job with your franchise research? Yes? Good. I may mention it *again* if the mood strikes me.

For example, even if you've set your budget for a franchise start-up that allows for lots of breathing room and have committed to only looking at franchises that fit it, doing a half-assed job on your franchise research could cost you *a lot* more money than you originally budgeted; as a matter of fact, you could go out of business during your *first year*. Think of James Pennington. It didn't take *him* long to blow through his money . . . and you know how good of a job he did with *his* franchise research.

The good news is that if you really *do* follow my step-by-step suggestions on researching franchises contained in this chapter, you'll learn how to do the following:

- Be a confident franchise buyer.
- Own the entire research process.
- Know when to walk away.
- Know when you're on the right track.
- Lower your financial risk.
- Increase your odds of success as a franchise owner.

So don't rush through this chapter. I know you're excited to start a business. Heck, I know that you probably want to be *in business* as soon as possible. (Tomorrow would probably work for you, right?) You may be finding it increasingly more difficult to get a good night's sleep these days because you're anxious and maybe even a little fearful. This is to be expected; you've probably never done this before. You're likely afraid that you'll make a mistake, and you may worry that you're going to miss something. You know in your heart that it's entirely possible that you'll fail and that you might lose your money. If I told you that you're exactly where you're supposed to be right now, psychologically, would that help ease your mind a bit? Yeah . . . I didn't think so. Would thinking about the thousands and thousands of franchise buyers that have already gone through what you're enduring (and who are now in business for themselves) help you relax a little?

Ok. I tried.

Let's do this.

The Research Steps

I'm now going to take you through—in order—all the franchise research steps that you'll need to take to guarantee that you'll make an informed, fact-based decision on investing in the franchise that you feel is the one for you. As you'll soon see, the steps themselves are not difficult; they'll just take some time. But it's going to be *quality* time.

1. Franchise Packet Delivery: What to Do

After you request information from the franchisor(s) in which you're interested, you'll receive a franchise information packet from them— either in the mail, electronically, or a combination of both. Read through the materials, and write down or highlight the areas where you have questions.

It's *incredibly* important to remember that the informational materials through which you'll be looking are marketing collateral. They're sales pieces. They're designed to sell you on the idea of buying that particular franchise. Now there's absolutely nothing wrong with that; you just need to remain aware of this while you're thumbing through the company's materials.

The information you receive or view online will undoubtedly have some nice photos that usually show amazingly happy franchisees that are strolling around—maybe even having fun—while working in their businesses. *Please remember* that you're experiencing franchise marketing techniques at their finest. What you *really* need to do is talk to some of the current franchisees and find out if they are, in fact, really that darn happy. Think about it from the franchisor's perspective: if you were trying to get prospective franchise owners all juiced about your offering, wouldn't you want to show pictures, and maybe even videos, of happy franchisees? As you go along in this chapter, continue putting yourself in the franchisors' shoes during each research step. Doing that will help keep things real.

The franchise brochure has actually been a source of aggravation for me over the years, and here's why: some prospective franchise buyers get so engrossed by the sales literature that they forget that they're only looking at *sales literature,* which requires a time-sucking intervention from yours truly (someone who *hates* wasting time.) So let me save us both time right now. You need to understand the following.

The franchise brochure is not the franchise business. I want you to *memorize* those eight words. Close the book for a couple of minutes. As a matter of fact, close your eyes, and start memorizing those words. See if you can find your happy place—your bliss—as you do it.

I hope that my friend Shashi Bellamkonda doesn't get mad when he reads this. (Shashi is the "Social Media Swami" for Network Solutions–a Herndon, Virginia-based company that specializes in helping small businesses get online.) Whenever I say the word *bliss*, I think of him because he gave me the following definition for it: "Bliss is a state of mind." Thank you, Shashi!

So, if bliss is a state of mind, you need to get in a fact-based one. What I mean by that is try not to let a bunch of happy-sounding words and the occasionally hypnotic pictures that you find in franchise brochures determine whether you should continue looking into it. That's because *the franchise brochure is not the franchise business.*

Here's something to ask yourself as you look at some of those pictures that seem to be showing *way*-to-happy franchisees who are heavily involved in their daily duties as small business owners; what are the chances that you'll be smiling like a freaking brochure model as you're busting your butt working in your franchise business?

A franchise brochure has nothing to do with the everyday realities of franchise ownership.

It's nothing but a tease. I compare it to some of the better beer commercials out there today—the ones that usually have good-looking guys and gals, both with perfectly coiffed hair, toasting to the good times and focused on some good clean fun in some type of high-class drinking establishment. The commercial, of course, is trying to get you (men) to believe that drinking *their* brand of beer will allow you to magically attract beautiful women that you've never seen (or met) before for a classy night out on the town.

In reality, a half hour after you and your buddies purchase this beer (to drink in the basement of your house), you'll probably be downing them like there's no tomorrow, too drunk to drive anywhere that there would be even a remote chance of meeting up with *any* six-foot-tall Norwegian women like the ones portrayed in the very commercial that just helped you empty your wallet.

So keep in mind when you're looking through online or offline franchise brochures that some of the words and pictures contained in them are meant to stir your emotions and help you convince yourself that you'll be a happy, productive, and wildly successful franchisee in that particular franchise business. Unless, of course, the brochure has a totally *different* effect on you.

(I hope you're wondering why I'm spending so much time showing you proper franchise brochure reading techniques. You'll find out; keep reading.)

Franchise brochures have prevented more people from buying franchises than almost anything else in the franchise industry. I know that sounds crazy because you'd think that a well-crafted franchise brochure would have the *opposite* effect—and sometimes a great brochure *can* help produce new franchise unit sales. But more often than not, a prospective franchise owner receives the brochure in the mail (or online), reads it (or scans it), and makes a decision about whether to pursue the opportunity *based solely on what was stated in the brochure.* Personally, I think it's very short-sighted, and here's why:

What if something about the franchise opportunity changed *after* the brochure was printed or posted online? For example, let's say that you were interested in learning more about a dry cleaning franchise that you found in an advertisement at one of the franchise opportunity websites that you visited. You liked the fact that it was less of an investment than some of the others, and you remember reading something about this franchisor related to how serious they were about the environment.

Then, a couple of days after you requested information from this franchisor, you received a packet in the mail from them. Their brochure was enclosed, so you immediately started reading through it. You were able to learn things about the company history, the total investment needed to start one, and more. But there was something *really* important that seemed to be missing in the brochure: the so-called green aspect of the business. In fact, there wasn't a single mention of anything related to the environment. You even found the company website, but it was not working properly. Both of these factors angered you because your focus was on green franchise opportunities, or at least on franchises that seemed to be interested in doing business in such a way as to not harm the environment. So what did you do next?

You threw the entire franchise information packet into your recycling bin. Game over for the dry-cleaning franchise that you *were* interested in. The franchise development representative even called and left a message for you to call back. You didn't. As you started your search for some other franchise opportunities, you said to yourself, "Boy, they really missed out. I would have made a wonderful franchisee." Really? I beg to differ. As far as I'm concerned, *you're* the one that missed out because you based your entire decision on whether to pursue the dry-cleaning franchise on the information that was *in their brochure* (or, in this case, the information that *wasn't* in their brochure). I understand that you're interested in franchises that seem to be environmentally friendly. That's great. But you may have blown it in this case, and here's why. Allow me to throw in a few what ifs:

What if the dry-cleaning franchise mistakenly sent you an old, out-of-date brochure? It's happened before. Is it possible that all of the old brochures weren't thrown out (or recycled, of course) at company headquarters? What if a new employee at headquarters started the same day you put in your request for information? Is it possible that this individual grabbed the wrong brochure?

The scenario I just described *can* happen. I realize that it's probably a long shot, but I wanted to give you an example that was easy to visualize. There were *two* mistakes made here:

1. The dry-cleaning franchise sent you the wrong brochure.
2. You never had a conversation with the franchise development representative.

Number 1 can definitely happen; but it can be fixed. The company can send you an updated brochure and resolve their website's technological issues (with an apology!).

Number 2 happens *way* too much. Real information gathering requires that you amass as much information as you can about the company so that you can make an intelligent decision. In this case, arranging a call with the franchise development director would've been the intelligent thing to do because it would have allowed you to learn the following about the franchise:

- The franchise would be immediately sending out an updated franchise information packet.
- The franchise was, in fact, *very* focused on being green; in fact, they would have sent you a list of 15 different ways that they were lessening the impact their business makes on the environment.
- The franchise would have provided the data to support their claims of being environmentally friendly.
- The franchise was only interested in awarding franchises to people who had the same environmental philosophies as they do.
- The franchise had plenty of availability for new franchises in your area.

However, you didn't learn any of this. Instead, you made assumptions based solely on what was stated and shown in a brochure. (As it turns out, it was the *wrong* brochure.) What if that dry-cleaning franchise was The One? I guess you'll never find out.

Here's the deal: if you don't want to accidentally pass up a franchise opportunity that could have turned out to be absolutely perfect for you, then you need to make sure that you've gathered enough facts *about* the opportunity to make a decision on whether to pursue it any further or to move on. All the facts you'll need *won't* be located in the brochure; you must talk to the franchise development representative! If you want, discuss any major concerns you have *first*. See how things go; you may be surprised.

2. The Call

I like to refer to the first scheduled phone call with the franchise development representative as *The Call*. It's an important one; the hour or so you spend on the phone with the franchise development representative has the potential to set the tone for future interactions with both the franchise rep and the company as a whole.

Before I get into what will likely take place during this call, this is a good time for you to think about who else you want to involve at this point in your franchise search. If you are married (or have a partner, live-in, etc.), you've obviously shared your goal of becoming a franchise owner. (Right? I hope so.) Assuming you have—and they're pretty much on board with the idea—their role in the business should have a direct correlation with their involvement at this stage of your franchise search. If they're going to be involved in the business's day-to-day activities, they need to be on the first call—and every other one—from this point forward (if possible). Even if they are only going to be involved part time, you may want them on this call, just so they can learn about the franchise opportunity a little more. If they are supportive but won't be involved in the business, they don't need to be on this call; however, it wouldn't hurt if they were.

In fact, the franchise development director may request that you both participate in the call, even if your spouse or partner won't be involved in the everyday business operations. I personally think that it's a good idea to include this person as early as possible because whatever you choose to do will ultimately end up being a family decision.

The first few minutes will usually consist of what I call Normal Phone Niceties (NPNs). The conversation will probably cover general topics such as meteorology (discussions about the weather), sports trivia (how your hometown or city's sports teams are doing), or maybe a discussion about the latest natural disaster. I guarantee the NPNs *won't* include politics. (If your franchise development rep *does* bring up politics, he or she is a big bonehead, and you should do whatever you can to move the conversation away from that subject.)

After the NPNs have subsided, it's time for you and the rep to get to know each other a little. He or she will ask some general questions—things like how you ran across their franchise opportunity or why you're attracted to it—things of that nature. They'll also want to know about your professional background in order to find out what you're bringing to the table. You'll receive questions about things like what your responsibilities are (or were, if you were downsized), how many employees you've supervised, and if you're looking for a new job at the same time you're exploring the idea of becoming a franchise owner. It's perfectly fine if you do happen to be job-hunting *and* looking for a business to own (I call it being on a dual-track). Tell the franchise rep! It's best to get everything out in the open, especially early on. Some people in my field may feel that franchise candidates would be wise to keep things close to their chests during this stage in the franchise exploration process. Not me. It's not like you're negotiating a multimillion dollar real estate deal. Be open and honest; there's really no need to play mind games.

The franchise representative will undoubtedly begin talking about their franchise offering at some point in the call. You'll get a brief overview, and then the rep will ask you if you have any questions.

You may only be able to ask a few during the first call; it just depends on the time factor. Sometimes, the first call is so introductory in nature that you don't have a chance to ask all of your questions. It's okay; just cover the topics that will help you decide whether you should continue learning about the particular franchise offering, such as the following:

1. Is there territory available in my area?
2. Are there any franchisees in my area? (If yes, find out how many and where they're located.)
3. Have your other prospective franchisees been able to obtain financing?
4. Have there been any failures in my area? (If so, find out what happened.)
5. What is the failure rate?

Feel free to add any other questions that are possible game-changers in your mind. In other words, what would you have to hear that would prevent you from having a second phone call with the franchise development representative?

After you work through the five questions I just gave you—and any others you may have thought of yourself—it's time to ask more general questions, such as the following:

1. How long has the franchise company been in business?
2. How long have you been with the company?
3. How many franchised units do you have open?
4. What qualities and abilities do you look for in a franchisee?
5. What is the total investment?
6. How long will your process take?
7. Do you offer financing?

You'll think of more, for sure. Just reading through the information packet and brochure will give you ideas for plenty of questions to ask the franchise development representative. Again, you want to make sure to ask the ones that are game-changers for you, before you ask anything else.

One more thing: while you certainly have the right to ask *any* questions you want, just be careful *how* you ask them. You don't want to come across like you're the lead detective in a murder investigation questioning a suspect; go easy. Try to make your questioning style conversational; don't just rattle off question after question to the franchise development rep. The same goes for when you're asking questions of the existing franchisees of the businesses in which you're interested. Remember: *this is not an inquisition*; you're just gathering some information.

It's really important for you to make a great first impression with the franchisor. Get to know the franchise director, and allow him or her to get to know *you*. Talk to each other about your families. Establish some rapport. If the opportunity turns out to be The One, then you'll be happy that you made a great first impression because *if the franchise team doesn't like you, you won't be awarded a franchise*. I know that you may find that hard to believe, especially because you've probably heard stories about how some franchisors don't have the most stringent requirements when it comes to awarding franchises. While it's true that some franchisors may not care that much about *who* is buying franchises—because they just want to *sell* franchises—it's still important to make a good impression. And if you follow the advice contained in this book and base your decision on investing in a particular franchise on the facts, you won't put yourself in a position to be taken advantage of by an unscrupulous franchisor.

By the end of your first call, you should be able to decide whether you want to continue learning about the franchise offer that was presented. The franchise development representative will ask you to gauge your interest level; if it's high enough, he or she will outline the next steps in their process, which may include the following things:

- Online webinars with your franchise rep
- Scheduled weekly phone calls with your rep for Q&A
- Group conference calls with current franchisees
- Franchisee calls and visits
- FDD review
- Discovery Day (a visit to franchise headquarters)

Sometimes, the first call convinces you that the franchise concept that really interested you at first glance isn't what you thought it was at all. And if you don't feel that it's for you, then there's pretty much nothing that the rep can say to convince you otherwise, so move on. This may sound like it's difficult to do, especially if the rep is incredibly nice, extremely professional, and just *good people*. And although you may like the person at the other end of the phone, you just don't like the concept behind the franchise they represent; it's just not right for you. This isn't the time to be a people pleaser or to just tell them what you think they want to hear. These representatives talk with 20 to 30 folks a week—sometimes more. They would rather spend their time working with people who are truly interested in purchasing their franchise. So this is not the time to feel guilty. Really. Don't worry about the franchise development department; they'll be fine. While these representatives may not like some of the things that I'm teaching you to do, none of them will be mad at me for telling uninterested franchise candidates to move on instead of wasting their time. I've found that the best franchise companies encourage their reps to move franchise candidates *out of the process* quickly anyway if their interest level isn't high enough. So promise me right now: no guilt. Find another franchise opportunity. Remember, this *has* to be about you.

Having said that, I've found that a good number of the folks I've worked with continued the process with the franchisor because there really wasn't enough specific information given on the first phone call to make a yes or no decision on whether to continue learning more. So unless you're totally convinced that the opportunity is just not right for you, I recommend taking the next step, which is formal application.

3. Formal Application

You're going to be asked to fill out a franchise application form, which you could be asked to do before or after your second call with the franchise rep. This multiple-page application requires that you disclose specific information about your professional background, education, financial information (use the net worth sheet you put together in Chapter 8), and there may even be what looks to be a psychological test. Some franchisors use specialized behavioral profiling tools that help them assess whether you have the right stuff for their franchise system.

Once you're done filling everything out, you'll need to sign it and send it back to franchise headquarters. The franchisor now has permission to do background and credit checks on you. They want to make sure that you're totally qualified to become a franchisee with their franchise concept if and when they decide to offer you a franchise.

One such tool, and probably the most frequently used, is Craig Slavin's Franchise Navigator. Created especially for franchisors, this survey tool identifies and quantifies the characteristics of who the top, mid, and poor performing franchisees are within any given franchise system. Existing franchisees are asked to fill out a survey, which is scored and sent back to the franchisor. Basically, this assessment helps franchise development executives hone in on their most successful franchisees' key behavioral traits. Once they know what those behavioral traits are, they can compare them to the results of the same survey that their *prospective* franchisees have filled out. So, in a perfect world, if you're a prospective franchisee taking the survey and your score is similar to those of the top-performing *existing* franchisees in the franchise system that interests you, then according to this tool, you have a good chance at being a successful franchisee, too.

Here's why the Franchise Navigator creator Craig Slavin thinks that more franchisors should be using it:

> The problem with most franchisors is [that] they don't know how to quantify who their "ideal" franchisee is and what that means. They tend to use only financial and geographic metrics and vaguely described requirements. However . . . just because someone can afford the airplane doesn't mean they should pilot it. In other words, just because someone can afford the franchise doesn't mean it is a good fit for them.

I agree 100 percent with Craig's assessment about fit being more important than financials. Craig goes on to explain:

> During the past 15 years of my 40-year history in franchising, I have focused on [the] metrics [that will] provide the highest predictive process for determining whether a candidate is a good fit—or not. We developed and launched Franchise Navigator in 1999, which is a Skills and Values Behavioral Assessment tool now used by almost 150 franchisors. We benchmark as many of the existing franchisees as possible; then using metrics—such as sales performance and operational compliance as graded by each of our franchisor clients—we create a Profile to which all inbound candidates are measured. This not only tells us if the candidate is a good fit to execute the business model; it also tells both parties, in advance, on what behavioral areas a franchisor needs to focus most to ensure the franchisee candidate's performance and satisfaction. As I have been saying for many, many years now—the very [elements] that affect success or failure in franchising have nothing to do with franchising, per se. [Rather], it is the Human Capital aspect that will affect success the most. You could have the best business model in the world; [however, it's just not going to work] if you have the wrong type of operator! So, [even more

important than the question] "Do they have the money?" [about the potential franchisor is the question]: Do they fit?"

Again, I'm in total agreement with Craig about having a great franchise business model and not having the right operators. The fit must be a mutual one. *A good franchisor only offers a franchise to folks that are financially qualified, have the needed skills for success, and are an all around great fit for them, their culture, and their vision for growth.*

Speaking of fit, would you like to see how you stack up against top-performing franchisees of several different franchises? Craig Slavin has made his popular Franchise Navigator assessment tool (which normally sells for $29.99), available to readers of this book, free of charge. Aren't you curious to see how you stack up with some very, very, successful franchisees? To access this free tool, just go to www.franchise-navigator.com/connectmesurvey.php.

Butterflies

You may start to get a little nervous at this stage in the process. Indeed, you may start to feel the fluttering of butterflies in your gut as you begin the physical process of filling in all the information required in the franchise application form. Usually, it's the act of sharing your private financial information that can really start to heighten those nerves. Writing down your assets and liabilities on a formal franchise application tends to slap you awake; reality may be starting to finally settle in a bit. You're starting to realize that you're not pursuing a job hunt; instead, you're embarking on something that may require you to write a big check. And once you write that check and obtain your small business loan, *you're* going to be the one who is 100 percent responsible for your business's eventual success—or failure. *Wow.* So, if you find yourself feeling a wee bit apprehensive as you're filling out all of this information, take a break. Go for a walk. Meditate. Do whatever you normally do to work through difficult things, and then come back and finish it up.

It's completely normal to start having second thoughts about becoming a franchise owner at this point. Look back at some of the other major decisions you've made throughout your life. I'll wager that you had some serious second thoughts about them, too. Walk through them again; see if you remember what you did to put them in perspective to help make your decisions. It takes a lot of chutzpah to do this, you know. (*Chutzpah* is a Yiddish word for *spunk*.) Not everybody is cut out to be a business owner. Some of us are better as employees, choosing to let others take all of the risks involved in owning and operating a business. Choosing to *not* become a franchise owner doesn't make you less of a person. It's just a choice—one that you may come to after figuring out what's best for you and your situation.

After you fill out and submit the franchise application, you'll be sent the Franchise Disclosure Document (FDD). This is an important document required by the Federal Trade Commission (FTC). Per the FTC website (http://business.ftc.gov/):

> Under the Franchise Rule, which is enforced by the FTC, you must receive the document at least 14 days before you are asked to sign any contract or pay any money to the franchisor or an affiliate of the franchisor. You have the right to ask for—and get—a copy of the disclosure document once the franchisor has received your application and agreed to consider it. Indeed, you may want to get a copy of the franchisor's disclosure document before incurring any expenses to investigate the franchise offering.

> The franchisor may give you a copy of its disclosure document on paper, via email, through a web page, or on a disc. The cover of the disclosure document should have information about its availability in other formats. Make sure you have a copy of the document in a format that is convenient for you, and keep a copy for reference.

> Let's review the FDD in general terms.

4. The FDD Review

In this section, I'm going to be giving you *very* general information on the FDD. *I am not an attorney, nor do I claim to be.* This is why you should discuss any and all legal aspects of a franchise investment with a competent franchise attorney—one who is familiar with franchise laws in your state.

The FDD is a fact-filled (I almost wrote fun-filled!) document that you get from the franchisor. It has very detailed and important information about every aspect of the franchise business you're investigating. *This is the most important document that you'll receive from the franchise company.* It may come in the mail, but most likely you'll be given an access code to use on the franchise company's website so that you can access the FDD at your convenience.

A word of warning here: occasionally, you'll run across a franchisor that doesn't choose to disclose the FDD until you visit their headquarters in person. Although it isn't too common anymore, this practice can be pretty unsettling. In my experience, there's a specific reason if the franchisor won't send you their FDD early in the process. There may be some negative information in the document that they would prefer to explain to you in person. The negative information may have to do with an abnormal amount of litigation, a sharp drop-off in franchisees, or anything else that you, the prospective franchise buyer, may deem to be a red flag.

If a franchisor insists on disclosing their FDD late in the process or in person only, I would walk away—unless they agree to send it immediately upon your request without argument.

To me, the decision to *avoid sending the FDD early on* is a bigger red flag than some of the things you may find *in* the FDD itself. That's because I believe in total transparency in business. I respect a franchisor who is willing to show both positive and negative things about their business up front because, in this day and age, prospective buyers are going to find out anyway. Franchisors that insist on dancing around issues they're having will find themselves selling fewer and fewer franchises as time goes on and as potential franchise buyers get smarter.

The reality is that no franchise is completely *without* problems. And as a franchise buyer, you have the right to know about these problems *way* before you invest your hard-earned money into the venture. As you get further into the franchise research process, you'll be able to easily get specific information about the problems that the franchisor may currently be having or may have had in the past.

The FDD itself is about 200 pages long; reading it is pretty darn tedious. It may actually end up being included on your personal top 10 list of the most boring things you've ever read. If you ever have problems falling asleep, the FDD is a great substitute for Ambien.

In all seriousness, the FDD can best be described as a painful combination of the following:

- Poorly written company executive biographies
- The franchisor's obligations/your obligations written in complex legalese
- Estimated franchise start-up investment amounts; numerous footnotes included at no charge
- A 30-page franchise contract that's excruciatingly difficult to read, Latin included

. . . and more!

A lot of franchisors are sending the FDD to you electronically these days. (It's not very green to keep printing out 200-page documents, now is it?) However, some still do send the printed version via U.S. Mail or UPS/FedEx (because the printed version is actually easier to read and go through.) Either way, there will be a receipt for you to sign and date for their records. Go ahead and sign it; then send it back to the franchise company. As I mentioned before, a growing number of franchise companies are starting to grant access to their FDDs electronically. Make sure you have enough ink in your printer because *you'll* want to print it out.

By law, the following 23 items must be listed in the FDD:

1. The franchisor, its predecessors, and its affiliates
2. Business experience
3. Litigation
4. Bankruptcy
5. Initial franchise fee
6. Other fees

7. Initial investment
8. Restrictions on sources of products and services
9. Franchisee's obligations
10. Financing
11. Franchisor's obligations
12. Territory
13. Trademarks
14. Patents, copyrights, and proprietary information
15. Obligation to participate in the actual operation of the franchise business
16. Restrictions on what the franchisee may sell
17. Renewal, termination, transfer, and dispute resolution
18. Public figures
19. Earnings claims
20. List of outlets
21. Financial statements
22. Contracts
23. Receipt

Here's what to do when you receive the FDD.

1. Print it out, read through it once, and take notes as you go along. (You can write on the pages if you want as it's yours to keep.) Be prepared for several hours of reading and note taking. *Several.*
2. Focus especially on the following items:

   A. **Franchisor's Business Experience**. You'll want to know the backgrounds of the executives at the franchise company as well as what they bring to the table, experience wise. Have they been in franchising for long? Have they led other franchise companies? How long have they been at this particular organization?

   B. **Litigation**. There could be a problem if there are a high number of lawsuits contained in the FDD. You need to figure out who's suing who. In other words: Were—or are—ex-franchisees currently taking legal actions toward the franchise company? or,

Are there lawsuits involving the franchise company suing the franchisees? Take good notes here; write down your thoughts and concerns as you'll be sharing them with the franchise development representative, the franchisees, and your franchise attorney later on in the process. As far as I'm concerned, it's absolutely necessary to note any lawsuits. Ultimately, a good franchise attorney will be able to advise you about any past or current litigation that's been disclosed in the FDD.

C. **Bankruptcy**. This section discloses whether the executives, or even the franchisor, have been involved in a recent bankruptcy. If so, it may be a cause for concern. For example, did a current executive start or involve themselves with a franchise concept in the past that went under? It will be disclosed here, so, if applicable, take notes, and save them for later.

D. **Earnings Claims**. Franchisors are not required to disclose franchisee earnings claims, which may include specific information about potential income or sales. If they do, the law requires that they have a reasonable basis for their claims and that they make the substantiation for those claims available to you, the franchise buyer. Twenty percent to 30 percent of the franchise concepts registered in the United States choose to make franchisee earnings claims. These claims may be in the form of individual franchise unit gross sales, gross sales broken down by years in business, or it may show gross or net profit figures. It's great if you're investigating an opportunity that *does* disclose earnings claims; you'll be ahead of the game because you'll have a good foundation upon which to build when you start calling existing franchisees to find out how much they're making. It's also fine if you're investigating an opportunity that does not disclose earnings claims. Personally, it makes no difference to me whether a franchisor discloses franchisee earnings or not. That's because even if a franchisor *does* show franchisee earnings, sales, or anything in between, franchise buyers still need to call existing franchisees and find out what they're seeing—and what they're making. By the way, always keep the following in mind: *Most of the answers to your most important questions are always going to come from the people that already invested their own money in the franchise you're interested in: the franchisees.*

E.   **List of Outlets.** The FDD lists all the current franchisees, including their names, addresses, and phone numbers; it is essentially a list of people that you'll be calling and maybe even visiting. It gets even better because there is also a list of all the franchisees *that have left the system* in the last 12 months. Now, *that's* cool. I'll show you why.

Do you remember those story problems you had to do in math class when you were a kid? I hope so because we're going to do a very important one right now! Take out your No. 2 pencils.

Let's say that the franchise concept you're considering has 100 *current* franchisees listed in their FDD. Let's also say that according their FDD, 14 franchisees have *left the system* in the last 12 months. Now please solve this: what percentage of franchisees listed have left the franchise system? You have five minutes to answer.

Please put your pencils down. What did you come up with?

If your answer is 14 percent, you're right. Fourteen percent of the franchisees have left the system in the last 12 months.

Now let's see how you do here with some bonus questions:

Bonus question #1: Do you think that 14 percent is a high number as it relates to this specific story problem?

Bonus question #2: How can you find out *why* 14 percent of the franchisees have left the system?

You have five minutes to answer those two questions.

Okay. Pencils down. What did you come up with?

The answer to bonus question #1 is: Yes. Fourteen percent is pretty high.

The answer to bonus question #2 is: You'll need to ask the franchise development representative why 14 percent of their franchises left the system in the last 12 months. You'll also need to see if you can wrangle some pertinent information about the franchisees that left the system from current franchisees. You should also try to get in touch with the people that left the system. Their phone numbers will be there, and even if some of the phones may be disconnected, it's still worth a shot. (If this is the case, you can always do a Google search of their names.) Once you locate a few, call them, and ask them what happened. They may have sold their franchises; they may have decided to not renew their agreements; or they might have gone under. If you can't get enough information this way, some of the *current* franchisees may have an idea as to what happened. Word gets around.

The five elements of the FDD I just pointed out for you—Franchisor's Business Experience, Litigation, Bankruptcy, Earnings Claims, and List of Outlets—are *really important*. They are the most crucial areas upon which you should focus on, especially early on, *because they'll help you get the real story*. And that's what you want. Of course, all 23 items will need your attention eventually, but for now, it's critical to make sure that you're a nice fit for the franchise(s) that you're considering at this juncture.

Here's what my Dad taught me about the FDD:

The FDD is *not* the business. It's just a combination of words and numbers. You're not buying the FDD; you're buying a franchise . . . a way to get where you want to go. To truly find out about the business, you need to call and visit the franchisees, and if things look positive and feel right, [the next step is to] visit franchise headquarters.

I'll add one more thing here: all the data contained in the FDD—that 200-page monster—isn't really all that important during the early part of your franchise information quest. First, you have to make sure that you can really see yourself running the franchise business in which you're considering investing. Then you need to talk to the franchisees, so you can make sure that you can make enough money, and that it's really right for you. Only then does the FDD become important. After all, if you don't feel that you're a fit for a particular franchise—if you just can't see yourself as the owner—then all the information contained in the FDD won't matter because you'll have moved on. So don't get too stuck on some of the contents in the FDD right now.

F. **Franchisee Validation Calls**. Once you have the list of current and former franchisees (garnered from the FDD), it's time for you to make contact with them. You may have another list from the franchise development representative as well. Sometimes, reps will send you over their own list of franchisees. In my experience, a really good franchise development representative will come up with some franchisees that he or she feels would be a good match for you. Maybe these franchisees come from similar backgrounds or circumstances as you. It's easy to find out why these are recommended franchisees to call; just ask! It may be that it is a customized list made up just for you, like I suggested in the preceding. Or it could be a list of franchisees that are very open to getting calls or visits from prospective franchisees and with which you'll be able to easily connect.

Now because your franchise ownership intelligence is growing at a really rapid pace, you probably don't need me to tell you that the franchise rep's list most likely includes mostly happy and profitable franchisees, right?

You've probably figured out by now that I'm a little on the skeptical side. It's served me well, so I've decided to stay that way. So, as I share this next point with you, I want you to know that I'm getting out of my *skeptical comfort zone* for a little while.

I highly recommend calling some of the franchisees from the list that your franchise development representative gives you. Because you're probably going to be a little uncomfortable calling *any* franchisees at first, you can look at these first few phone calls and e-mails as practice ones. You'll still get lots of great information, and, at the same time, you'll become increasingly comfortable asking some of the 40 great questions that I'm about to give you. Just be aware that these franchisees are probably used to getting lots of calls from prospective franchisees, so the answers you're getting will likely come at a rapid-fire pace. Well, *some* of them. That's because several of the questions that you're about to get have been taken from deep inside The Franchise Kingdom's vaults and have only been used by a few hundred people.

After you've called a few of the franchisees from the franchise development representative's list, you can then open the FDD and start choosing franchisees to call—*randomly*. I recommend calling a minimum of 10 to 15 from different parts of the country. Making this many calls is a lot of work; you won't be able to get a hold of all of the folks you're trying to call at first, so you'll be leaving messages and maybe even trying to contact them via e-mail. (To get their e-mail addresses, go to the main franchise website, and look up the franchisees by location.) And once you do connect with them, you can plan on spending an hour or more on the phone.

Use the questions that I'm about to give you as a starting place, and add more as you go. The answers that you receive from the franchisees will help you determine if you're a good fit for the franchise concept and provide you with the crucial information you'll need to make an intelligent, fact-based decision on whether to become a franchisee of the franchise you're considering. And remember not to rush through these calls!

Forty Questions to Ask Current Franchisees

1. What is your professional background?
2. How did you find out about this franchise opportunity?
3. How long did it take you (from start to finish) to make your decision about this franchise?
4. How long have you been in business?
5. What was your total investment, including any hidden or unexpected costs?
6. Was the franchisor's training adequate?
7. Do you feel that you've received all the tools you need to handle the day-to-day operations?
8. Were you able to open your business in a reasonable amount of time?
9. Who selected your location (if not home-based)?
10. Can you describe a typical workday from start to finish?

11. Is your role as a franchisee what you expected it to be? If not, what's different?
12. Were you aware of any competitors before you invested in your franchise?
13. How much and what type of competition is there? Are they good? How are you better?
14. Is it difficult to find and retain employees? Where do you find them?
15. How do you rate the franchisor's product?
16. Does the franchisor's product (even if it's a service-business) give you some significant advantages in your market area?
17. Are you satisfied with the cost, delivery, and quality of your products?
18. Do you have any repeat business? More or less than you originally thought?
19. Do you have to hit a minimum sales quota?
20. How is the franchisor's marketing?
21. Does the franchisor have a local website or web page established for you?
22. Are you permitted to set up your own website?
23. Is the franchisor using social media marketing?
24. Do you pay into a marketing or advertising fund? How much? Do you feel that it's worth it?
25. Does the franchisor provide ongoing training?
26. Does the franchisor have field personnel that make in-person visits?
27. How do you feel about the franchisor's support? How long does it take for you to get a response when you need help?
28. Is the franchisor's technology current and trouble-free?
29. How long did it take you to break even?
30. What were your gross sales in years one, two, and three?
31. What kind of profit margin do you have?
32. Are your income expectations being met?
33. If you had the opportunity to do this all over, would you invest in this franchise?
34. Do you have any growth plans? Will you be adding another unit or more space?
35. Are you aware of any real unhappy franchisees? If so, who and why?

36. What do you wish you would have known before you invested in the franchise?
37. What is your favorite part of this business? Your least favorite?
38. Do you have any input into the franchisor's operational or management decisions?
39. If I was a really good college buddy who was interested in this franchise for my area of the country, would you recommend it? Why or why not?
40. Are you comfortable with me calling you for help and advice if I invest in this franchise?

Those are my Top 40; you'll add more of your own as you go along. Try to ask as many of those questions as possible. I know that it seems like it's a lot to ask of current franchisees; yes, they're really, really, busy. Heck, they're trying to run their own businesses, so *they* can make money. Use your best judgment with each one. Sometimes you can only get to about half of the questions, so, if you can, try to arrange a second call to ask the rest. If the person is too busy for another call, he or she might be amenable to answering the rest of your questions via e-mail. However, it's best if you can get them on the phone again because this will allow you to start building rapport and establishing a bond.

See if you can get to know them a little more on the second call. Maybe back off a little from your list of questions. Building a comfortable relationship with a few of the current franchisees is an important thing to do. Not only will the franchisees be more open with you if they like you, but they may even offer to be a sounding board for you if you decide to open a franchise and need some extra support in the beginning.

Another benefit to establishing good relationships with some of the franchisees is that it will make it that much easier to ask them if you can spend a day with them at their business. Better yet, if you're really good, you could get yourself *invited* to their franchise business so that you can see firsthand what it's like to be a franchisee. If you have an opportunity to spend the day with a current franchisee, do it! Spare no reasonable expense for a chance like this.

Think about it: instead of relying on brochures, PowerPoint presentations, and other miscellaneous information that you've received from the franchise development team, you can witness for yourself what a day in the life of a franchisee *really* is like—no guessing or daydreaming about what you *think* it would be like to be a franchisee of this particular franchise. *Just do it.*

I'd like to go back to the franchisee validation calls. (They're called validation calls because you're validating what you've read in the FDD and what you've seen and heard up until this point.) You should really be taking great notes during your calls because doing so will help you stay organized. Make several copies of the sheets with the questions that you'll be asking them, and write down the date, time, and the franchisee's name and location on each. Believe me; after calling and asking numerous questions of 10 to 15 different franchisees from all around the country, you'll be glad that you recorded that information. It will make things a lot easier for you when you sit down and compare the answers that you were given. Plus, if you have more than one call with any of them, it'll be that much easier to keep track of your conversations—including when and where you left off.

One more very important thing about calling franchisees is that if you happen to be looking into a franchise offering that has locations in your geographic area, you'll be tempted to call or visit them right away—very early on in the research process. I know that you're excited about the idea of becoming a franchise owner, and you want to jump in and learn all you can from the very beginning—and that's great. It may be even more exciting knowing that there are a couple of franchisees right in your area and that you could just drive over and snoop around a bit.

But don't do it! Here's why: You're an amateur:

- You don't have a clue about the actual business model yet.
- You don't even know if it's the right fit for you yet.
- You probably have no idea of territory availability.
- The local franchisee will know that something's just not right with you because it's pretty obvious that you're not really a customer. Any questions you'd ask would be the wrong ones.

- You don't know the situation; this franchisee may be in the middle of a major dispute with the franchisor.

This goes for something as innocent (in your mind) as just a phone call to the franchisee that has a location five miles away. Don't call *the local franchisees* early in the process. Save it for later. The best time to call or visit a local franchisee of the franchise you're interested in exploring is *after* you've called (and maybe even visited) some others farther away. That's because by then you'll have learned a ton about the franchise, and you'll be superconfident; you'll know what to look for and ask. Kind of makes sense, huh? So don't give into temptation. Stay away from the local franchises until you know what the heck you're doing. Okay? *Call them last.*

How to Ask the Money Question

The most uncomfortable part of the franchise research process has to do with money. Sooner or later, you're going to want to get a good idea of how much you'll be able to make as a franchisee of the franchise concepts you're investigating.

Think about it; why the heck would someone who's never met you (and who may live halfway across the country) want to share his or her franchise business income information with you?

I actually don't have the answer, but I do know this; they probably *don't* want to share their private information with you.

Unless, that is, you know how to ask.

It's all in the approach. Remember when I suggested that you try to bond with the franchisees as you're talking with them on the phone? And that arranging a second call with them would be really beneficial in trying to do just that?

That's because it's going to be a lot easier to ask the "how much money do you make?" question if you've established some rapport with the franchisee as opposed to asking like this:

Billy: Hi there. My name is Billy Beenthere. I'm calling from the Boston area, and I'm looking into buying a Spicy Subs franchise. How much money did you make in your first year in business?

Do you think Billy was able to get his question answered?

If your answer was no, you'd be right. Why *would* that franchisee of Spicy Subs want to answer Billy's question? After all, he really has no idea who it really is on the other end of the phone. And with Billy's approach, I'll wager that this franchisee doesn't really care, either. Heck, Billy didn't even ask for his name!

This franchisee doesn't care who's on the other end of the phone because there was no bond established between them on the call. It was just two strangers talking to each other. There was no give and take. Billy's approach was cold, and he asked the money question way too fast.

Let's meet Carol Correct. Carol is a student of relationship-building. She knows that she has to take it slow in order to get personal information from someone. She also knows that she has to make sure that the person she's going to ask is comfortable with her. In short, Carol also knows the importance of timing.

Here's how Carol asks the same question:

Carol: Hi Jim. I'm thinking about becoming a fellow franchise owner of Spicy Subs, and I was hoping to ask you a few questions to see if maybe I would be a good franchisee candidate for them. Is this a good time to talk?

Do you think that Jim will at least stop for a moment to consider if he can spend some time on the phone with this fine lady now? Or at least arrange a better time?

Let's assume that Jim makes the time to talk to Carol. Carol's questions may include "How did you end up becoming interested in Spicy Subs?" "What is your business background?" "Are you happy with your choice in the franchise that you now own, and why or why not?"

She goes down her list of questions and gets her answers.

Notice that she's asking some open-ended questions early on, which prompts Jim to give more than yes or no answers. This helps Carol get a feel for him and, more important, for the franchise in which she's interested.

But there's something that Carol *hasn't* done: she's hasn't asked a thing about his income.

Now Carol can still stumble here. (Remember, this is her first phone call with this franchisee.) She may find herself bonding incredibly well with Jim. Who knows; maybe they've been on the phone with each other for an hour already, and he really doesn't seem to be trying all that hard to get off the phone. *Carol may be feeling comfortable enough right now to ask Jim how much he's making.* But she needs to wait. Carol needs to schedule a second phone call right now.

This may be frustrating for Carol because she really wants *and needs* to know how much she'll be able to make. If her ROI isn't enough for what she's willing to invest in that franchise, than she'll need to move on to another opportunity. The other opportunity may end up being a different franchise concept, or she may even decide to get another job. My point is that she needs the information.

The second phone call, which she formally scheduled, went like this:

Carol: Hi Jim, it's Carol. I'm calling back as promised. Is this still a good time?

Jim: Sure, Carol. Were you able to talk with some more franchisees since our last call?

Carol: Yes, I'm getting a lot of great information!

Jim: Fantastic! What other questions can I answer for you?

(At this point, Carol is scanning through her list of questions and carefully chooses which other ones to ask. She asks them and finally gets to the one she really needs answered.)

Carol: Jim, if one was to buy a Spicy Subs franchise, how much could one expect to make in the first year?

Jim: Well, Carol, in my case, I didn't make much in the first year . . . and I didn't expect to, but I brought in $35,000 in my second year, and almost $75,000 in my third.

That wasn't so bad, huh?

Did you notice the approach that Carol used to ask her most important question? She asked it in the third person—in a very detached way. Jim didn't feel at all threatened because Carol wasn't really asking about *his* income. Notice as well that Carol didn't even refer to herself in the question, either. She asked "if *one* were to buy a Spicy Subs franchise." Amazingly, Jim did disclose his own personal financial information, and he was perfectly comfortable doing so. And it's not like Carol tricked Jim into answering her question; if he didn't want to answer it, he wouldn't have. The point is that Jim must have felt *some* type of bond with Carol and that he could trust her with the information he was giving.

Now this technique of asking important questions using the third person won't always work. Sometimes, franchise owners clam up. They get paranoid. They may think that you're an IRS agent. (Now that's what I call paranoid!) Or it may be that they're just really private people. It's okay. I'm confident that if you talk to and establish a bond with enough franchisees, you'll get all the answers you need.

Speaking of *bonding*—by this point, you've hopefully found a couple of franchisees with whom you felt pretty comfortable and who are within driving distance of you. If so, call a few of them back, and arrange an in-person visit—at a time that's convenient for *them*. Remember that they have their own businesses to run, so be really flexible with them. If they're willing to let you spend the day—or even a few hours—at their place of business (or if it's a B2B franchise, a day in the field with them), you need to jump at the chance to do it. It can be a game-changer in the sense that you'll really be able to see what your potential future franchise business will look, feel, smell, and taste like. You'll also have the ability to ask franchisees questions face to face. You've probably heard the phrase "the eyes are the windows to the soul." It's true; look into the eyes of the franchisee or franchisees with whom you get to meet and ask questions *before* you make your decision on whether to become a franchisee yourself.

The franchisees that you visit will fully expect you to ask lots of questions, so fire away. They'll probably come very naturally at this point because you've already gathered lots of information from your other franchisee validation calls. Of course, seeing how the business runs in person will present an opportunity to come up with even more questions. It's important that you take as many notes as possible during an in-person visit; there's no way you'll remember all or even most of what you discussed with the franchisees.

Your intuition should also be coming into play by this point. In other words, how does it feel when you first walk into the franchisee's place of business? It will usually either feel right or it won't. Sometimes the operation may not feel quite right immediately, but it kind of grows on you after a few minutes. That's perfectly okay. Just trust your gut during these visits.

Remember that it's best to visit more than one franchisee. Even though most successful franchise businesses will have lots of uniformity, individual franchisees are, well, individuals. Therefore, their management styles will be different. Plus, it's always better to get more than one perspective before making a decision on anything, especially something as potentially life-changing as this. Believe it or not, every franchise establishment that you visit will feel different.

Now it's absolutely fine if you're only able to make one in-person visit. Don't sweat it. Making even one in-person visit puts you *so* far ahead of most franchise buyers, like James Pennington; I don't recall James arranging to visit any of the franchisees with whom he talked. As a matter of fact, he didn't visit one of the pizza franchise's locations until his Discovery Day at corporate headquarters. A one-hour, in-person visit with a franchisee isn't really enough (especially with members of the franchisor's executive team in tow!).

If possible, visit franchises in person *way* before you have to make a decision on whether to invest in the franchise. The fact-finding stage of the franchise research process is really the time to do it, because there's going to be way too much emotion involved as you're nearing the end of the process.

G. **Results Calls.** After you feel that you've talked to enough franchisees (and hopefully visited one or two of them in person), it's time to share what you've learned—along with any concerns you may have—with the franchise development representative. If you've been staying organized like I suggested, it should be relatively easy to come up with a list of questions to ask the franchise development representative.

One of your first questions will probably be about franchisee income. You may want to verify what you've been hearing from the franchisees who were kind enough to tell you about their own experiences. Now this may sound a little strange, but unless the franchisor has made an earnings claim on their FDD, their representatives cannot discuss franchisee earnings with you. It's not that it's illegal; it's just that if earnings figures are to be given, they must be done via the FDD (specifically in item 19 of the document.)

Therefore, this part of the research process can be a little frustrating. One would think that it would be fairly easy to answer a simple little question like "How much can I make as a franchisee of your organization?" After all, if you're about to invest $100,000 or more into *their* franchise, you'd think that they would gladly answer your question, right? But think about it. If you asked your representative that question and he or she replied, "You can easily make $40,000 in year one," wouldn't you feel angry if you make something closer to $10,000? As a matter of fact, do you think you'd be angry enough to sue them for misleading you?

It won't ever get that far, though; not with you, anyway. That's because you already *have* your answers. They've come from one or two places:

1. The FDD
2. The current franchisees

And because you now know exactly how to research a franchise, you're not going to have to experience the frustration of finding out how much you can make—like most other franchise buyers who have no clue what they're doing. (I'm trying to change that!)

As I mentioned, it should be relatively easy to come up with a list of questions to ask the franchise development representative based on your conversations with the franchisees. Don't be shy; ask away. Franchise development representatives are used to getting peppered with questions. And just like when you talked to franchisees, remember to take detailed notes.

Something important to keep in mind during and after you conversations with franchisees is that about 80 percent of the ones with whom you spoke should be *happy*. Even the best franchise systems have unhappy franchisees; some people can't be pleased, no matter what. You probably got that sense from one or two franchisees you met. Some people like to complain and to place blame. As I stated in an earlier chapter, no franchise system is perfect.

However, your goal should be to find a franchise opportunity that you feel gives you an above-average chance of being a successful franchisee, is affordable, and is one that you can easily visualize yourself owning.

There's one other thing that relates to your conversations with the franchisees, and it's pretty important. Did you get the feeling that they were similar to you as you talked with them? Did any of them have similar backgrounds to you? Were they easy to talk with? Or were you really uncomfortable talking to them . . . even on the phone? Were they just not your kind of people? If you were able to pay one or two of them a visit, how did it feel to be with them? Did you like having face time with them, or was it kind of painful?

Lots to think about, huh?

Here's even more: The following is a very special list of questions that I've put together that you can (and *should*) ask the franchise development director in addition to the ones you're already asking. The great thing about this next series of questions is that you can also ask them of the franchise executive team if you end up visiting franchise headquarters.

- What is your franchise system's failure rate? (This is something that an experienced franchise development representative should know. If not, they should at least be willing to get that information for you from whoever has access to it.)
- What types of people have you found to be especially successful as franchise owners in your system, and what types of people have performed below average?
- Can you describe a perfect franchisee for your opportunity?
- What are some of reasons you have turned down prospective franchisees?

- Can I have some specific examples of problems that your franchisees have experienced and how your support team has jumped in to help out?
- Are you looking to acquire any other franchise concepts?

The franchise development representative may not be used to answering some of the tougher questions that you've been asking. (That's because most franchise buyers don't have this fine list of questions like you do!) It's okay; just remember that this is *all about you*. You're trying to do everything in your power to *lower your risk*, so you can *make money*, and *own what you do*. The next chapter is designed to show you how to do all three.

11

Loans, Legalities, and Luggage

"If you can't ride two horses at once, you shouldn't be in the circus."
—American proverb

By NOW, YOU'VE made quite a bit of progress in your efforts to become a franchise owner. You've talked with and hopefully visited current franchisees of the franchise you're seriously considering. You've shared some of your findings and concerns with the franchise development representative. You've read the FDD and have gone through it with the franchise development representative.

This means that you only have a couple more things to do before you get to your Decision Day. Congratulations! Now let me ask you something: how well can you multitask? You're going to have to do some of that in this phase of the franchise research process. There are several areas to cover here:

1. You're going to have to start gathering information on small business loans.
2. In terms of legalities, you'll want to start looking for a competent franchise attorney to help you decipher the FDD and eventually the franchise contract (if things get that far).

3. You may be invited to what's called a Discovery Day. These take place at the franchisor's headquarters in most cases, so you should start digging out your luggage. You'll have an opportunity to meet the executive team, and they'll have the same opportunity to meet you. If they like you, you'll be offered a franchise. If you like them and the opportunity, you'll be moving toward your Decision Day.

But first things first. Let's talk about how you're going to get some money. . . .

Loans

"A bank is a place that will lend you money if you can prove that you don't need it."

—Bob Hope

You're now at the point where you should be thinking about how you'll obtain financing for your franchise business. Now before you say, "Joel, I haven't even decided to go through with it yet," just stay with me. It doesn't matter if you've made a yes decision on a particular franchise or not; you still need to start the loan application process. Lately, it's become quite a chore to obtain small business financing, and it could take a lot longer than you think to get your loan approved, which is exactly why I want you to start *now*. Even if you ultimately decide not invest in the franchise(s) on which you're focused, you'll be way ahead of the game when and if you find another one. Plus, it never hurts to learn how the loan process works.

Lenders are inherently conservative, so the less risk they have, the better they feel about loaning you the money needed for a business of your own. Another important thing to understand is that each lending institution has different criteria for loans. Of course, your current debt, credit ranking, and asset base are all factors in this equation. About the only thing set in stone from a lender's perspective is that you must have a proven record of paying your bills on time.

There are a number of ways to obtain financing for your own business. I'm giving you a basic overview here; however, it's crucial that you find finance options that can work for *you*. I'll discuss some in detail in the following.

Small Business Administration (SBA) Loans

The U.S. Small Business Administration has several different programs for small business owners. Instead of my explaining exactly what the SBA does here, I'll save some time and direct you to their website: www.SBA .gov. Here, you can read what they have written about these programs and their role in each. Consider the following excerpt from SBA.gov:

> The SBA does not make direct loans to small businesses. Rather, SBA sets the guidelines for loans, which are then made by its partners (lenders, community development organizations, and microlending institutions). The SBA guarantees that these loans will be repaid, thus eliminating some of the risk to the lending partners. So when a business applies for an SBA loan, it is actually applying for a commercial loan, structured according to SBA requirements with an SBA guaranty. SBA-guaranteed loans may not be made to a small business if the borrower has access to other financing on reasonable terms.

As you can see, the SBA is not the actual bank; rather, it's the *strength behind* the bank. The SBA loan guaranty requirements and practices can change as the U.S. government alters its fiscal policy and priorities to meet present economic conditions. The percentage of the loan amount that the SBA guarantees can move up or down depending on economic conditions. Your lender will tell you what the current percentage is if you're curious.

The SBA offers several different types of loans. If you'd like to see which are currently being offered, simply visit the SBA.gov website. Several new sections have been added, all of which are designed to make the loan process a lot less complex. You'll even be able to find out which lenders in your local area are considered SBA-Preferred Lenders. Just go to www.sba.gov/loans-and-grants (Disclosure: I write a monthly blog post on franchising for the SBA.gov website. Just go to www.community .Sba.gov and look under "The Industry Word.")

Lots of franchise owners go this route, and I've found the SBA to be pretty franchise friendly. Now, there's no guarantee that the SBA will approve your loan just because you're investing in a franchise business; it's just that the franchise business model inherently brings a lot to the table that a typical lender will like, such as the following:

- **A track record.** There are (usually, except in the case of a brand new franchise opportunity) other franchisees who are in business and who are using the same business model that you're telling the lender you'll be using.
- **Brand recognition**. Sometimes the fact that the franchise offering brings with it an established brand name can effectively tilt the odds in your favor.

Lenders have access to The SBA Franchise Registry, which includes listings of franchise systems whose prospective franchisees may receive a more expedited loan process when applying for financial assistance from the SBA. It's not mandatory for franchisors to get listed on the Franchise Registry, though, so be sure to ask the franchise development representative if his or her franchise opportunity is listed.

Home Equity Loans or Lines of Credit

The folks with whom I worked from 2002 to 2008 had an option available to them that isn't used as frequently at the present time: the home equity loan. That is because, as of this writing, residential real estate prices across the United States are pretty low, so franchise buyers may not have lots of equity in their homes.

In this scenario, you could use a certain percentage of the equity you have in your home as collateral for a loan. For example, if your home has an appraised value of $400,000, and you owe $100,000, a percentage of your equity can be used for whatever you want. Lots of people tap into their home's equity to pay off their high-interest rate credit cards, do some home improvements, pay for their children's college, and, yes, invest in a business of their own. In a home equity loan, the borrower gets a check for the amount requested.

A home equity line of credit (HELOC) is a little different; in this scenario, you're still using the equity in your home for collateral, but it's in the form of an open credit line, and it usually has a time frame of five years. You get a checkbook and can write checks as needed up to the amount approved (your credit limit.) In both cases, you *may* be able to write off the interest paid to the lender, which is a great thing. Make sure you consult your tax advisor, who may also be your CPA, to see if this applies to you.

Speaking of taxes, you also need to start learning about business taxation. Your small business will be taxed on its profits based on how it's set up, that is, the business entity (S-Corporation, LLC, Sole Proprietorship, etc.). For example, I consulted with my business attorney and accountant before deciding how to set up my business. I didn't really know what entity to use. I had no idea about things like self-employment and payroll taxes; I also knew nothing about business liability issues and how to go about protecting myself and my family from frivolous lawsuits and things of that nature. I certainly didn't just want to guess on the best entity for my business.

Fortunately for me (and for you), my good friend Barbara Weltman is a great resource for issues on small business taxation. Barbara has written several books on small business-related tax issues and also has a weekly radio program. You can visit her website, www.barbaraweltman.com, to check out all of the resources that she's made available. While you're there, make sure that you sign up for Barbara's "Idea of the Day." These short daily e-mails provide finance tips and strategies, but, more important, you'll receive important reminders about when taxes and tax filings are due. It's really easy to forget some of the tax-related things that are due throughout the year, especially when you're distracted by the daily demands of running a small business.

Family and Friends

One way to get a loan for your franchise is through a family member or maybe even a close friend.

For example, Barry Brokeda has always wanted to own his own business. As a matter of fact, his entire family has known this for years. That's because Barry isn't exactly shy when it comes to sharing his long-term plan; Barry wants to be a millionaire someday, and that's pretty much all he talks about. Barry is smart enough to know that he'll need to become a small business owner of some type in order to increase his odds and realize his dream. There's one problem, though; Barry is broke.

It's not like Barry is afraid of hard work; he held down two restaurant jobs all through high school. He's saved some money, too. The problem is that $15,000 isn't enough for what he has in mind.

Enter Uncle Harry. Uncle Harry is a very successful small business owner. He's owned a chain of auto parts stores in the southern part of the United States for the better part of 20 years. Uncle Harry is loaded. He also visits his sister (Barry's mom), a couple of times a year and always makes the time to sit down with his nephew, Barry, to talk about school business. Barry loves the man and wants what he has (loads of money!).

Barry is scheduled to graduate from college this year and, during one of Uncle Harry's visits, shares that he really doesn't want to look for a traditional job. Of course, Uncle Harry knows this and makes Barry an offer: "Barry, if you can find a business in which you really, really, think you could do well, let me know; I'll look into it myself, and if I feel it's a good one, I'll back you."

Barry gives his good old uncle a bear hug, thanks him profusely, and starts setting his sights on a couple of restaurant chains (franchises) that he's been casually checking out on his own time.

Barry starts investigating these franchises more closely, using a lot of what he's learned in college to do so. He disqualifies one of the two after finding out that the CEO had a rather sketchy background. (He was accused of embezzlement in his last corporate position.) He ends up settling on a 50s style diner called Dine and Dash. It's a fairly young concept, but Barry really feels that it could be a winner. He has visited several franchise locations and really likes what he sees. He calls his uncle, and he tells Barry to arrange a meeting with the franchise development representative.

Before the meeting, Uncle Harry started nosing around a bit, trying to see what he can find out about the Dine and Dash restaurant chain. He discovers that there are 30 of these franchises open, which he feels is acceptable considering the franchisor has only been around four years. He asks his business attorney to see if he can find any dirt on the company and its executives. He finds none. Uncle Harry flies out to meet his nephew and the franchise representative in Des Moines, Iowa, because that's where Barry's family lives, and Barry wants to open a business locally.

The meeting goes pretty well, and it looks like Uncle Harry may end up opening up his checkbook to help Barry get in business for himself, that is, until Uncle Harry receives a very disturbing phone call from his attorney. The attorney lets Uncle Harry know that he thinks his long-time chief financial officer (CFO) has just been arrested for some type of financial scam. As if that news wasn't bad enough, the attorney shares that it looks as though this CFO has been manipulating the books at Uncle Harry's company for years and that he may have stolen hundreds of thousands of dollars. Uncle Harry hurriedly leaves the meeting, saying that he has an urgent business matter to take care of and flies back home.

Barry apologizes to the franchise representative and assures him that they are very interested and will get back to him soon.

A few days later, Uncle Harry calls Barry to apologize about abruptly leaving the meeting and goes on to share what's happened. Barry asks his uncle if there's anything he can do to help and is told that "there is really nothing you can do." His uncle also tells him that until things straighten themselves out, he's not going to be able to back him on this business venture or any other. Barry, of course, understands and wishes his uncle good luck.

Barry knows that it's over. He's really angry. He knows that his uncle would have backed this venture! But now, his dreams are shot. He calls the franchise development representative to share the news, to which the representative replies, "Why don't you just try to get a small business loan from a bank?" Barry explains that because he's still in college, he hasn't been able to amass any assets, and he doesn't feel that a bank would want to loan him any money (especially the type of money needed for a full-service diner).

Barry's correct in this assumption; a 24-year-old who's about to grad-uate from college isn't really someone who a bank would take seriously. Remember when I shared with you that banks want you to have skin in the game? Well, they also want you to have collateral, and it's unlikely that a "Barry" would have any at this stage in his life. It may not seem fair to turn down a sharp, energetic student like Barry, but that's just how things work.

Admittedly, that tale was an extreme one; but I'll bet that a scenario very similar to that one has happened to someone, somewhere. When you approach a family member or even a close friend for money, just remember that they're going to be in the driver's seat from the moment they agree to it. That could get downright frustrating.

You should also know that asking a family member or friend for money is going to be a little weird. There's a huge difference between *thinking* about asking someone close to you for a pretty substantial sum of money and actually sitting down and *doing* it. It can get uncomfortable.

Now, just so you know, there are two totally different degrees of uncomfortable.

First, there's the "I'm thinking about getting into business for myself, someday. Would you ever consider loaning me some money if I find something that's interesting?" hypothetical question. Those conversa-tions tend to be pretty laid-back, and you may get a response like this:

"Sure. If you find something that's really interesting and has some potential, I'd look at it."

The second type of conversation involves you asking for a specific amount of money: "Remember when you said that if I ever found a great business opportunity to let you know, and you would maybe loan me the money? Well, I think I've found it! It's right up my alley, and I would only need around $100,000 or so from you to get it going. Could you loan me that kind of money?" A conversation like that is *a lot* more serious than the first one. But reading about it just doesn't capture the essence; you should try it sometime. It's something that you won't soon forget. One of the responses you may get will undoubtedly include a request for you do produce lots of specific information about the opportunity as well as data on what you've been able to learn about it. And this particular reply may be a little more common:

"Well, I know that I told you that I'd consider loaning you the money for a business. It's just that the economy has been so unpredictable lately. Also, we just had to replace both of our cars, and you know that we've been trying to sell our house. I'm sorry; it's nothing personal, it's just that your timing is bad. Maybe next year," blah blah blah.

The other thing that can occur—something that I've seen happen numerous times with several franchise candidates with whom I've worked—is this: the potential lender doesn't approve the franchise concept that the person asking for the money has chosen. In many of these instances, the uncle or friend gets involved way too late in the process and is, therefore, forced to undergo his or her own franchise research process a bit too hastily.

The other thing that happens in cases like this is that the potential lender ends up hearing something—usually negative—from a friend or business associate concerning the franchise business and puts the kibosh on the deal without even verifying if whatever has been said is actually true. It's really too bad when that happens; it's certainly not fair to the person asking for the money, who's spent a lot of time and energy learning about the opportunity. That's why I insisted on meeting—or at least talking with—*everybody* that would be involved in the potential franchise purchase or operation. If the money person wouldn't agree to meet or talk with me via phone before I presented some opportunities, it was game over. There was no way that I was going to spend hours on end working with someone who had an inaccessible financial backer. The folks who worked with me had to do things my way, or I wouldn't work with them. I'm still that way today in all my dealings. I figure that if you're going to come to me because you feel that I have the knowledge and expertise you crave—and feel very strongly that you'll derive tremendous benefit from working with me—then you have to let me do what I do best.

Now I don't want you to think that it's *impossible* to open a franchise with money from a family member or friend; you'll just have to be really good at managing the process. That means that you'll have to involve your backer early and often. You'll need to talk frequently with him or her during the entire process; doing so will keep them mentally in the game. Bring this individual with you when you pay a visit to a franchisee of the franchise that interests you. Arrange a conference call with your backer, yourself, and the franchise development representative, and try to bring your backer to Discovery Day. (There will be more on that in a bit.) He or she will need to develop a certain level of comfort before they can open up the checkbook. It's up to *you* to keep your backer engaged. And if you want to be a franchise owner badly enough, you'll find a way to do it.

Just for your information, I can only remember one time during my 10 years as a franchise broker that a financial backer actually ended up writing a check out to invest in a franchise for the buyer. Would you like to know how it ended? No . . . you don't.

In summation, it *is* possible to invest in a franchise with someone else's money. It doesn't really happen all that often in my experience, but don't let that deter you. After all, just because *I* haven't seen it happen a lot doesn't mean that it doesn't occur at all. I can only share what I know and what I've seen firsthand. So go ahead; prove me wrong. Become a franchise owner using a family member or rich friend's money. Because if you *do* manage to convince one of these individuals to back your venture into franchising, you've proven one really important thing about yourself: you're a great salesperson, and you'll be able to use that skill no matter what type of franchise you choose.

Borrowing Money from Yourself

It can be done, you know. In order to do this, you'll need to have a nice sum of money sitting *somewhere* against which you can borrow. So the obvious question is this: if you already have a nice bit of money sitting *somewhere*, why not just use it to pay for your franchise start-up? After all, there wouldn't be any interest if you had enough money to pay for the entire up-front investment, and that alone could be worth the price of admission. (You would save thousands of dollars in interest.) The little bump in the road—and the reason why you can't use that money all at once—has to do with *where the money is sitting*. (Hint: it's not sitting in a certain Scandinavian country's bank vaults.)

The reason that you can't use it all at once is that it's sitting in a retirement account. It's either in a 401(k) or an individual retirement account (IRA), and you're probably not yet at the age where you can start taking it out without serious penalties. Bummer.

But you *may* be able to tap into a portion of it for your start-up franchise without penalty if you use what are called *rollover as a business start-up plans* (ROBS). These plans have to do with something called the Employee Retirement Income Security Act (ERISA) of 1974. I'm not going to get into the details of these plans; suffice it to say I've had a couple of franchise buyers use them over the years who claimed to be very comfortable borrowing money to start their franchises using the ROBS plans.

A word of caution, however: the IRS has been looking rather closely at these plans for a few years now, and, so far, their focus seems to be on the paperwork portion. If you choose to borrow money for a start-up business in this way, make sure that the firm who's administering it knows what the heck they're doing.

I'll tell you what I tell everyone that asks for my royal opinion on these plans: I'm perfectly okay with franchise buyers using them in the following cases:

1. They are only using *a portion* of their retirement money.
2. They are looking at an *affordable* franchise.
3. They have talked to others who have used a ROBS plan.

After all, it is their money to begin with; they should have a right to use it as they wish. If you'd like more information about ROBS, check out my website www.franchisebizplans.com.

Long-Shot Loans

Years ago, I advertised my franchise services in the classified section of Cleveland's only newspaper, *The Plain Dealer*. I would usually get one to two calls a week from local area residents who were interested in learning about franchise ownership. Half of the folks who called seemed to be more interested in finding out how to get the money to buy a franchise and didn't really understand how small business loans work.

For instance, when I inquired about how much of their own money they would be willing to use, some of these folks would tell me that they didn't have *any* money to use toward a business; that's why they needed a loan. I would gently share with them that in order to *get* a loan, the banks would need them to put a portion of their own money in, too. After about 10 seconds of complete silence from the other end of the line, I would ask them if they knew anyone that could loan them money for a business. The answer was almost always no, so I would thank them for contacting me and tell them to call me if anything changed. Sometimes, as I was moving the phone away from my ear to hang it up, one more question was asked of me, and it bears mentioning in this chapter: "Aren't there government grants available for people that want to start a business?"

My answer was always the same: "I'm not really sure, but I've never met anyone who used one to start a business. Let me know if you find one."

That was my way of saying that there's pretty much no way in heck that you're ever going to get any type of government grant to start up a franchise business. Now maybe you're saying to yourself, "Joel . . . dude, you're being so negative. You're so harsh. How do you know? Maybe there are grants out there to start a business."

You're right. I'm sorry. Maybe there are some government grants available. They're probably sitting in a highly protected bank vault located somewhere in Washington, D.C.

Seriously now; you may *read* about the availability of government grants, or hear about them from hawkers like Matthew Lesko, "The Question-Mark Guy." However, if you really think that you're going to get enough money from a government grant (if you can even get a grant) to start a $200,000 franchise business, you really need some serious help. It's not going to happen, so get it out of your mind. Forget about it. No way.

A discussion on long-shot loans wouldn't be complete without the mention of venture capital funding. That's right; there are actually prospective franchise buyers who think that a venture capital firm would want to talk with them. After all, they do have money to loan—right?

Well, actually not exactly; they have money to *invest*. Big difference. Banks *loan* money. They find numerous ways to minimize their risk, including one that you already learned about; SBA loans. If you remember, the SBA is in the business of *guaranteeing loans* that are made by the banks. Banks use the SBA to lower their risk.

Venture capitalists *invest* money, usually in riskier investments, and have an equity stake in the companies in which they invest. Lots of high-tech companies use venture capital to keep themselves afloat until they have real breakthroughs. These company execs are willing to share in the ownership of their companies and a pretty large percentage of their profits because this approach lowers their overall risk.

However, venture capitalists are not interested in helping Bill and Sally realize their dreams of opening a CruiseOne or Dairy Queen franchise because there's just not enough money to go around. They want to get in on the big deals, like the ones that involve entire franchise *chains*. So unless you're thinking of doing that, there's no need to spend any time searching for a venture capital firm to help you fund your franchise business.

You now have some basic information on the types of loans that are out there, and the bottom line is this: unless you're going to pay cash for your franchise business, you're going to need a small business loan. *So start looking around now.* Talk to some local lenders in your community, and get a feel for what the current lending environment looks like. You should also find out how long the entire process—from when you apply for a loan to when you can get your money—will take. That way, you'll know when to jump in and present your business plan and apply for your franchise loan.

That's right; you're going to need a formal business plan. We'll tackle that next.

You Need a Plan

> *"The general who wins the battle makes many calculations in his temple before the battle is fought. The general who loses makes but few calculations beforehand."*
>
> —Sun Tzu

You don't just need a plan; you need a *franchise business plan*, to be exact. Even if you decide on one of the loan alternatives I mentioned, like using a portion of your retirement funds, you should really have a roadmap of sorts. There's a saying that goes something like this: "If you don't know where you're going, it's kind of hard to get there." I probably butchered that quote, but hopefully you get the gist of what I'm saying.

So what is a business plan? According to my friend Tim Berry, founder of Palo Alto Software, a business plan is "any plan that works for a business to look ahead, allocate resources, focus on key points, and prepare for problems and opportunities" (www.bplans.com). It's also almost always required by banks that you're requesting money from for your franchise business start-up. It's something that you really need to do right.

I asked Tim to share his thoughts about franchise business plans for you, my readers. Here's what he told me:

Out in the real world, your franchise business plan is a tool that helps you better control your own destiny. It lives mainly on your computer, not as a document. It helps you keep track of strategy, priorities, goals, specific steps, tasks, responsibilities, and of course basic business numbers. It's the first step in the planning process, which is regular plan review [that allows] you to track progress, highlight the unexpected, and manage change. It [highlights] the relationships between different parts of the business, who's responsible for what, and when, and what you need to change as you go along. Think of the planning process as steering—making regular small course changes to keep you en route to your desired destination.

The key points in your franchise business plan are your review schedule, list of assumptions, strategy summary, major milestones with dates and names and budgets, and basic numbers—including projected sales, cost of sales, gross margin, expenses, profit and loss, and cash flow.

Then Tim shared with me what the banks are looking for when they look over a business plan for a franchise:

When a bank asks for a business plan, [they] want a document that's a convenient summary of the key points of the business. [This should] include highlights like what you sell, into what markets, through what channels, with what sales and marketing strategies. [It should also let them know] who's in charge of this business, and what experience the people in the team have.

But most of all, a bank is looking for stability, reliability, and responsibility in a business plan. They want to see a good credit history, both business and personal, and assets to cover loans and reduce risks.

An important caveat here: don't confuse the document for the bank with your *real* business plan. The real plan lives on your computer and is something you update regularly to help you manage better. The document you give to the bank is a snapshot of what the plan was on the day that document was printed, plus some dressing, descriptions of the team, the history, the product, the market, and so on—and as a courtesy to the banker, helpful descriptions of your business.

I mentioned that Tim Berry founded Palo Alto Software, a company for which I'm an affiliate partner (which means that I make a couple of bucks if you buy it through my website). Now, Palo Alto is a great company, but as good as some of the business plan software is, it can't actually write up everything that you'll need, nor does it plug in the numbers for you. (How could it? They have to be *your* numbers.) What the software does do is allow *you* to plug in the information that you've gathered (or are in the process of gathering) and then connects it all together, so you have a finished product that you can present to a lender with total confidence.

If you'd like to check out this brilliantly devised software (which happens to be the best-selling business plan software available) just go to www.franchisebizplans.com. (As of this writing, you can buy it and try it; Business Plan Pro comes with a 60-day money back guarantee.)

Another resource that's available for you, the prospective start-up franchise owner, is the Small Business Development Center (SBDC). Small Business Development Centers are administered by the SBA and are usually partnered with colleges or universities. They provide free educational services for small business owners and aspiring entrepreneurs. Just go to www.asbdc-us.org/ to find the closest office near you; they have counselors that should be able to assist you with your business plan. I've also found SBDCs to be great sources for other important things that you'll need to start your franchise, like which banks to go to for small business loans, as well as names of local accountants and attorneys that specialize in small businesses.

There's one more resource that may be available for your business plan that may be only a phone call or two away.

If you feel that you've made a couple of friends during your franchisee validation calls—you know, the people who've told you to call them if you needed some more help—then this may be a good time to make good on those favors. It's perfectly okay to call one or two franchisees back and ask them if you could use their business plans. Think about it; you'd be able to customize them to your local area and plug in your own numbers. I bet that the folks at the SBDC could help you do that. I'd even bet that the business plan software about which you learned a little could do the job, too. Try it. The worst thing that could happen is that they say no. The best thing that could happen is that you get one of these and have a nice little jump-start on things.

A Little More Legal Learning

> "The minute you read something and you can't understand it, you can be sure it was written by a lawyer. Then, if you give it to another lawyer to read and he don't know just what it means, then you can be sure it was drawn up by a lawyer. If it's in a few words and is plain and understandable only one way, it was written by a non-lawyer."
>
> —Will Rogers

I purposely chose not to go into too much detail regarding the FDD. First off, while important, the FDD is just a big, fat document. Like the franchise brochure, it's a physical (or virtual, if it's online) piece of information that you get to read and eventually decipher. Now, because I'm assuming that you aren't an attorney that specializes in franchise law, there's no compelling reason for you to go through the entire document acting as though you are. That's the second reason that I didn't go into too much detail about it. The franchise attorney that you're going to hire will go through the FDD with you and can explain it far better than I ever could.

There's another reason why I didn't get too anal about all the intricacies of the FDD; I don't want *you* to. I want your focus to be more on *the human side* of things. I'm referring to the interactions that you're hopefully having via phone and in person with the people that have already taken the risk: the actual franchisees.

This is really where you're going to get to the truth and be able to get a feel for how good the franchisor is. If you haven't talked with or visited with enough franchisees, then get cracking! You'll be glad you did.

The process of writing this book has reminded me of one very important thing; I don't have all the answers. I can only teach you what I've learned myself and try to weave all of the important things about franchise ownership into not-too-boring-paragraphs. And in keeping with the theme of me not having all of the answers, I want to now introduce you to three attorneys of the franchise kind. These gentlemen *know franchising*. One of them is my own attorney, who has been incredibly helpful to me and almost everyone I've ever helped get into business. The other two are individuals with whom I've interacted with online and over the phone for a few years now. Like me, they are engaged in helping to protect future and current franchisees. I asked these men—Jack Kurant, Rush Nigut, and Charles Internicola—to share their thoughts and perspective on the FDD, especially in regard to the areas on which you should be focusing. Here's what they had to say.

Jack Kurant, Managing Partner of Wachter Kurant, LLC, in Cleveland, Ohio, shared this:

In reviewing the FDD, prospective franchisees should thoroughly examine, understand and verify, to the extent possible, the various fees, expenses, royalties and charges.

In addition, the franchise agreement—[which is] usually attached as an Exhibit to the FDD—is the most important item for the prospective franchisee. [This] is the "contract" that binds both the franchisor and franchisee, [the document that] delineates both parties' rights and obligations. The franchisee's attorney should review and explain this.

Finally, before signing the franchise agreement, the franchisee should fully understand all of the franchisee's obligations, including non-competition provisions that extend beyond the end of the franchise agreement and the extent of personal liability of the principals of the franchisee.

Rush Nigut, Attorney/Shareholder, Brick Gentry, P.C., in Des Moines, Iowa shared this:

In my franchise agreement, I always point to the trademark indemnification provision as a point to negotiate. My goal is to always obtain trademark indemnification (including the payment of any attorney's fees expended) for a franchisee. This means [that] I want the franchisor to contractually obligate themselves to stand by their name and protect the franchisee from lawsuits involving trademarks of the franchisor. A federal court lawsuit is an expensive proposition. Therefore, a franchisee definitely does *not* want to end up in court defending the marks of the franchisor at their own expense. After all, if the franchisor can't stand by their name, what are they really selling?

I [also] recommend checking the franchisor's litigation history. That includes not only a review of the FDD but also a Google search and perhaps even a check of the various court websites where the franchisor does business. Franchisees [should] directly ask the franchisor about whether any recent litigation is pending that is not included in the franchise disclosure document, since the FDD may not be updated to reflect new litigation—and prospective franchisees may not necessarily become aware of a new lawsuit just by reading the FDD.

Look closely at the franchise system, including intellectual property. Study the franchisor's system. Is the intellectual property independently developed or does it closely resemble other systems? Do patent, trademark or copyright infringement issues exist?

Also, examine the trends of the Franchisees. Is the number of franchisees on an upward or downward trend? Are there a lot of transfers and terminations? An abundance of [these trends] often indicates a troubled franchise system.

Charles Internicola, ESQ., of Decker Decker Dito & Internicola, LLP, shares this perspective:

When representing a "prospective franchisee"—whether an individual, husband and wife or family members looking to "purchase" their first franchised business—the one thought that always comes to mind is that my clients are about to take a big step that will impact their financial and "personal" well-being for many years to come. While I'm a proponent of franchising and believe in the tremendous value and potential that it presents to individual franchisees, I am also mindful and well-aware (as you should be) that all franchise opportunities are not the same. Some franchisors are comprised of sincere and hardworking management with solid and valuable business systems, while others are poorly managed and comprised of business systems that, over time, will only fail. [Therefore], the "due diligence" process of evaluating and selecting the right franchise opportunity is a critically important task and one that should not be taken lightly.

When evaluating and reviewing the FDD, prospective franchisees must understand that [this] is a document prepared by the franchisor—and the information contained therein may, in many instances, be generic and not objectively verifiable. While all of the material is relevant and should be reviewed with an experienced franchise attorney, some of the initial FDD disclosures that prospective franchisees must evaluate (even before hiring an attorney) relate to those FDD disclosures that (a) provide some insight into "profitability" and (b) are susceptible to some form of independent verification.

Also, make sure that you look at FDD Item 6: "Other Fees." [This will give you a bit of] insight into "some" of the almost guaranteed fees and expenses that will be charged to you on an on-going basis. These fees are important to evaluate since they will have a direct impact on your business's "profitability". [Some of these] "ongoing" fees include royalties, advertising fund fees and local advertising mandates. [You always want to verify] them with the franchisees [with whom] you're talking.

■ ■ ■

The best thing about reviewing the FDD with an attorney who knows what to look for is the fact that you're working with an attorney who *knows what to look for*. In other words, you don't want to hire a general attorney for this important task. Don't even *think* about asking your attorney uncle or friend to look things over if they don't have any experience with franchise documents and franchise contracts. This is *much* too important a decision for you to get free advice that's not relevant to franchising. *This is not the time to be cheap*. It won't usually cost you more to work with an attorney who's well-versed in franchising; however, I guarantee that it will cost you more in the end to work with one who's *not*.

By the way, you don't need to involve an attorney until you're really close to making a decision. In fact, you *will* be wasting your money if you meet with a qualified attorney too early in the franchise research process. You don't need a lawyer until you're just about ready to pull the trigger.

That's usually right before you attend a Discovery Day or immediately after. Now, about those Discovery Days . . .

The Discovery Day

You'll need your luggage for this special day because this is when you travel to the headquarters of the franchise in which you're seriously considering investing. You'll get to see the operation in action and will finally get to meet your franchise development representative and the rest of the executive team. You'll also get a tour of the facility and the chance to spend some time in all the different departments. You may even get to visit one or two franchises that are located in the vicinity of headquarters.

The Discovery Day is one of, well, discovery. It really should be called Meet the Franchisor Day. But it's also a "meet the prospective franchisee day," in the eyes of the executive team at franchise headquarters. And it's an, "I'm Close to Getting Paid a Nice Commission Day" for your representative, who's really (as you've undoubtedly figured out by now) a salesperson. This individual has been working with you and answering all of the great questions that you've been asking for a couple of months by now; he or she doubtlessly wants you to visit headquarters so that you'll move toward making a decision. Of course, the franchise company's CEO wants you to visit, too; after all, the franchise system could be one step closer to adding a new franchise unit and, with it, a nice-sized check for the franchise fee as well as the possibility of receiving a nice future royalty stream from you if you do in fact become a franchisee.

In most cases, you'll need to get *invited* to the franchisor's Discovery Day. The franchise development representative will officially invite you if he or she feels that you've got the right stuff and are in a position to make a yes or no decision—either during your visit or a week or two after, at most. From the franchisor's perspective, *the right stuff includes your skills, financial wherewithal, and the fact that there's a territory available in your local area.*

Most of the time, you'll be expected to pay for your own travel expenses although some franchisors do pick up some or all of the tab in the form of a reimbursement if you do, in fact, become a franchisee. I feel that it's a nice gesture on the franchisor's part to offer that, so if you are serious about the opportunity, take them up on it.

Now, assuming that you *do* receive an invite for a Discovery Day, you're probably going to notice a difference in the way that your franchise development rep is communicating with you before your visit; things may start to feel a little more intense. That's because in his or her mind, things are starting to move in one direction: toward The Decision. Well, actually *two* decisions—both of which will take place after your Discovery Day.

The first decision will come from them: the executive team will need to decide if they feel that you'd be a good franchisee and, if so, approve you. If they do so, your franchise representative will call you a day or two after your Discovery Day visit and formally tell you that you've been approved as a franchisee and that they'd love to have you as one. It's a great phone call to receive.

The second decision will, of course, be yours; The Decision to accept their offer and become a franchise owner.

To start preparing you for *your* part of The Decision, the questions that your franchise representative starts to ask in the days leading you up to your Discovery Day visit may not be as open-ended as you've become accustomed to. They may instead include queries such as the following:

- Are you looking at any other franchises or other business opportunities?
- Is your spouse, partner, or significant other *totally* on board with you?
- Have you had a formal conversation with your bank?
- Do you need to talk to any more franchisees?
- Will you be ready to move forward one to two weeks after your Discovery Day visit?
- Do you have enough liquid cash available for the franchise fee?

After hearing (and answering) a few questions like that from your franchise development representative, don't be surprised if you start having second thoughts about becoming a franchise owner. Most huge decisions in life involve backpedalling; it's simply human nature. You may start questioning the wisdom of your decision to become your own boss in the first place. Maybe you'll go to that *job-hunting place* located somewhere in your subconscious. Maybe getting a nice, stable, well-paying job with a guaranteed two-week vacation wouldn't be so bad after all. Hopefully, you'll be able to walk through *that* dark tunnel and remember why you're looking at becoming a franchisee to begin with. I'll admit that writing a check for $30,000 to some franchise company that you really don't know *that* much about can sound kind of daunting (even more so if you hadn't read this fine book.) But come on now, you can do this. Remember, at this point, we're only talking about *a visit to franchise headquarters*. But it *is* time to get serious.

This next section is really important:

> I don't recommend traveling to the franchise company's headquarters unless you're at a point in the process in which you feel that you have a good handle on the franchise concept and that you're convinced that it's the right fit for you and you for it. *You are also really serious about becoming a franchisee of this franchise and are ready to go out and get a loan, if needed, meet with a franchise attorney, and write that check for the franchise fee when the time comes.*

I've had franchise candidates ask me if they should attend a Discovery Day "just to see the operation in person." My answer was always no because there are only two reasons to attend a Discovery Day:

1. Because you've been invited to it
2. Because you've pretty much decided that this is The One

Now some members of my industry disagree with #1. They feel that if you're invited to a Discovery Day, you should just go. That will allow you to see for yourself just how good an operation it is and really give you a feel for things. I suppose it's fine if you subscribe to that school of thought; that particular outlook just so happens to be a first cousin of one with which I'm very familiar and have a bit of experience (which I'll describe now).

I had some great teachers when I was in the car business many years ago. In addition to meeting and greeting car buyers on the sales floor, I also had to answer sales calls (via phone) that came in throughout the day from folks who wanted to know if we had certain vehicles on hand—things such as specific colors, engine sizes, stuff like that. Some of the calls were of the "I want your best price" variety.

When I was brand new in the car business, I was very eager to supply these potential car buyers with our best price on whatever vehicle they were seeking. After all, I just wanted to sell a car! My sales manager certainly appreciated my enthusiasm, and, because he got paid a percentage of whatever I sold, he, too, wanted nothing more than to sell a car. So I didn't really understand why—when I walked into his office with the name and phone number of a hot prospect—he wouldn't just give me the automobile franchise's best price.

Even though he made me really, really mad at times, Joe Stokar—my first sales manager—taught me more about sales and the psychology behind it than anyone ever has. Whenever I would walk (run) into his office with a hot phone prospect, Joe and I would end up arguing. That's because, as I said, he never gave me a price to quote when I called these folks back. "But Joe," I would say, "all they want is our best price, and if I give it to them, maybe they'll come in and buy the car!" Joe's response was always the same: "Joel, if you *do* give them the price, they'll never come in." I asked Joe what I should do, and what he said changed everything for me as a brand new salesperson.

"Get them in here, Joel." He explained that anyone could give a price to someone that's shopping by phone. He told me that I was there to sell cars, not give prices. Amazingly—and with Joe's help—I was able to come up with several methods to get them into our store. Once they were in front of me, I could show them around the dealership, introduce them to the service manager, the parts manager, the owner, and even Joe. I could ask them some great questions face to face, which ended up helping me find the right vehicle for their exact needs. *And they were able to see what they were buying.* I sold a lot of cars using this approach.

When was the last time you made a major purchase—whether it was a car or even something like a major appliance? Did you see it in person before you bought it, or did you just buy it online or over the phone? Didn't you want to see, touch, and even smell the last car your bought? Didn't you want to take a test drive? If you had to replace your washing machine, did you just *look* at a picture of one on the Best Buy website? I'll bet that you went into the store and touched it; you even had the salesperson explain all the cool features before you bought it. Right?

Sales professionals will tell you that they would prefer to have the prospective buyer *in front of them* when they're pitching their product or service. Do you think it's possible that a franchisor's franchise development team would want you in front of *them*, too? Now, I'm not suggesting that anything underhanded or manipulative is behind a simple invite to their Discovery Day. But they *do* want an opportunity to meet with you face to face so they can show you what they've got. They want you to be sold on their opportunity, and they want to sell you a franchise.

By this time, you should have talked to and visited with plenty of franchisees. You've gathered just about all the data you need and should have a pretty good idea if this is the franchise for you. You've found out what it's going to take to apply for and receive a small business loan. You've started to think about getting a franchise attorney. (This is the multitasking part I mentioned earlier in this chapter.) The Discovery Day visit should really be a final validation of what you've been able to learn about the concept.

As I said, you'll be able to meet not only the person with whom you've been interacting for probably a couple of months now, but the entire team. You'll spend some time with the following people:

- Franchise development director
- CEO/president
- Operations director
- Marketing director
- Director of information technology (IT)
- Director of training
- Field support manager
- Accounting manager

You'll be able to see for yourself what the entire team brings to the table. Remember, the franchisor is charging *you* a royalty every month for all that's being provided—some of it by the very people that you're meeting during your Discovery Day visit. So feel free to ask each of them some questions. Have they been with the organization long? What's special about it? What types of problems have some of their franchisees had that they've been able to solve? You'll find that it will be easy to think of more questions to ask.

You'll also be able to see some of the franchise's systems and technology at work. You'll be impressed (or you should be). In conversations with franchise candidates after they return from a Discovery Day, systems and technology are almost always the things about which they're most excited. Sometimes, the systems and technology are so outstanding that it's very hard to *not* want to become a franchisee with the organization. For example, I've heard the following things:

"Joel, their technology is off the charts!"

"You should see how they do their direct marketing. I've never seen anything like it."

"They have a system for *everything*."

"Joel, you weren't kidding; everything is absolutely state of the art."

"These guys rock."

Now, you need to realize as you're going from department to department that they're checking *you* out, too. Most franchisors don't want just any schlub becoming a franchisee. A good franchise company will only award a new franchise if they feel the candidate:

- Has the right skill set
- Has the financial capability
- Will follow their system
- Will make them money
- Fits in

When I say *fits in,* I'm talking about your ability to mesh with the culture that currently exists there. Every company has a certain culture and unique personality. There's a certain feel that permeates a business's overall structure. And it usually starts from the top, which is why it's important for you to meet the CEO. What is he or she like? Are they on the stiff side or fairly laid back? Does this person seem to be really smart? Can you see why he or she is the CEO? What about the management team? What were they like when you met with them? Was everyone pretty much on the same page, or did you get the sense that there could be some conflict going on? Did you feel that you'd be able to easily ask anyone at headquarters for help if you needed it? The bottom line is whether these are the type of people with whom you'd like to partner.

I realize that it's kind of hard to know for sure whether these truly are the folks with whom you'd want to work. For that reason, I have something that you can do that may help you get more comfortable with them if you're not all the way there after your visit:

Call in one more marker. That's right; call one of the franchisees whom you've gotten to know and ask them how *they* feel about the member (or members) of the executive team about whom you aren't quite sure about. If this franchisee doesn't really know the person in question, ask this franchisee who does, and then call *them.* Don't stop; keep calling franchisees until you get your answers. As a matter of fact, keep calling the franchisees until you get *all* of your answers. Don't worry about calling them too much. This is about you. Remember, you've become an intelligent franchise buyer, and you're after the facts!

You may find this hard to believe, but *some* franchisors are better at selling franchises than they are at supporting them once they've been sold. But you needn't worry about becoming a franchisee with one of *those* organizations; that's because you've been doing your franchise research exactly like I've suggested here, so you're not going to let a lousy franchisor take advantage of you.

Time to Get Feelings Involved

Up to this point, your franchise research has been centered on fact gathering. The franchise development representative of the franchise concept in which you're interested the most has been providing tons of information for you to digest. You've digested it and have taken the necessary steps to make sure that the information you've received was valid by asking the franchisees. After all, they're the ones who are living this business every waking minute, and they've already invested their money into this franchise business opportunity. You've taken what you've learned from the franchisees back to the franchise development director (during the results call), and have gone through most of the FDD. You have become a franchise fact-gathering *machine*.

However, all the facts in the world can't compete with what you actually *feel* about the opportunity. It's important to remember that we've all been given something called intuition, an awareness of sorts. It's something that we as humans feel, and it has nothing to do with previous knowledge, data, or cold, hard facts.

Attending a Discovery Day can provide great insight into just how good of an operation this franchisor has. You may not know it while you're visiting, but you're actually collecting data all day long. It's being processed in your brain for later retrieval. It's great to have even more facts at your disposal as a way for you to make your final decision. However, all those facts that you've gathered during the past couple of months aren't going to matter at all if things just don't *feel* right.

The Decision on whether you'll *become a franchise owner* with this particular franchisor will ultimately come from your gut. Even if you've always considered yourself to be incredibly datacentric—and you think that every decision you've made up until now has been based on the facts that you've been collecting—I have to tell you something: they haven't been, you only *think* they have.

I want you to do the following exercise: think of something that you went ahead with in the past and ended up regretting in the long run. Maybe it was that new job that you just *had* to take that ultimately turned into a dysfunctional mess. (I did that once or twice.) It could have even been someone that you decided to date when you were younger who turned out to be a stalker post-breakup. (Yep, did that, too.) Do you remember the feeling you had inside when you were debating on whether to take the job or ask this person out on a date? It may have been on the subtle side; of course, it could have been really loud.

"Don't do it!"

Well, either way, that was your intuition talking—your inner voice telling you that you were about to make a big mistake. But you made the conscious choice *not to* listen to it. Do you remember reflecting back on those poor decisions and saying some of the following things to yourself:

"I should have known."

"Why didn't I just listen to that voice inside my head?"

"I *knew* it!"

Well, you *did* know. You probably even had some factual information to work with, but you didn't trust your intuition (or you simply chose to ignore it), and look how things turned out.

When it comes to The Decision on whether to move forward with a franchise opportunity, you really need to be aware of that inner voice. It may appear during a phone call or an in-person visit with a franchisee. It may show up while you're on one of your calls with the franchise development director. It may start chattering while you're visiting headquarters. Be aware.

Of course, things may feel really right during your Discovery Day visit and during other parts of the franchise research process. It's important to trust your intuition when it's *positive*, too! I've had candidates tell me, "Things felt really right when I was at headquarters, Joel." Or "This franchise opportunity has felt like a match from day one." I used to love it when candidates would tell me that; it meant that my process was working.

Toward the end of your Discovery Day visit, your franchise representative will sit down with you and ask how you feel about things. (See? Even *they're* talking about feelings!) They may even want to know if you'd be ready to move forward if the executive team approves of you. You'll also receive a specific time frame in which you'll need to make your decision, and you should be aware that it's usually a short one.

The day is soon approaching on which you'll need to make a yes or no decision. That day is called Decision Day—and, amazingly, it's the title of the next chapter. Ready?

12

Decision Day

"Using the power of decision gives you the capacity to get past any excuse to change any and every part of your life in an instant."

—Anthony Robbins

YOU MAY FIND it strange that the person who's been teaching you exactly how to do your franchise research, who's been pushing you to make sure that you leave no stone unturned while doing it, is now the one telling you that enough's enough.

That's right; stop right now.

Now, to be fair—I'd totally understand it if you wanted to make another call or two to one of the franchisees of the business opportunity you're considering—just to make sure that you haven't missed something. I'd even understand it if, after hours of tossing and turning one night, you decided to fire up your laptop and do a Google search for *Blankety-blank franchise lawsuits*, just to make *sure* you didn't miss anything. It's just that you don't have to. That's because you've read this book.

You've learned about the origins of the business model of franchising. There's something to be said about going back in time for a bit and finding out how something started. It tends to give us a real appreciation for some of the struggles that those before us endured. Don't you wonder what it would have been like to be one of the first franchised car dealers back in the dirt road days?

I taught you everything you need to know about what a franchise business *really* is and what it includes. Franchising has a lot of advantages, and you've learned about all of them. But first I had to share some of the things that you may have heard about franchising—in other words, those nasty myths. Hopefully, you won't fall for the "franchising is easy" or "everything is all set up for you, because it's a turnkey business" rumors that I cited. You know that everything won't be automatically set up if you become a franchise owner and that whatever the franchise is—being a small business owner is *never* easy.

You've been engaged in real risk-lowering activities although you may not have known it. The mere fact that you went over to the www .takethefranchisequiz.com website and spent some time finding out if you do, in fact, have the right basic personal traits and characteristics for owning a franchise type of business is one way that you've done so. Most prospective franchise owners don't take the time to see if they're even a fit for the mostly rigid, rule-following, franchise business model.

The self-assessment activities in which you immersed yourself helped you hone in on your top professional skills and ascertain your most dominant personal characteristics and abilities. But you didn't stop there; you learned how you'd be able to apply what you learned about yourself to some of the different categories that exist in franchising today. In other words, you learned how to completely customize your search for the best franchises *for you*. Specific examples were provided that gave you plenty of food for thought. *You successfully lowered your risk* by making sure that you matched the opportunities to the person: *you*.

Speaking of risk, I hope that you learned a few things about how *not* to buy a franchise after reading James Pennington's story. Here was a guy who—at 50-something years old and after finding himself downsized for the third time in the last 10 years—didn't feel that he had it in him to do the *interview shuffle* one more time. So instead of looking for a new job, he decided, after seeing an advertisement one day, to start looking for a franchise, so he could control his own destiny and have a shot at a decent retirement.

James's motives were certainly pure; he simply wanted the best for himself and his family. It's just that he didn't know how to go about choosing the right franchise for himself; and, once he thought that he had found it, he really had no idea how to go about his franchise research. The end result: James lost $300,000, had to lawyer up, and then had to go find a job. Ugh!

You then learned exactly how to figure out a budget for your franchise business, so you wouldn't set yourself up for financial disaster (similar to that which James endured). You were also schooled in the different types of small business loans that are available and how to approach a lender. I'm thinking that the importance of having a turbocharged franchise business plan wasn't lost on you in the least bit. You discovered something incredibly crucial about investing in a start-up franchise: in addition to having working capital readily available, you need to set aside some living expenses for the first several months (at least) that your new business would be in operation. (If you only knew how many new franchisees don't do this.)

I truly feel that it was worth it for me to open up a veritable can of worms with regard to some real truths concerning the franchise brokerage industry. Doing this allowed you to see why most franchise brokers and consultants offer their franchise matchmaking services for free. I shared that there were certainly some good franchise brokers out there and then gave you my must-ask list of questions to use before you agree to engage in their services. (Feel free to ask some of the questions, even if you're already using one of these services.)

In this book, I've laid out the most thorough, step-by-step franchise research techniques that have ever been assembled. If you follow my franchise research steps to the letter, there's no reason that you won't be able to make an intelligent, fact-based decision on a particular franchise.

My intuition tells me that I've adequately convinced you that investing in a franchise is *way too important* for you to accept any free advice from your well-meaning, but totally unqualified attorney friend or uncle who knows about as much about FDDs and franchise contracts as you do. (And maybe even less!) Why *wouldn't* you go out and find a franchise attorney?

You were able to attend a Discovery Day without even having to pack your suitcase, park your car at the airport, and get frisked by the Transportation Security Administration (TSA). That's because I walked you through one and gave you the chance to find out about some of the things that you'd experience if you were ever invited to one and ultimately chose to attend it. And, because I haven't yet given you a reason to *not* believe what I've been teaching you thus far, you wouldn't even *think* of attending a Discovery Day unless you were pretty darned convinced that the franchise opportunity being offered was the right fit for you and you for it. Right?

So that brings us here. If you:

- Are convinced that you have a franchise personality
- Are only looking at franchises that are truly a match for *you*
- Didn't skip *anything* while doing your franchise research
- Are being *careful* about your financial exposure and have some money set aside
- Have *met* the CEO *and* the franchisor's executive team
- Are *only* going to obtain a loan that makes sense for *you*
- Have found *an attorney that knows franchising* inside and out
- Have the *backing of your family* and so on

Then—and *only then*—are you prepared to make a decision. Now I can't obviously make it for you, but I'm trying like heck to make sure that you've done everything you need to get ready for your Decision Day.

Do This and This

As your search for a franchise begins winding down (or winding up, depending how you look at it), you're going to find that things may not go in the order that you think they will. They also may happen sooner than you'd assume during the franchise research process. Every franchisor does things a little differently in regard to their franchise sales process.

For example, I suggested that you should start approaching lenders to see what they're offering, loanwise, earlier rather than later. One of the reasons for doing this simply has to do with timing. If you decide to become a franchisee of the opportunity at which you've been looking, you're going to want to open your new business as soon as humanly possible. It's going to be an exciting time in your life, and believe me, you'll be chomping at the bit to get moving! It may take 45 to 60 days from the day that you formally apply for your loan for you to actually receive the check. Of course, the franchise development representative knows this, and he or she could start encouraging you to start applying for one as soon as there's a feeling in the air that you're starting to get pretty serious.

Naturally, applying for a small business loan at your local bank probably won't go very well unless you've prepared a franchise business plan to present to your lender, which is something that your franchise development director knows. That's why it's pretty likely that you'll be asked to start working on a business plan for your franchise business at the same time that you're doing your franchise research.

Now it can sound pretty overwhelming to be doing these two things—writing up a business plan and applying for a small business loan—while you're also immersed in some serious franchise research. But it's not really that bad because you've been following my advice and have made a few friends. These new friends to whom I'm referring are the one or two franchisees with whom you've really connected—the ones that have said things like the following:

- "Don't hesitate to call me back whenever you want if you have more questions."
- "If you need to know *anything*, just call."
- "If you'd like to drive up here and spend a day or two with me in my business, please just let me know and we'll make it happen."

I want you to call these franchisees back, even if you think you'll be uncomfortable doing so, and find out the following:

- Where they ended up getting a loan and what kind it was
- How long it took to get the money
- If they had a formal business plan and, if so, who helped them write it
- If you can borrow their business plan

I've taken the liberty of repeating these so you'll do it!

Now they may or may not share their business plan with you; some franchisees are more private than others. But if you can convince these individuals to send you as much of their information pertaining to loans and business plans as possible, then you can count on saving tons of time. Try to visualize how great it would be if you were able to get a copy of *their* business plan—and all you had would have to do was replace their numbers with your own. If you recall, I already let you know about some people who could help you with the numbers; CPAs and Small Business Development Centers (SBDCs) are the two that I suggested.

If a franchisee is generous enough to share his or her loan and business plan information, it wouldn't hurt to show this individual how much of a class act you are. Plus, who knows? You may have to reach out to them again for something else. Here's what you can do:

Call the chamber of commerce that's located closest to this franchisee, and tell them that you really want to show your appreciation for something that a local business owner did for you. Ask the person at the other end of the phone for the names and phone numbers of a couple of the better restaurants in town. Then find these two restaurants online, see which one looks nicer, and call them. Tell them you want to buy this franchisee and his or her partner, significant other, or spouse, a gift certificate in an amount that will cover a very special dinner. Buy it from them, and send it to the franchisee, along with a thank you note. Make sure to include your name. I guarantee that this simple gesture will be greatly appreciated and remembered long after their desserts have been eaten.

The other thing you need to focus on now that the research phase is really over is arranging a franchise document review with a competent attorney whose main job is to protect you. You need to know exactly what you're getting into if you become a franchisee. That's why you'll want to make sure that you have a thorough understanding of the following:

- The FDD
- Your obligations as a franchisee
- The obligations of the franchisor
- Business entities
- Legal remedies of both parties
- The franchise contract
- Any red flags

Because I know that you're *totally convinced* that you need to sit down with an attorney familiar with franchising in order to protect yourself—and also to make sure that you have a complete understanding of all things legal—all you have to do now is locate one.

One way to do so is by getting a direct referral. Because most of the franchise candidates with whom I worked lived locally, I felt that—in my particular case—it was really important for me to have as my go-to person a local attorney who was very familiar with franchise law. I gave Jack Kurant's name (of Kurant Wachter CO., LPA) to every prospective franchise buyer I could when it was time for them to get some legal guidance regarding their FDDs and franchise contracts. My dad had worked with Jack and told me that he liked and trusted him. I met him and felt the exact same way. I wanted to work with someone who would help *protect* my franchise candidates. Jack fit the bill then and continues to do so now.

There are several other places where you can get attorney referrals. If you're working with the SBDC, their counselors may know of one. Your lender probably knows some business attorneys and business attorneys know franchise attorneys. A local franchisee of a noncompeting franchise business probably knows of one as well.

If those ideas don't work, check out the resource section of this book; I've included some legal resources there.

When you do end up finding an attorney, you'll want to ask these questions before you agree to engage his or her services:

1. Do you regularly review franchise contracts and FDDs?
2. Are you up to date with our state's franchise laws?
3. Will you recommend the proper type of business entity to set up in order to protect us?
4. What will you charge for your services? (I'm not going to even attempt to suggest what you should pay for a franchise document review. Some attorneys do it by the hour, while some have a set price for doing it.)

In most cases you'll send the franchise documents to your attorney ahead of time via mail; you may even drop them off in person if the office is close to you. Your attorney will need some time to go over the documents and will call you to set up a convenient time to meet. Unless there's anything out of the ordinary in the FDD or contract—such as excessive fees, tons of lawsuits, or anything else that looks suspect—your attorney's role during the meeting is really to make sure you understand the FDD and the franchise agreement and then to make sure that you understand what your obligations are as a franchisee. Find out what the best and worst case scenarios are; you need to know. In addition, your attorney may discuss the types of business entities that are available to you. Corporations, LLCs, and Subchapter Ss are the most common ones; it depends on several different things, all of which your attorney will explain to you. That's really all you'll be discussing with him or her because anything more than the things I mentioned would probably be overkill.

For example, you may end up meeting with an attorney whose ego gets in the way and who starts making suggestions that really have nothing to do with why you hired this person in the first place. Your attorney may all of a sudden seemingly alter his or her personality right before your very eyes and become a "business adviser." All sorts of suggestions and ideas may start to be thrown around so furiously that you may wonder if this is the same attorney who you shook hands with only moments ago. I remember one situation in which my candidate was referred to an attorney, and things didn't go so well. My candidate was looking at an opportunity and simply needed the attorney to go over some documents. My candidate told me a story about how this individual basically went off on some type of weird tangent, something to the effect of, "Are you sure you need this company to help you do this business? Do you really want to pay them royalties? Why don't you just do this on your own?" Now, because my candidate never asked this attorney for his opinion on the opportunity or on franchising in general, he was definitely caught a little off guard. My candidate also told me that after this attorney was through with his tirade, he told him thanks, but no thanks, and ended up going to another one—which worked out just fine.

If your attorney starts to go all business adviser on you—unless the information they're providing is highly relevant to the reason you're there for in the first place—gently (if at all possible) move the conversation back to the FDD and the contract. That will usually work. Otherwise, you may have to explain to this person that you only came to get a franchise document review, and that's really all you want at this point, and just ask a question about the FDD to move things back to the original conversation that you had only five minutes earlier. If that doesn't work, you'll have to get creative. And how you do *that* is totally up to you.

Now exactly *when* you invest a little money into a franchise document review varies. I've had franchise candidates meet with their attorneys a week or so before they were scheduled to go to Discovery Day. I've also had people make an appointment in advance for a few days after they return from a Discovery Day. Either approach works as long as you keep one thing in mind: don't hire an attorney until you're pretty darned sure you're going to invest in a specific franchise. If you do, you're just throwing away your money. There's absolutely no need to get any legal advice regarding franchise ownership until you're *about to become* a franchise owner.

It's Time to Be a Decider

"Courage is being scared to death… and saddling up anyway."
—John Wayne

"Every beginning is a consequence—every beginning ends something."
—Paul Valery

You knew that this day would come. Although you may not have thought about it too much while you were *beginning* your search for franchise opportunities, you probably started to right around the time you filled out some franchise applications, at which time you had to disclose your personal financial information. That's usually when reality sets in.

While Decision Day is nothing to sneeze at in terms of its place on the serious scale, there's a lot to be said about doing enough right things *before* you're at the point at which you need to make a major life decision like this. It's not like you're going into this blindly (unless you've skipped every chapter in this book, and started right here!). Even if you've only done 80 percent of what I've gently suggested throughout this book, you're light-years ahead of almost every prospective franchise buyer that's out there looking for his or her opportunity right now. By making only a miniscule investment, you've been able to learn exactly how to properly select and carefully research franchises. But you're still nervous. It's okay; being nervous is just another part of this process. Actually, if you're *not* nervous on Decision Day, something's drastically wrong with you. *You're supposed to be nervous.* Becoming a franchise owner *will* change your life. But that's what you wanted, right?

Or are you having doubts? Again, you *should* be. It's just not normal to not have them. An important question to ask yourself is: What are you having doubts *about*? Are some of the following questions dancing around in your head?

What if I Don't Have the Right Skills to Run This Type of Franchise Operation?

If you've only been focusing on franchise opportunities that are a match for your top skill sets, you have nothing to worry about. Right?

What if the Folks at Franchise Headquarters Are All Compulsive Liars?

Some of the questions that I've provided for you to ask the folks at headquarters may not be welcomed with open arms. They're doubtlessly tough questions to ask and even tougher to answer, and they're designed that way for a reason: to flush out the truth. They usually do. However, if you end up saying yes to an opportunity on Decision Day, and it turns out that the entire franchise team at headquarters lied to you about everything concerning the franchise opportunity, get your franchise attorney on the phone as soon as possible. You may end up *owning* the entire franchise operation.

What if I Missed Something?

It's entirely possible that you may have missed something. If you did, I highly doubt that it would be something big enough to put you in a state of financial Armageddon. If you're really that paranoid about missing something, reread this book. Review your notes. Meditate.

What if the Franchise in which I'm about to Invest Experiences Some Type of Public Relations Disaster?

Then it does. What I'm trying to tell you here—in my usual, gentle way—is that there are certain things that you simply cannot control. For example, let's say that a fellow franchisee decides to attend the National Basketball Association (NBA) All-Star Game drunk, dressed in a see-through toga that has the franchise logo embroidered all over it and proceeds to get chased around the basketball court and gets Tasered, and it's caught on national television. (Hey, it could happen.) In a case like that, most franchisors would immediately contact a PR firm and have them assist with damage control. That's what you're paying for, every month, with your royalties.

What if I Run out of Money?

You could, you know; it does happen. Interestingly enough, however, the people who run out of money before their franchise business becomes profitable are the ones who didn't have enough money to invest from the beginning or weren't savvy enough to set any money aside that they could use if need be. Of course, these are the same people who most likely didn't do the type of intensive franchise research that you just did, which means that they never found out from the existing franchisees how long it would take to break-even. The bottom line? Stash some money.

What if I Pick a Lousy Location?

Both parties (you and the franchisor) have to agree on the location. Find someone local who really has a good grasp of the commercial real estate market. Ask your attorney, your accountant, or even your lender. They all know commercial realtors as well as owners and managers of shopping centers. When it comes to deciding on location, combine what you've learned with your intuition. Just know that sometimes locations *do* turn out to be less than stellar. Make sure that you understand your lease before you sign it, and find out if you can break it in order to move someplace better.

Can I Get out of My Franchise Contract if I Don't Like It?

Not really. Franchisors aren't in the business of awarding franchises to folks who "want to see if things work out." (And franchisors shouldn't be either.) Investing in a franchise business should never be done in a half-hearted way. It's a contractual arrangement that is usually about 10 years in length. But, if you really do want to get out of it, you actually do have some choices:

1. The franchisor could *buy it back* from you. (Be aware that this is a rarity.)
2. You can *sell it to someone*. (Check your franchise contract to see how it would work.)

3. You could just *walk away*. Of course, this means that you would lose your investment and experience the sheer ecstasy of being sued by the franchisor, the leasing agent, your vendors, and other miscellaneous entities. Suffice it to say—this isn't the most appealing option.

What if I Lose My Money?

Obviously, this is the biggest fear of them all, and it's a valid one. That's because even if you do everything I've suggested in this book to lower your risk, it's still possible to lose your money. Franchises get cold. Market conditions change. Recessions happen. Populations shift. Natural disasters occur. People get sick. Businesses get sued. Employees steal. Stuff happens, folks.

Now, if all you're thinking about day and night is the (albeit real) possibility that you may lose your money if you buy the franchise on which you've been focused, you may not be ready to become the owner of a franchise—or any other type of business for that matter. I'm serious; if you and I were working together, and you told me that you were really concerned about losing your money in the franchise in which you were seriously considering investing, I would tell you not to do it. I've already shared with you that it's perfectly normal to be nervous about becoming a franchise owner. However, if you find that you're constantly losing sleep over it, and you're way beyond nervous, then you really need to take a step back because becoming a franchise owner may be too risky for you at this point. If you're just not ready to take the risk *now*, then it's *okay* to take some more time and see if you can work through your fears. Just be honest about your feelings with the franchise development representative. Your relationship with him or her should be comfortable enough by now for you to ask for a little more time.

However, if you really don't feel that there's anything you'll be able to see or hear that will allay your fears about losing money, then it's time to walk away. But you needn't feel that you're walking away in defeat; it takes a lot of courage to admit that you're just not ready to do something this big. Some people have found that the mere *idea* of going into business for themselves is great. However, when it comes time to complete the act of physically writing a large check to do so, combined with going out and getting a bank loan, signing a long-term commercial lease, and so on, it is a bit too much for them to handle.

There's a huge difference between opting *not* do something because you feel that it's too risky and going forward with something that you *know* is too risky for you but doing it anyway. One is pretty darned smart, and the other one is just stupid. (You may have some examples of both locked away somewhere in your brain's memory cells. This may be a good time to do a search.)

As I mentioned in the last chapter, it's incredibly helpful to have lots of facts at your disposal. I've provided a wealth of proven strategies and techniques for you to use in order to get them. If you've been putting in the time and effort needed to do things right—and have really followed everything that I've laid out in this book—then you should feel very confident going forward. As a matter of fact, if there was an award available for fact-gathering, you'd be in serious contention for it. I'm serious; very few people know how to correctly find, research, and invest in a franchise that's truly right for them.

This is the bottom line:

You need to base your decision to become a franchise owner on all the facts that you've been able to gather up until now, combined with what your inner voice or intuition is telling you. If both of those are in alignment, you'll know exactly what to do.

I trust your judgment. And you should, too.

Final Thoughts

I'VE SAID IT COUNTLESS times throughout this book, so it bears repeating one last time: becoming a franchise owner isn't for everyone. Not only do you have to have the right personality characteristics for a business model that demands strict adherence to rules and procedures, but you also need to be comfortable with the idea of taking on risk in order to reach your professional and personal goals. You'll also have to have enough money available to not only invest in the franchise of your choosing, but also to allow some breathing room during the cash-poor, start-up phase.

For some, franchise ownership is something that they find interesting to learn about, but it kind of just ends there. Some folks only think about becoming a franchise owner when they lose their jobs; others already have jobs but hate them so much that they're having sick thoughts about what they'd like to do to their current bosses. For other folks who have always wanted to work for themselves, it's an idea to be explored—one that they're hoping turns out to be the answer that they've been seeking.

My hope is that, if it turns out that you *are* right for franchise ownership (and that franchise ownership is right for you), you follow every suggestion that I've made in this book. In a perfect world, I want nothing more than to see you become a successful franchise owner. I'd love you to be able to have the freedom and control to do the following:

- Grow your business
- Create new jobs in your community
- Become a business leader in your area
- Involve your children or grandchildren in your business
- Build equity in your franchise business
- Create wealth for yourself and your family
- Become an advocate for franchising

If you do end up becoming a franchise owner, make sure that you go into the experience with complete awareness of the fact that your business will have its ups and downs and that there could be some interesting twists and turns included when you least expect them. It's not going to be easy; you'll be working harder than you ever have before. Your stress level will enter the red zone—a lot. You may even doubt your abilities if your new franchise business ends up taking longer than you projected to break even and start to show a profit.

The great thing about owning a franchise business—heck, about owning *any* business—is that you really are in charge, (for the most part.) It's very empowering to know that you can't be fired . . . that a boss can't ask you to step into his or her office to have a little chat ever again . . . *because you're the boss.*

"But, Joel," you might be thinking, "If I become a franchisee, I know that the franchisor makes all the rules, and I also know that they could terminate my franchise contract anytime they want. So, I'm really not in charge."

You're wrong. Who's opening up the door to your franchise business every day? Who's doing the hiring and the firing? Whose name is on the commercial lease and the small business loan papers? Who's the one trying to grow the business?

You are. You're the franchise owner. All you did was buy someone else's business system so that you could take a shot at your dreams. Sure, you have to follow the rules; so what? Does that make you any less of a business owner? And yes, the franchisor could terminate your franchise contract—and you with it. But, if you're growing your business, that means you're sending in bigger and bigger royalty checks to your franchisor. If that's the case, then why would they *want* to terminate your franchise contract? Franchisees are the lifeblood of a successful franchise concept. The good franchisors want to keep their franchisees happy. To prove that what I just wrote isn't just theoretical hogwash, I've provided some proof.

The Franchise King's Franchisor-Franchisee Happiness Rule:

*A Franchisor with 300 Really Happy Franchisees Will **Always** Outperform a Franchisor with 300 Mostly Unhappy Franchisees*

If you choose a franchisor that has happy franchisees—most of whom are making money—then there's no reason that you can't be a happy money-making franchisee either!

Just do the right things and be patient while your new franchise business ramps up. If you get stuck, call the franchisees that you befriended during your franchise research; they'll help you. Call the franchisor if their answers don't seem to be working; but don't wait too long. Don't be like James Pennington, who, for whatever reason, didn't reach out for help until it was way too late and instead tried to figure out everything himself. (*That* worked out well, huh?) In other words, don't let your ego get in the way of staying in business. As much as you'd like to think that you do—you *don't* know everything.

If, by chance, you decide that franchise ownership just isn't in the cards for you, it's okay. At least you only had to invest the price of this book in order to find out. Others had to spend way more than that.

But, if you do become a franchise owner—and a successful one—it may turn out to be the best decision you've ever made in your life.

—The Franchise King, Joel Libava
July 17, 2011

A Royal Collection of Resources for Franchise Buyers and Franchise Owners

I'VE ASSEMBLED a collection of resources that all franchise buyers and owners should check out. These resources are all small business- or franchise business-related and are worthy of your time. Enjoy, and pass them on!

Franchise Websites

www.franchisedirect.com

http://franchising.alltop.com

www.spring-greenfranchiseblog.com

www.topnewfranchises.com

www.franchising.com

www.americasbestfranchises.com

http://franchise.business-opportunities.biz

www.franchise.org

www.frandata.com

www.franchise.com

www.franchisehelp.com

www.redhotfranchises.com

www.greenfranchisedirectory.com

www.dailyfranchisenews.com

www.franchisetimes.com

www.franchisessentials.com

www.stopsellingstartclicking.com

www.franchiseopportunities.com

www.thefranchisehandbook.com

Small Business Websites and Blogs

www.smallbiztrends.com

http://community.sba.gov

www.openforum.com

www.smallbizdaily.com

www.smallbusinessadvocate.com

www.bizsugar.com

http://small-business.alltop.com

http://yourbiz.msnbc.msn.com

www.carolroth.com

www.jonathanfields.com

www.timberry.com

http://blog.guykawasaki.com

www.bloggertone.com

www.barbaraweltman.com

www.allbusiness.com

www.businesspundit.com

www.ignite-vp.com

www.therisetothetop.com

www.entrepreneur.com

www.smallbiztechnology.com/

www.business-opportunities.biz

www.jimkukral.com

www.barrymoltz.com

www.ivanwalsh.com

www.networksolutions.com

www.solobizcoach.com

www.money.cnn.com/smallbusiness

http://smallbusiness.foxbusiness.com

www.smartmoney.com

www.searchguru.com

www.blogsforsmallbusiness.com

www.smallbizlabs.com

www.smallbusinessfinanceforum.com

www.thesearchguru.com

www.fastcompany.com

www.paypal.com

www.cheapdomain24.com

www.businessweek.com/small-business

www.smallbizsurvival.com

www.seobook.com

www.bplans.com

www.builttosell.com

Marketing

www.copyblogger.com

www.ducttapemarketing.com

www.kitchentablecompanies.com

www.drewsmarketingminute.com

www.kherize5.com

www.influentialmarketingblog.com

www.marketingprofs.com

www.marketingprofessor.com

www.tengoldenrules.com

www.steverubel.me

www.hubspot.com

www.aweber.com

www.infusionsoft.com

www.constantcontact.com

Social Media

www.chrisbrogan.com

www.socialmediaexaminer.com

www.briansolis.com

www.socialmediaexplorer.com

www.marismith.com

www.lizstrauss.com

http://socialmediatoday.com

www.problogger.com

www.scottmonty.com

Public Relations

www.spinsucks.com

www.sandersonpr.com

www.shankman.com

www.perkettpr.com

www.davidmeermanscott.com

www.shonaliburke.com

www.edelman.com

www.crt-tanaka.com

www.regancomm.com

www.sspr.com

Legal

www.lawkkwt.com

www.rushonbusiness.com

www.newyorkfranchiselaw.com

www.lawyers.com

www.smallbusinesslawfirms.com

www.myfranchiselaw.com

www.attorneypages.com

www.ftc.gov

Attention Franchise Buyers!

Would you like to work with me? I provide very personalized franchise advisory services for those interested in exploring the idea of becoming franchise owners. Contact me for more information.

If you're at the "I'm thinking about becoming a franchise owner" stage, I can provide all sorts of guidance. If you've already started looking at franchise opportunities, I can help you figure out if you're on the right track and coach you along the way, helping to make sure that you're not missing anything.

If you've already decided on a specific franchise, I can be your sounding board, while at the same time providing some last-minute tips that will enable you to protect your interests. If you're working with a franchise broker or consultant, I can assess whether *your* interests are being kept front and center or if the possibility of a $15,000 commission paid to your broker are keeping them on the back burner.

My services are designed to do one thing; help you lower your financial risk. If that sounds appealing, please feel free to contact me. Let's talk.

Joel Libava

E-mail: thefranchiseking@sbcglobal.net

Phone: 216-831-2610

Web: www.thefranchiseking.com

Twitter: @FranchiseKing

Facebook: TheFranchiseKing

YouTube: www.youtube.com/franpro1

If you found me *because you purchased this book*, make sure you mention it. I'll knock off the retail price of the book for any advisory services that you purchase.

Index